BORUTO
-NARUTO NEXT GENERATIONS-

VOLUME 10

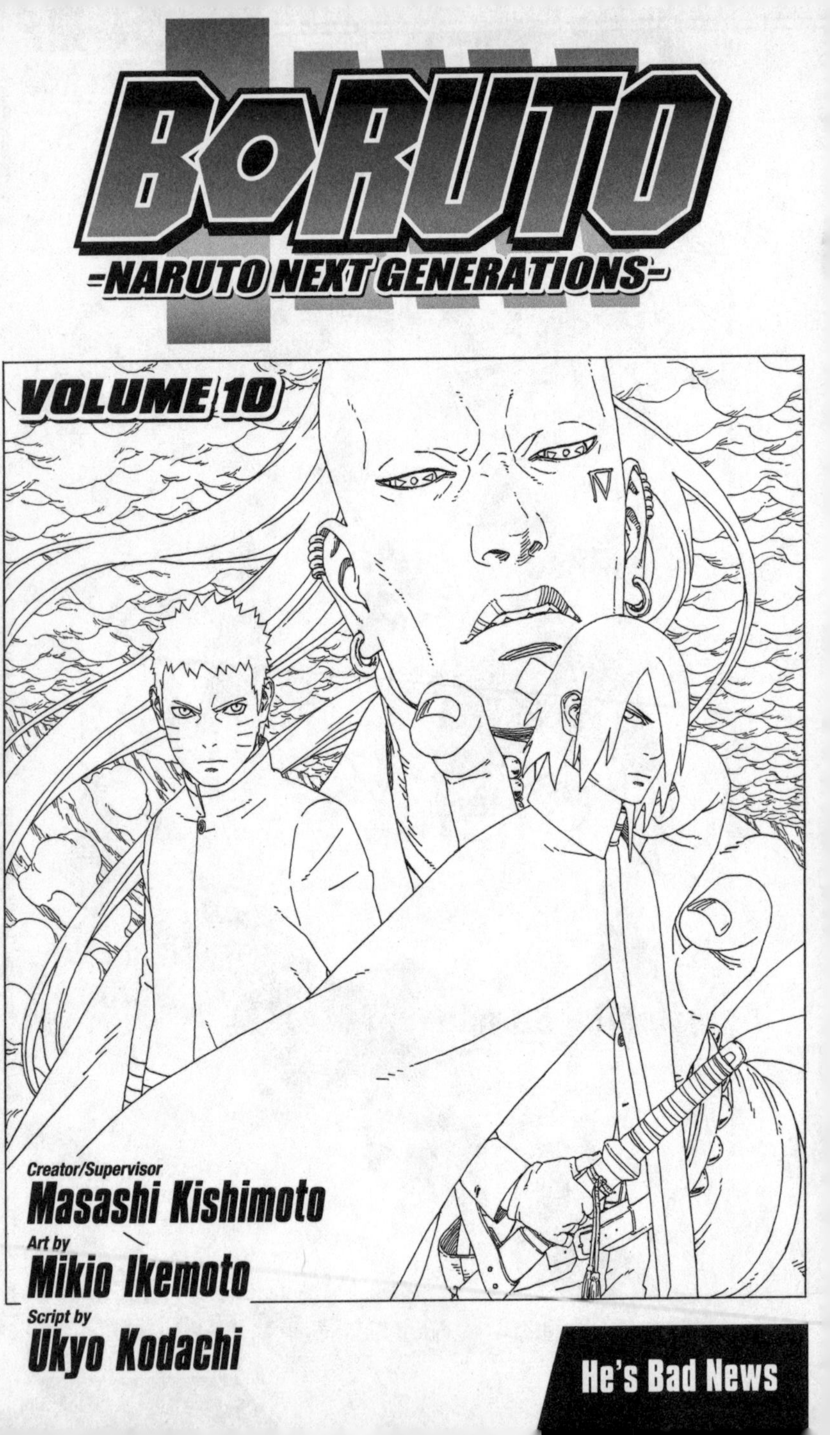

Creator/Supervisor
Masashi Kishimoto
Art by
Mikio Ikemoto
Script by
Ukyo Kodachi

He's Bad News

BORUTO -NARUTO NEXT GENERATIONS- CHARACTERS

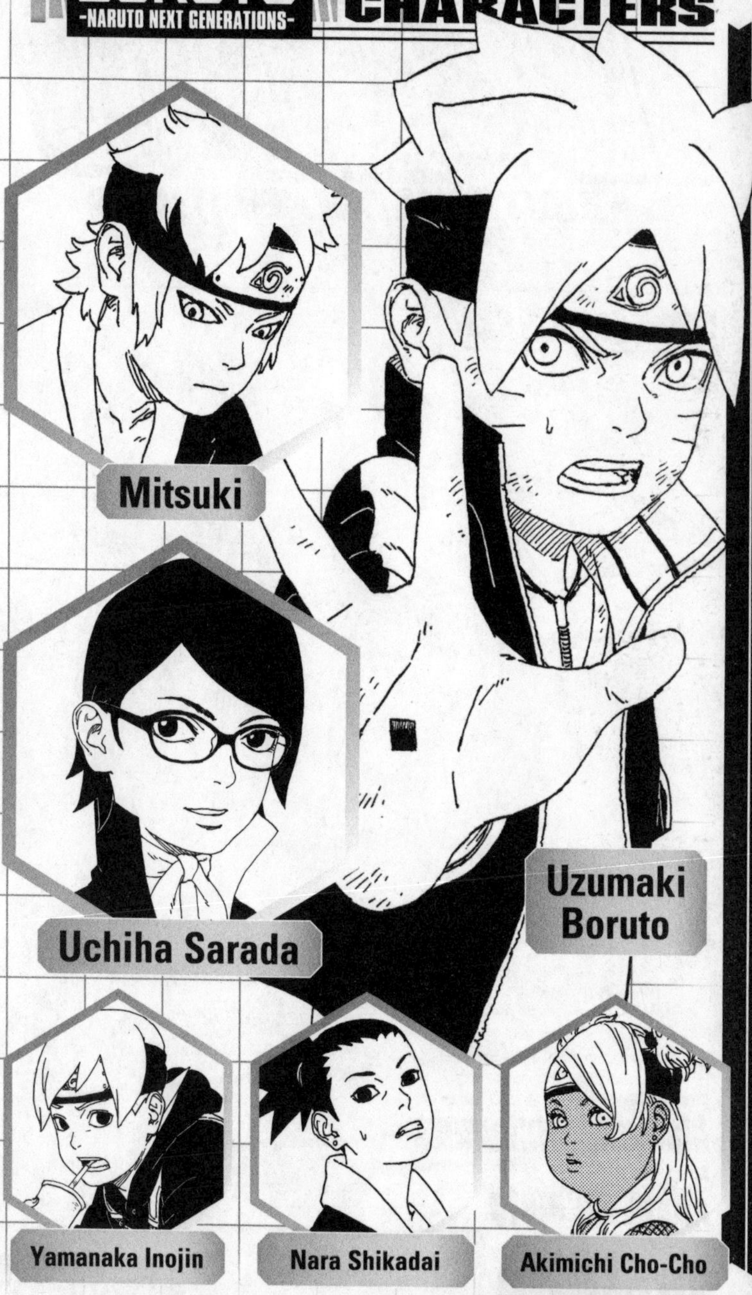
Mitsuki
Uzumaki Boruto
Uchiha Sarada
Yamanaka Inojin
Nara Shikadai
Akimichi Cho-Cho

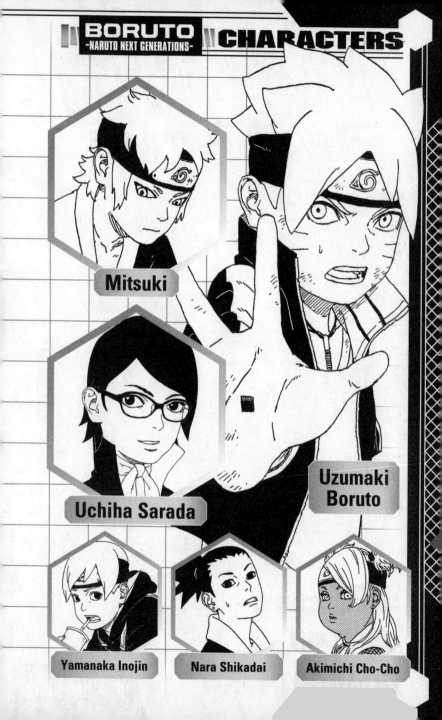

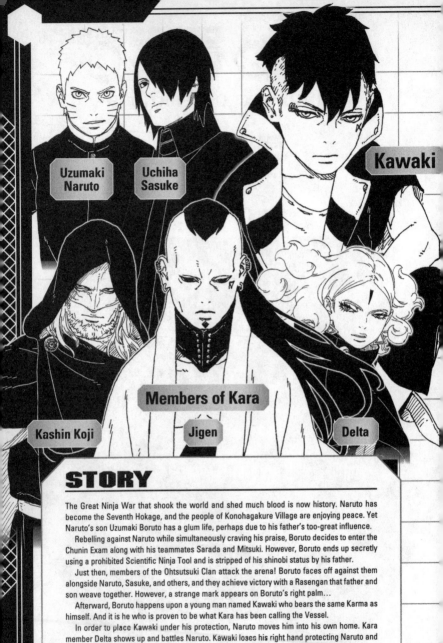

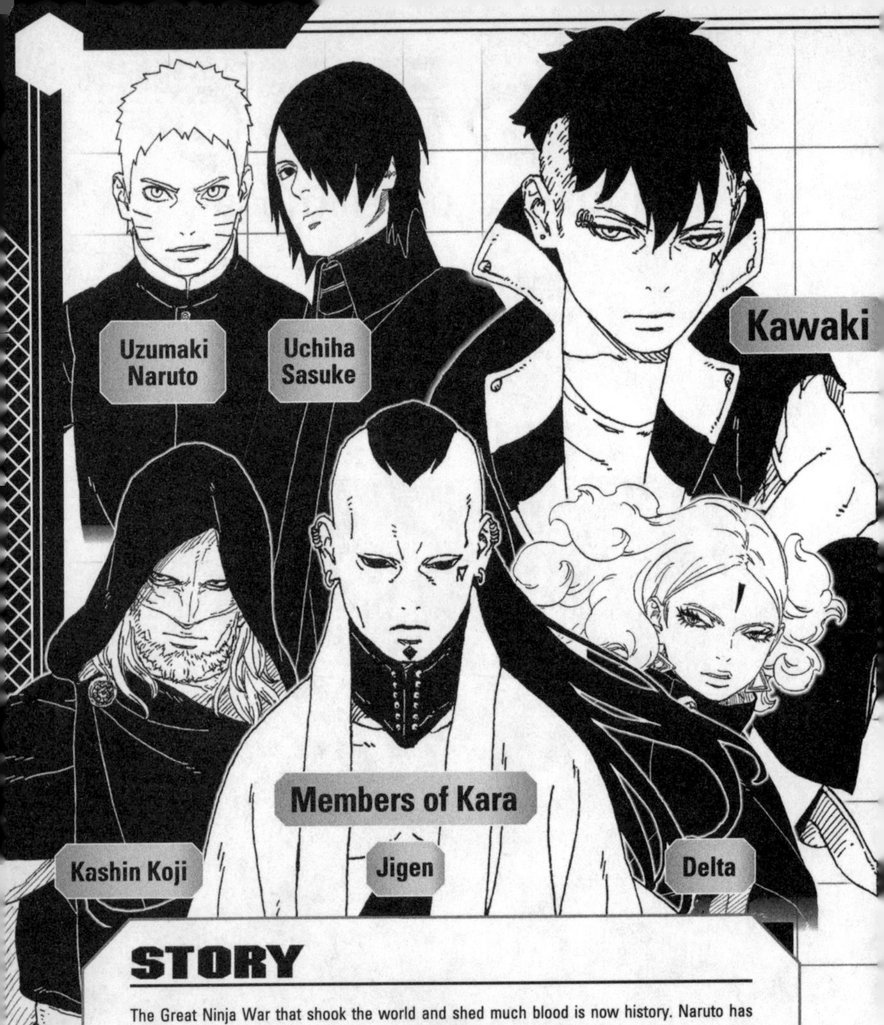
Kawaki
Uchiha Sasuke
Uzumaki Naruto
Members of Kara
Delta
Jigen
Kashin Koji

STORY

The Great Ninja War that shook the world and shed much blood is now history. Naruto has become the Seventh Hokage, and the people of Konohagakure Village are enjoying peace. Yet Naruto's son Uzumaki Boruto has a glum life, perhaps due to his father's too-great influence.

Rebelling against Naruto while simultaneously craving his praise, Boruto decides to enter the Chunin Exam along with his teammates Sarada and Mitsuki. However, Boruto ends up secretly using a prohibited Scientific Ninja Tool and is stripped of his shinobi status by his father.

Just then, members of the Ohtsutsuki Clan attack the arena! Boruto faces off against them alongside Naruto, Sasuke, and others, and they achieve victory with a Rasengan that father and son weave together. However, a strange mark appears on Boruto's right palm…

Afterward, Boruto happens upon a young man named Kawaki who bears the same Karma as himself. And it is he who is proven to be what Kara has been calling the Vessel.

In order to place Kawaki under his protection, Naruto moves him into his own home. Kara member Delta shows up and battles Naruto. Kawaki loses his right hand protecting Naruto and his daughter Himawari. However, he is given one of Naruto's prosthetic hands and starts feeling at ease with life in the Village…

B O R U T O

-NARUTO NEXT GENERATIONS-

VOLUME 10
HE'S BAD NEWS

CONTENTS

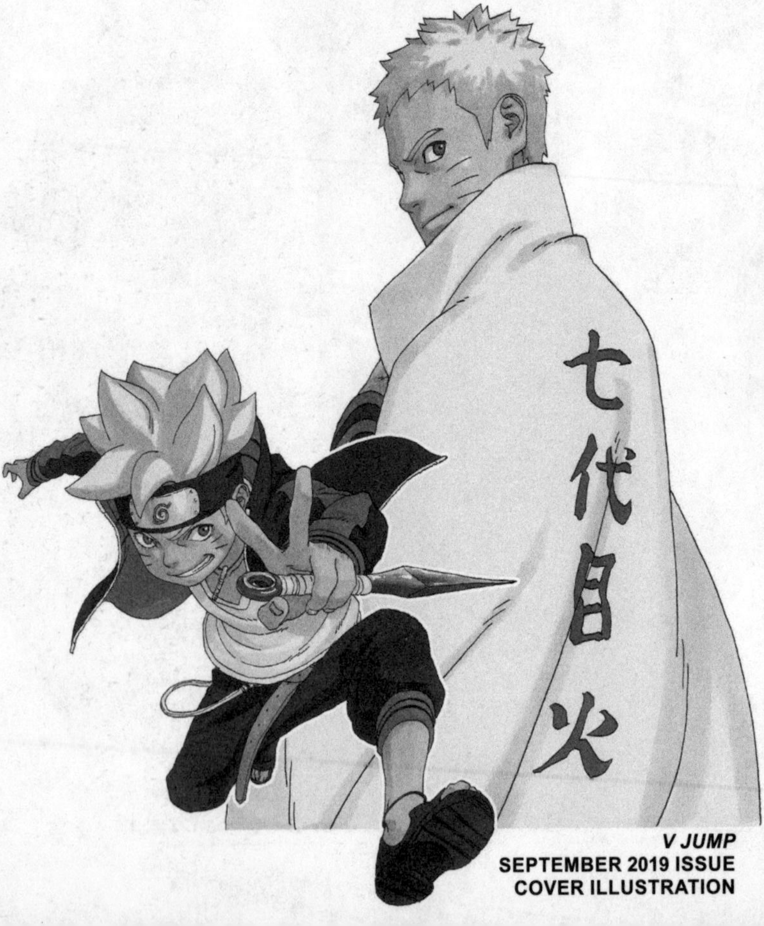
七代目火

V JUMP
SEPTEMBER 2019 ISSUE
COVER ILLUSTRATION

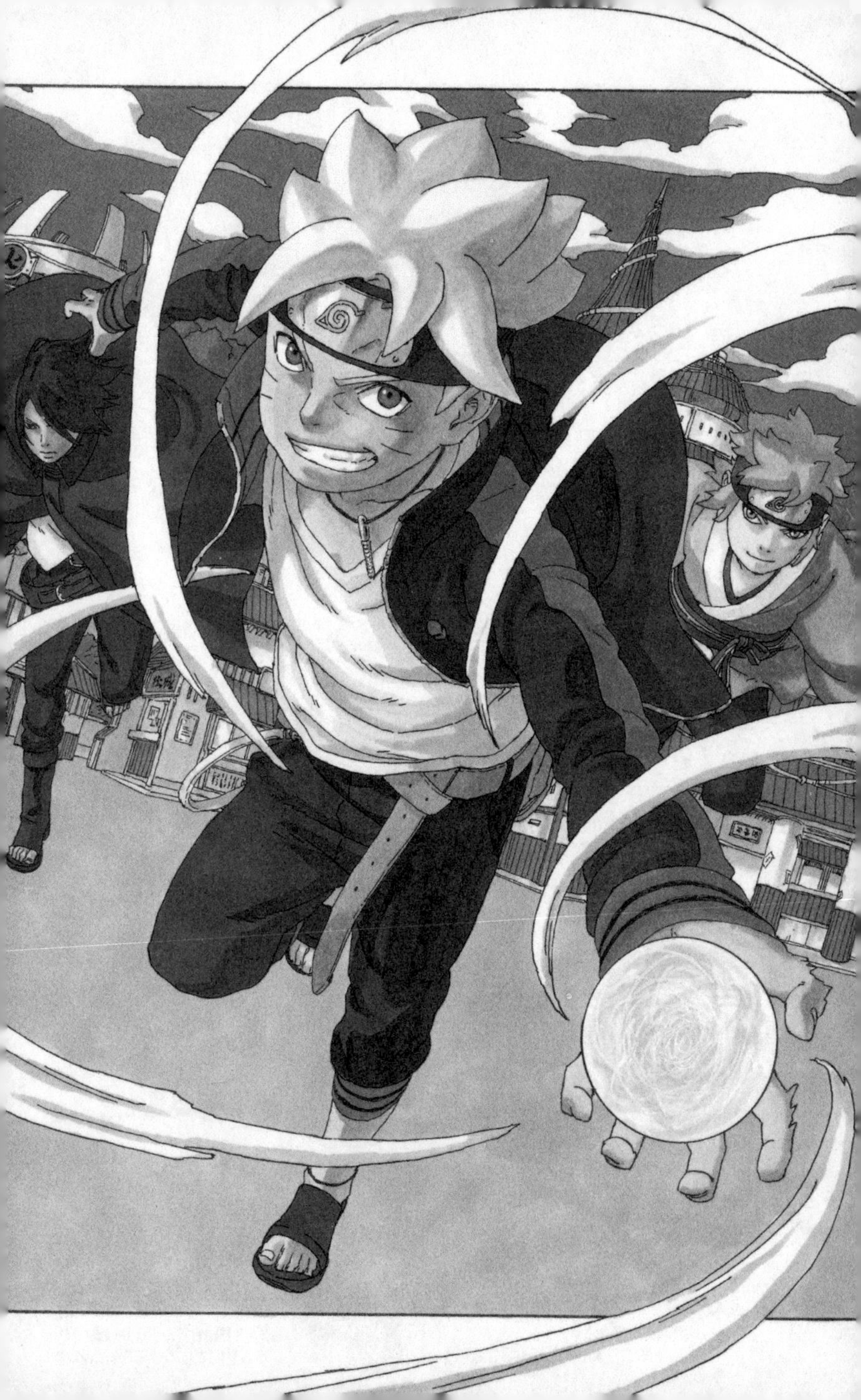

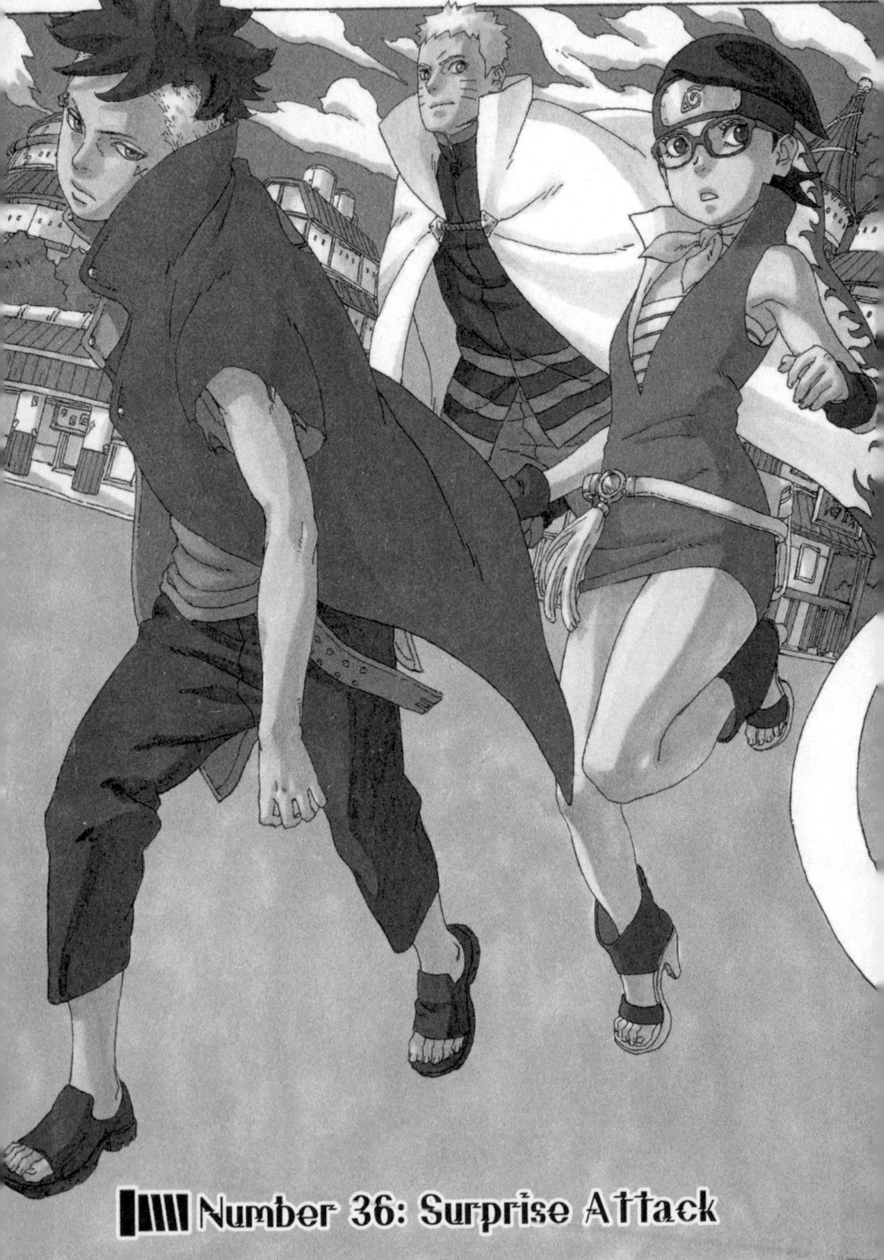
Number 36: Surprise Attack

BORUTO

-NARUTO NEXT GENERATIONS-

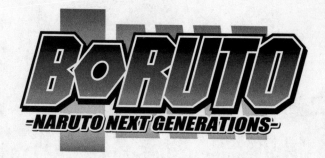

VWOOOOO O
忍
TAK TAK TAK TAK TAK TAK
FSH
ZSH
WHA ?!

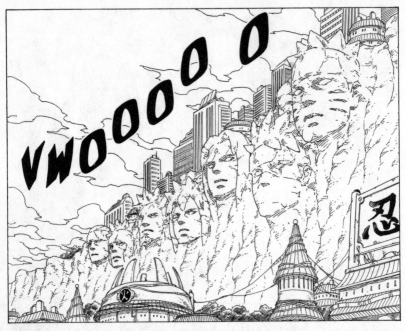

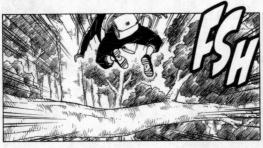

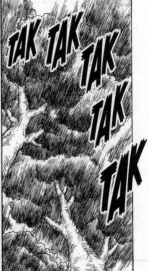

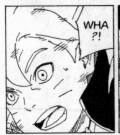

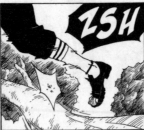

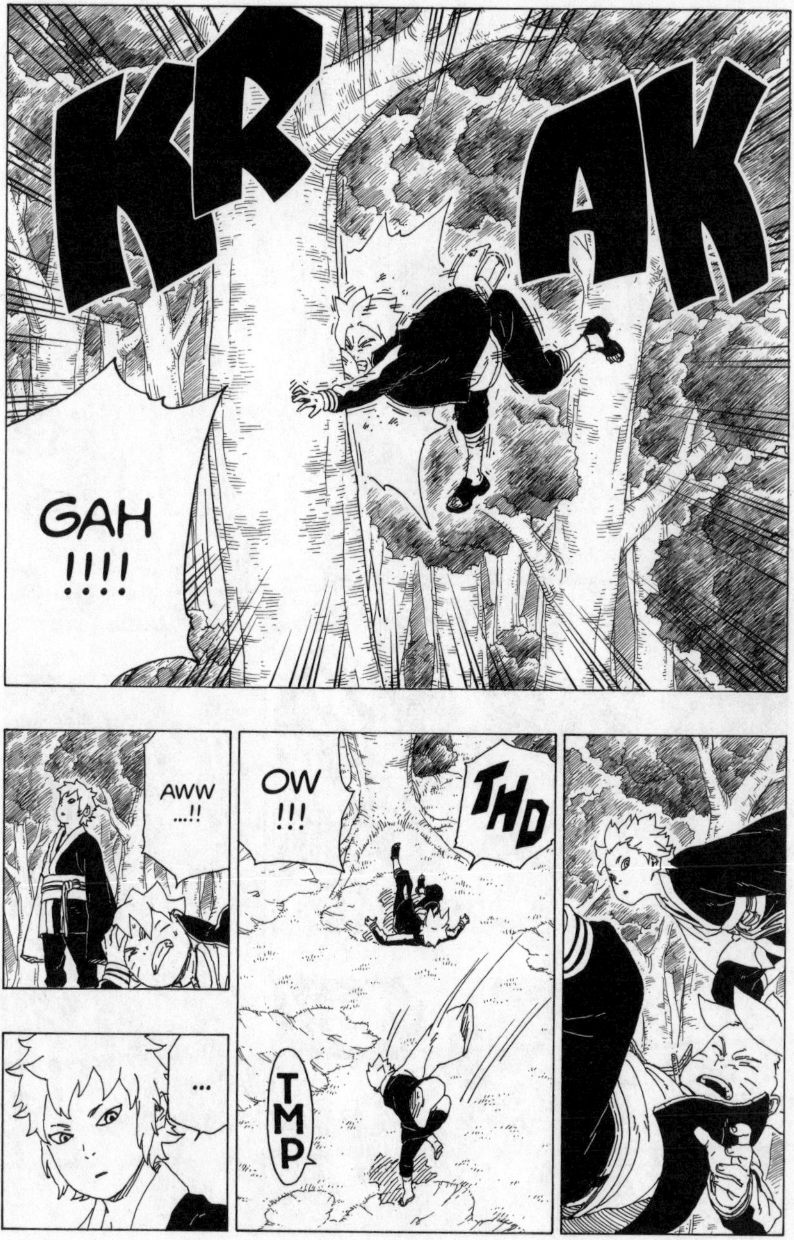
KRAK
GAH !!!!
THD
OW !!!
TMP
AWW ...!!
...

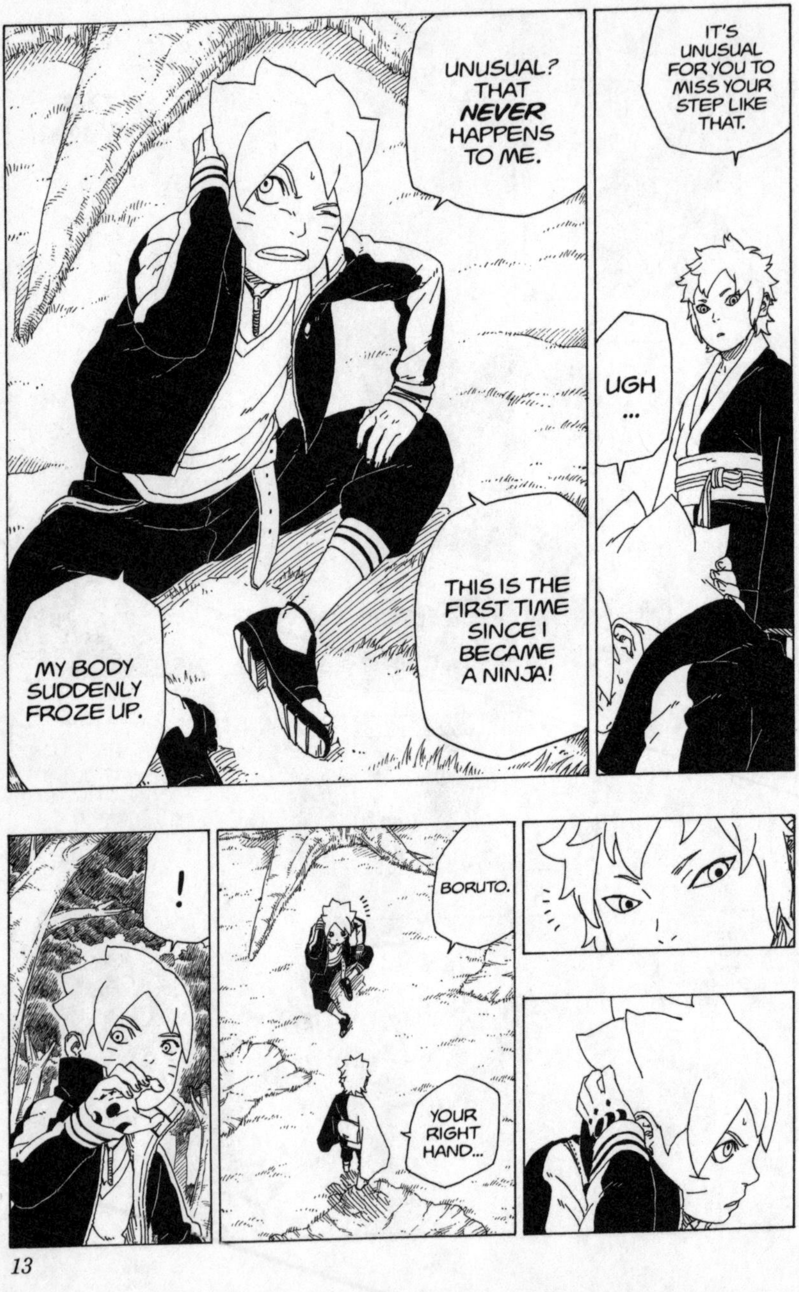
IT'S UNUSUAL FOR YOU TO MISS YOUR STEP LIKE THAT.
UGH ...
UNUSUAL? THAT NEVER HAPPENS TO ME.
THIS IS THE FIRST TIME SINCE I BECAME A NINJA!
MY BODY SUDDENLY FROZE UP.
BORUTO.
YOUR RIGHT HAND...
!

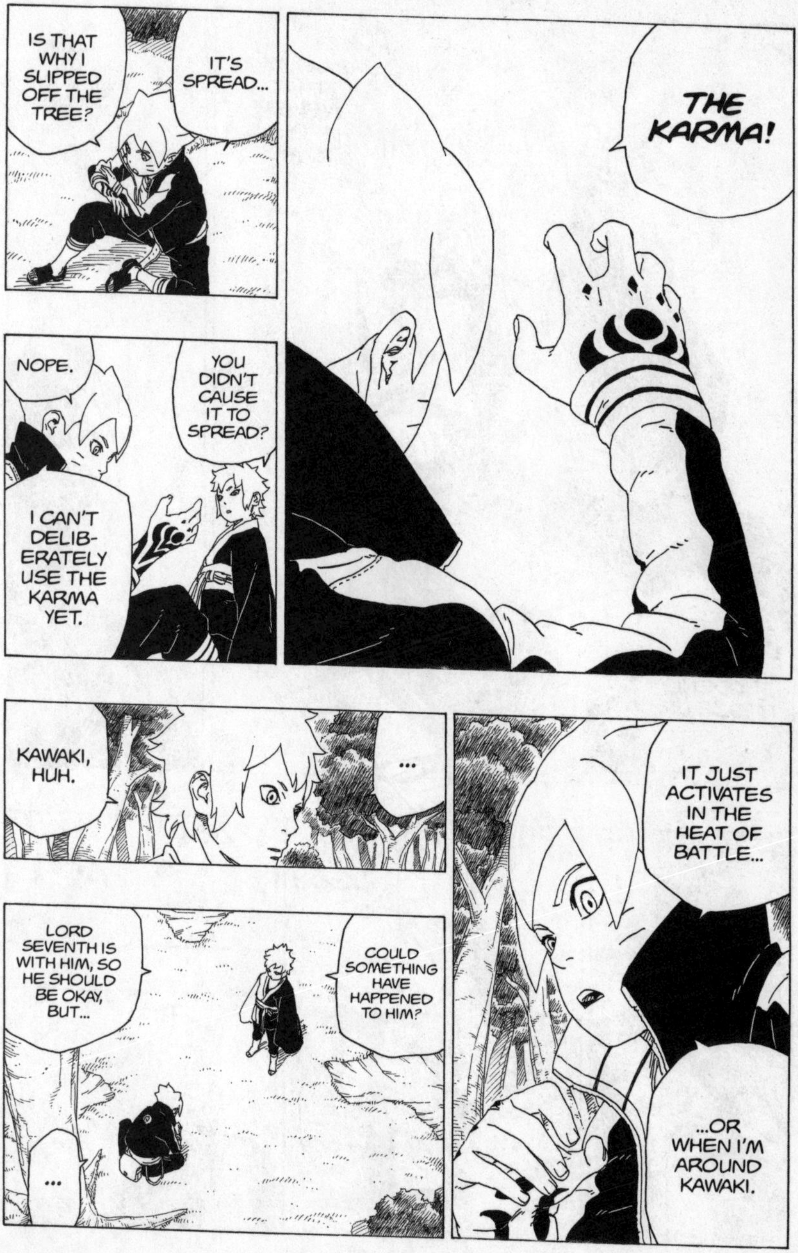
THE KARMA!
IT'S SPREAD...
IS THAT WHY I SLIPPED OFF THE TREE?
YOU DIDN'T CAUSE IT TO SPREAD?
NOPE.
I CAN'T DELIB-ERATELY USE THE KARMA YET.
IT JUST ACTIVATES IN THE HEAT OF BATTLE...
...OR WHEN I'M AROUND KAWAKI.
...
KAWAKI, HUH.
COULD SOMETHING HAVE HAPPENED TO HIM?
LORD SEVENTH IS WITH HIM, SO HE SHOULD BE OKAY, BUT...
...

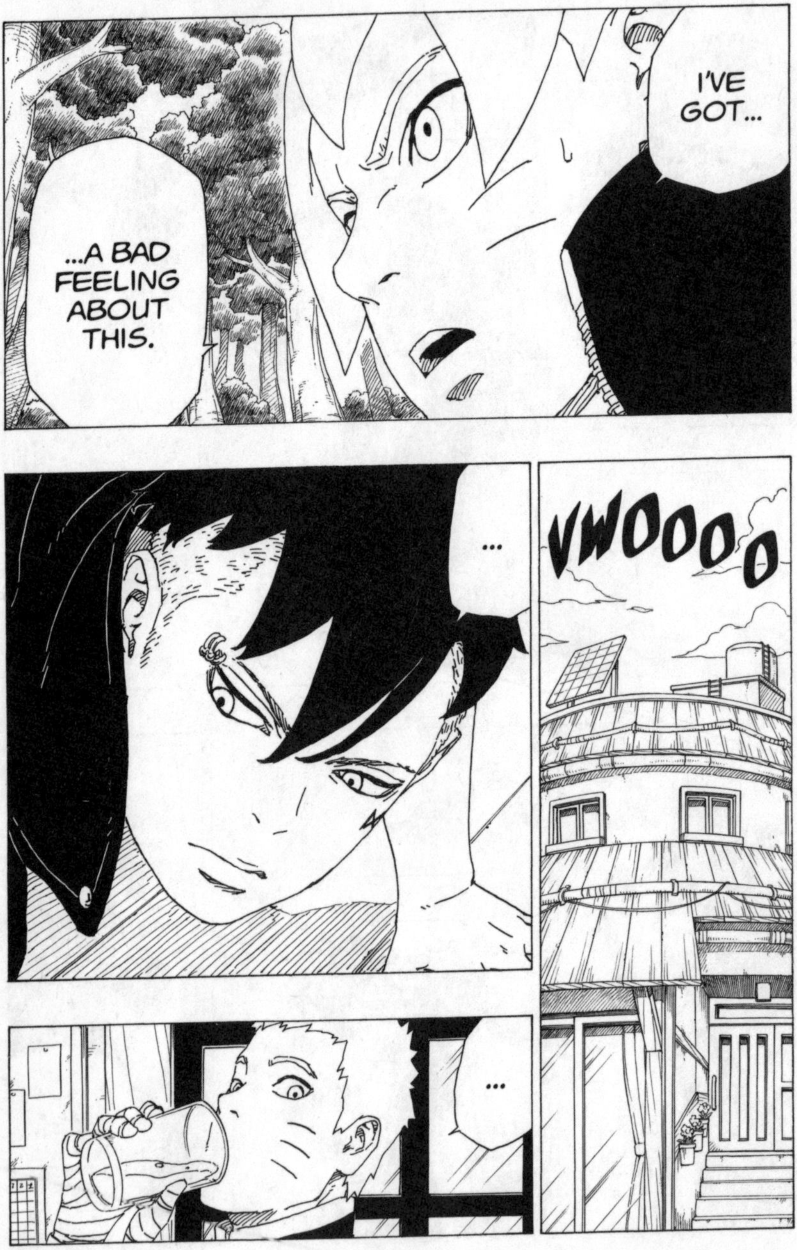
I'VE GOT...
...A BAD FEELING ABOUT THIS.
VWOOOO
...
...

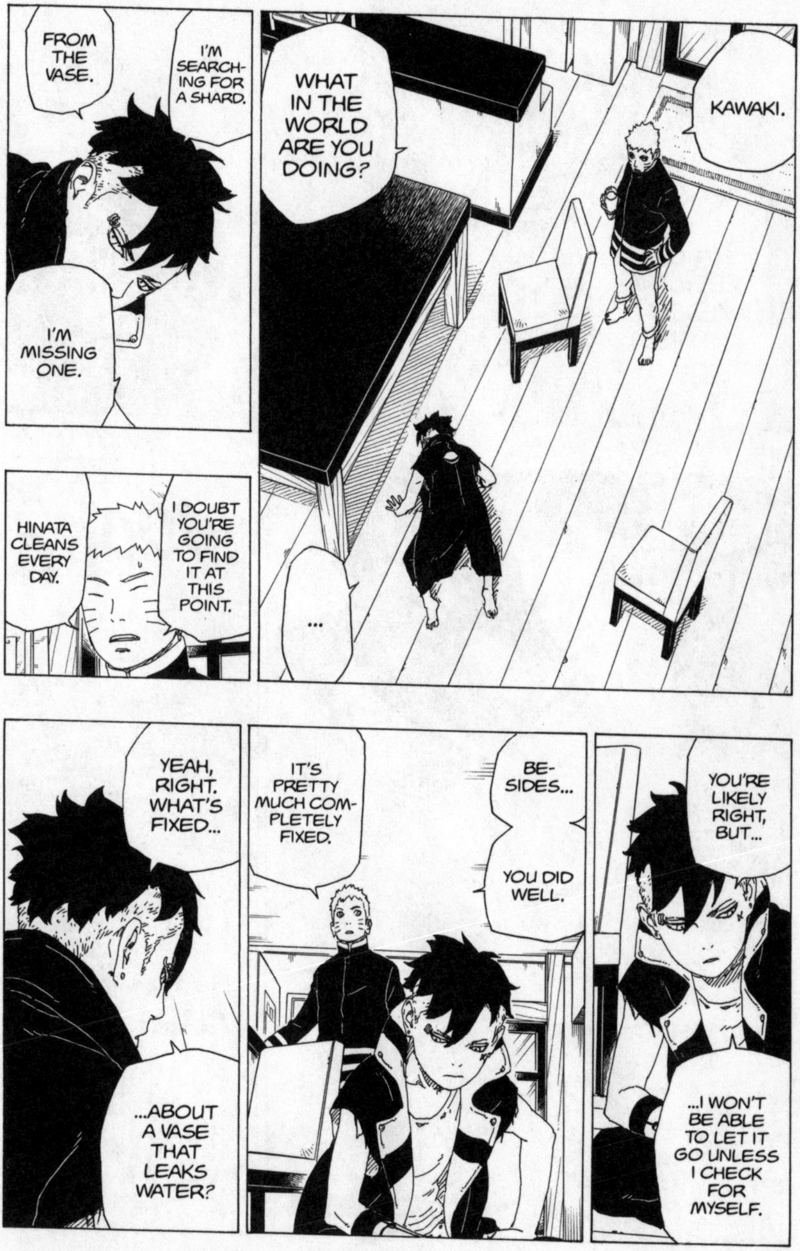
KAWAKI.
WHAT IN THE WORLD ARE YOU DOING?
...
I'M SEARCH-ING FOR A SHARD.
FROM THE VASE.
I'M MISSING ONE.
I DOUBT YOU'RE GOING TO FIND IT AT THIS POINT.
HINATA CLEANS EVERY DAY.
YOU'RE LIKELY RIGHT, BUT...
...I WON'T BE ABLE TO LET IT GO UNLESS I CHECK FOR MYSELF.
IT'S PRETTY MUCH COM-PLETELY FIXED.
BE-SIDES...
YOU DID WELL.
YEAH, RIGHT. WHAT'S FIXED...
...ABOUT A VASE THAT LEAKS WATER?

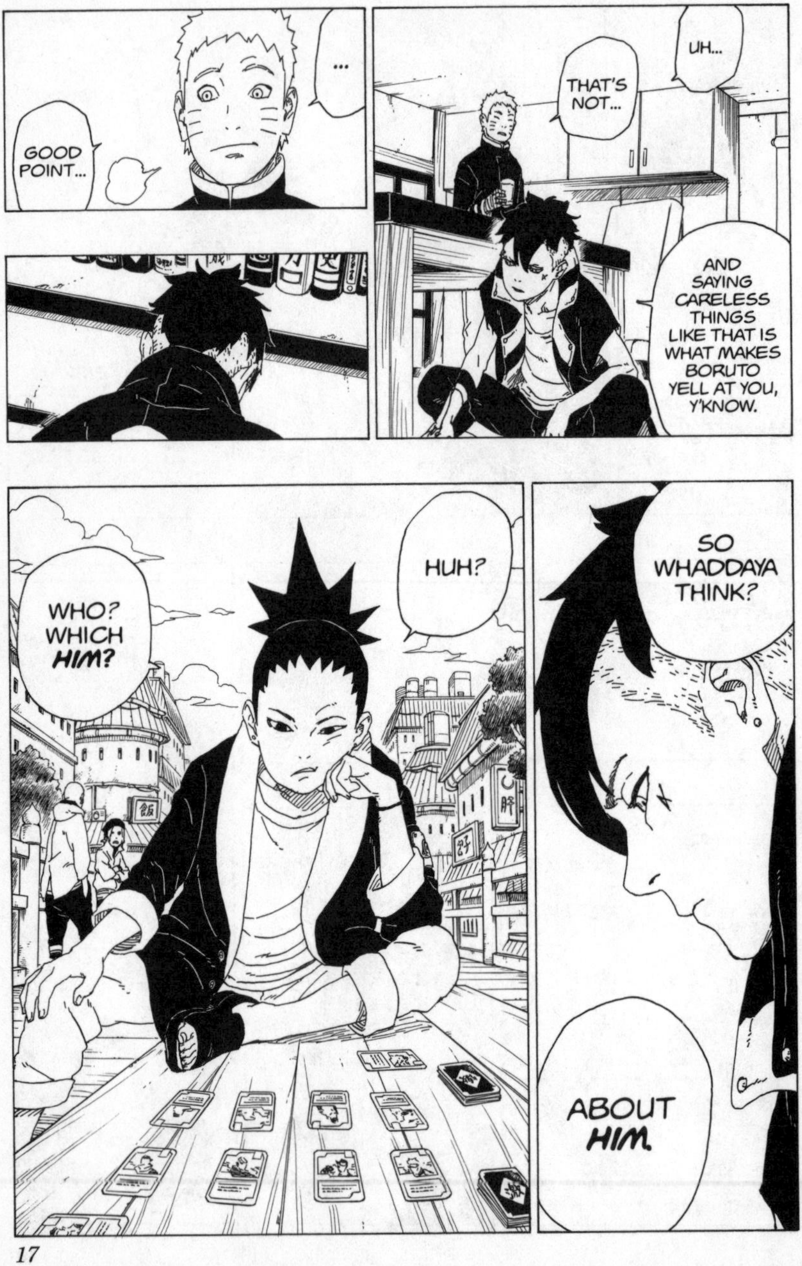
UH...
THAT'S NOT...
AND SAYING CARELESS THINGS LIKE THAT IS WHAT MAKES BORUTO YELL AT YOU, Y'KNOW.
...
GOOD POINT...
SO WHADDAYA THINK?
ABOUT *HIM.*
HUH?
WHO? WHICH *HIM?*

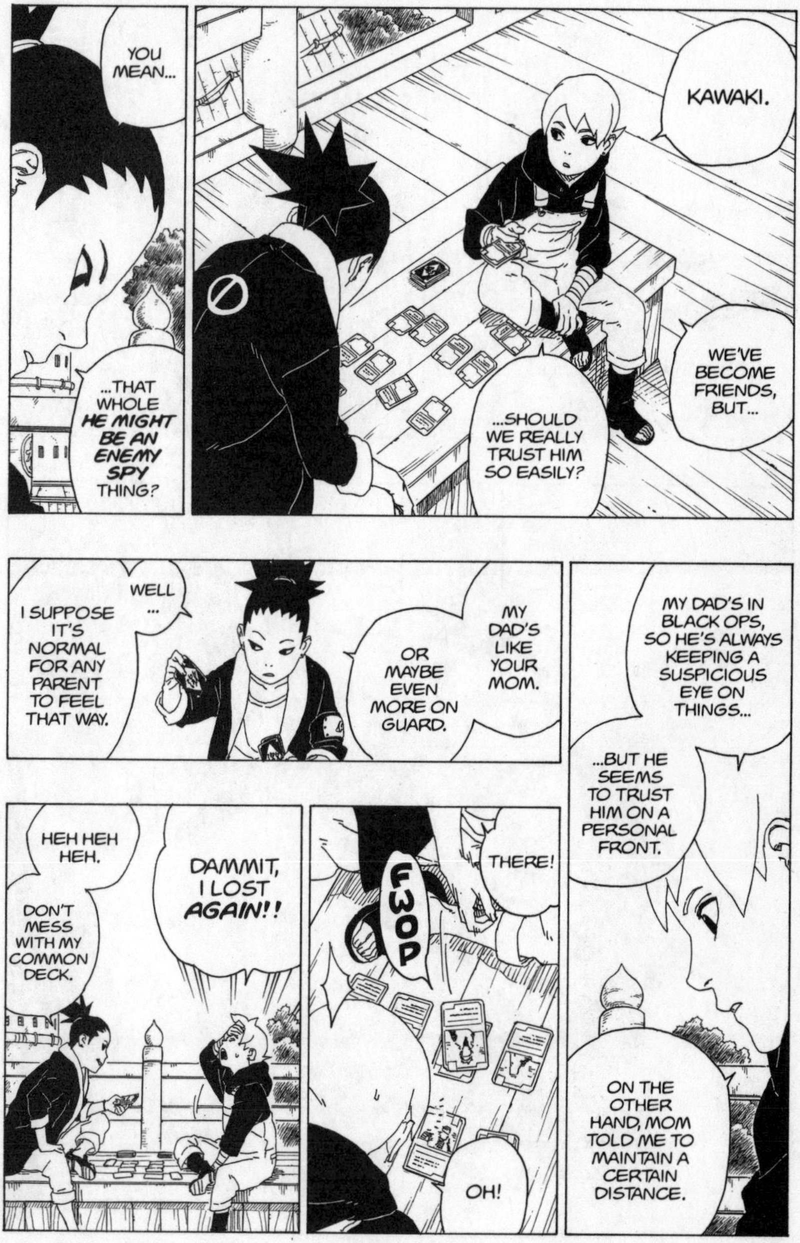
KAWAKI.
WE'VE BECOME FRIENDS, BUT...
...SHOULD WE REALLY TRUST HIM SO EASILY?
YOU MEAN...
...THAT WHOLE *HE MIGHT BE AN ENEMY SPY* THING?
MY DAD'S IN BLACK OPS, SO HE'S ALWAYS KEEPING A SUSPICIOUS EYE ON THINGS...
...BUT HE SEEMS TO TRUST HIM ON A PERSONAL FRONT.
ON THE OTHER HAND, MOM TOLD ME TO MAINTAIN A CERTAIN DISTANCE.
MY DAD'S LIKE YOUR MOM.
OR MAYBE EVEN MORE ON GUARD.
WELL...
I SUPPOSE IT'S NORMAL FOR ANY PARENT TO FEEL THAT WAY.
THERE!
FWOP
OH!
DAMMIT, I LOST *AGAIN*!!
HEH HEH HEH.
DON'T MESS WITH MY COMMON DECK.

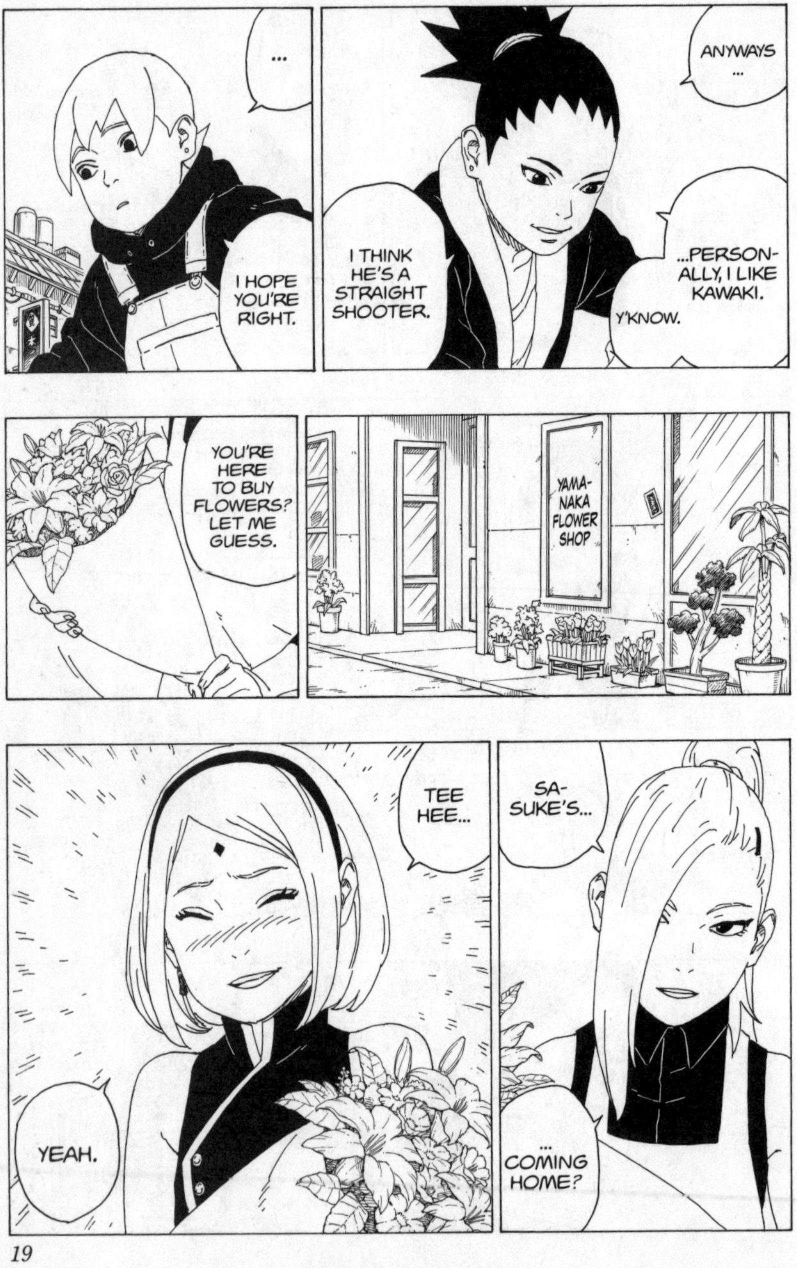
ANYWAYS ...
...PERSONALLY, I LIKE KAWAKI.
Y'KNOW.
I THINK HE'S A STRAIGHT SHOOTER.
...
I HOPE YOU'RE RIGHT.
YAMANAKA FLOWER SHOP
YOU'RE HERE TO BUY FLOWERS? LET ME GUESS.
SASUKE'S...
... COMING HOME?
TEE HEE...
YEAH.

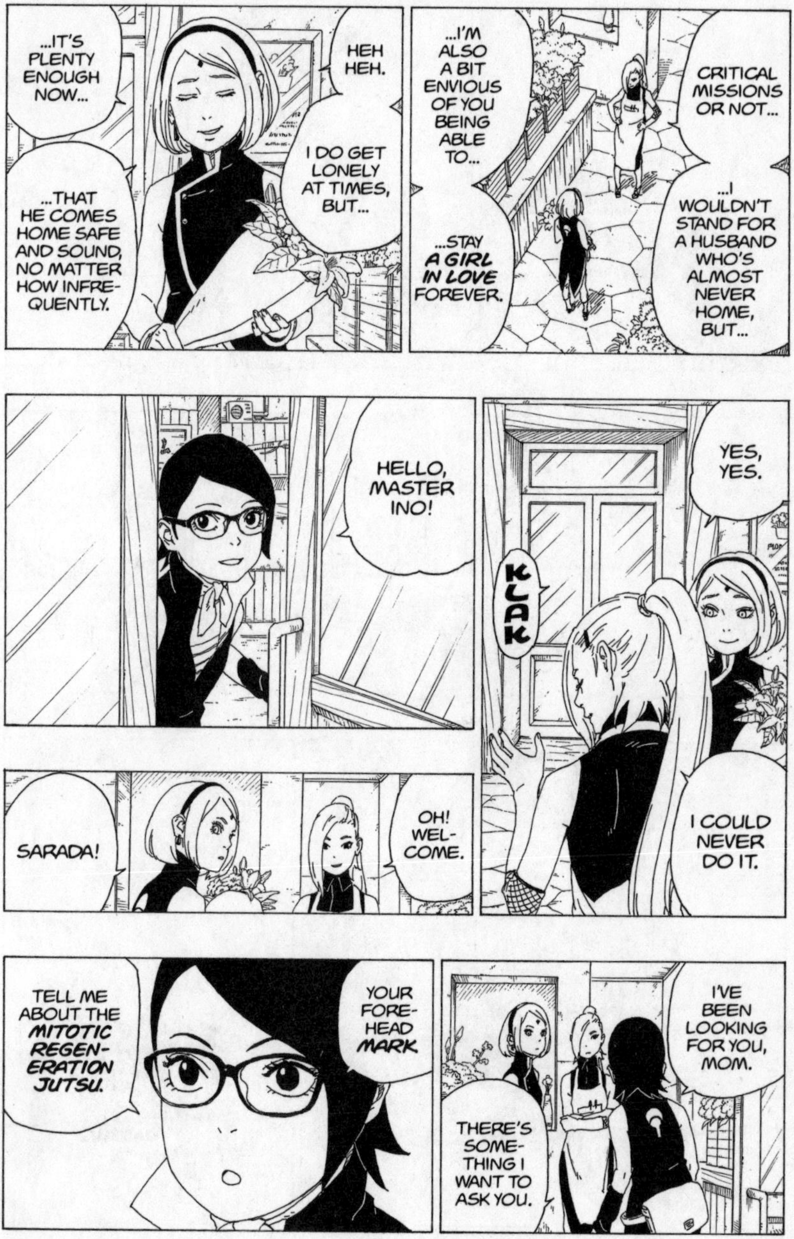
CRITICAL MISSIONS OR NOT...
...I WOULDN'T STAND FOR A HUSBAND WHO'S ALMOST NEVER HOME, BUT...
...I'M ALSO A BIT ENVIOUS OF YOU BEING ABLE TO...
...STAY *A GIRL IN LOVE* FOREVER.
HEH HEH.
I DO GET LONELY AT TIMES, BUT...
...IT'S PLENTY ENOUGH NOW...
...THAT HE COMES HOME SAFE AND SOUND, NO MATTER HOW INFREQUENTLY.
YES, YES.
I COULD NEVER DO IT.
KLAK
HELLO, MASTER INO!
OH! WEL-COME.
SARADA!
I'VE BEEN LOOKING FOR YOU, MOM.
THERE'S SOME-THING I WANT TO ASK YOU.
YOUR FORE-HEAD *MARK*
TELL ME ABOUT THE *MITOTIC REGEN-ERATION JUTSU.*

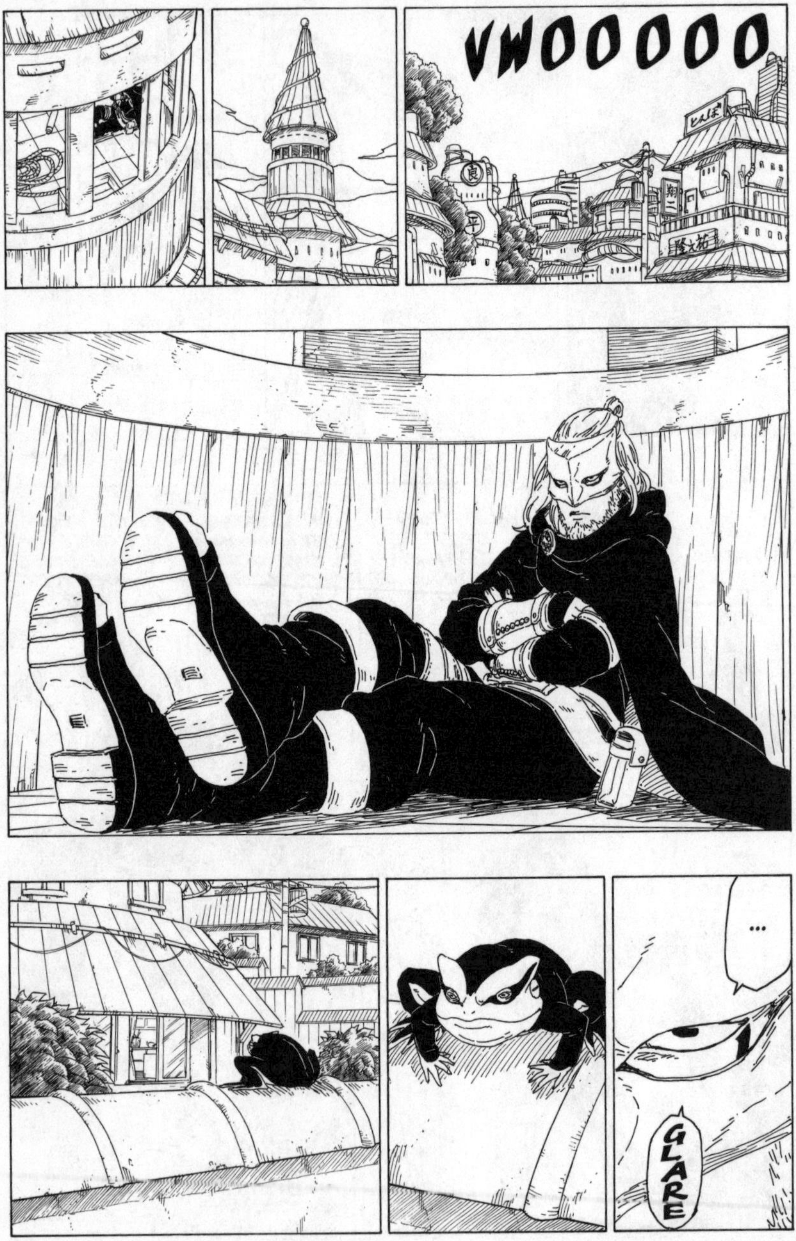
VWOOOOO
...
GLARE

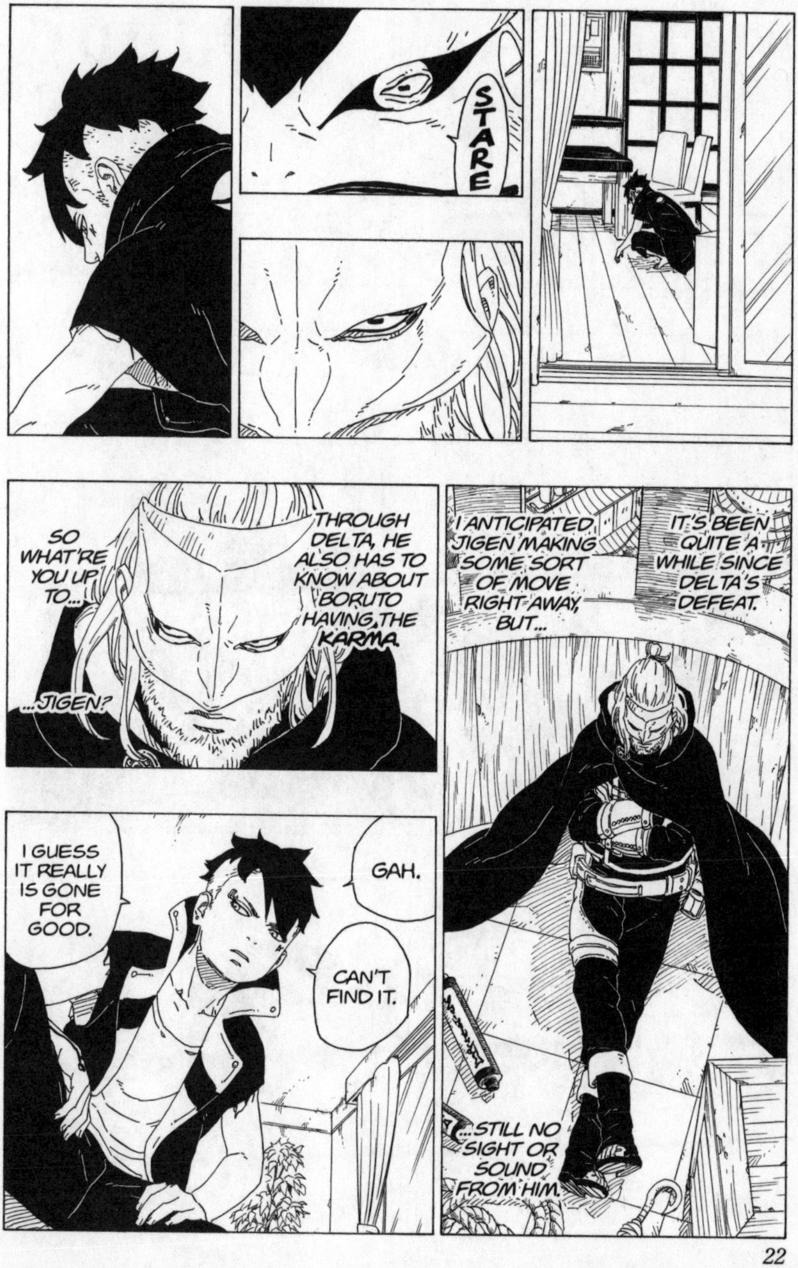
STARE
IT'S BEEN QUITE A WHILE SINCE DELTA'S DEFEAT.
I ANTICIPATED JIGEN MAKING SOME SORT OF MOVE RIGHT AWAY, BUT...
...STILL NO SIGHT OR SOUND FROM HIM.
THROUGH DELTA, HE ALSO HAS TO KNOW ABOUT BORUTO HAVING THE KARMA.
SO WHAT'RE YOU UP TO...
...JIGEN?
GAH.
CAN'T FIND IT.
I GUESS IT REALLY IS GONE FOR GOOD.

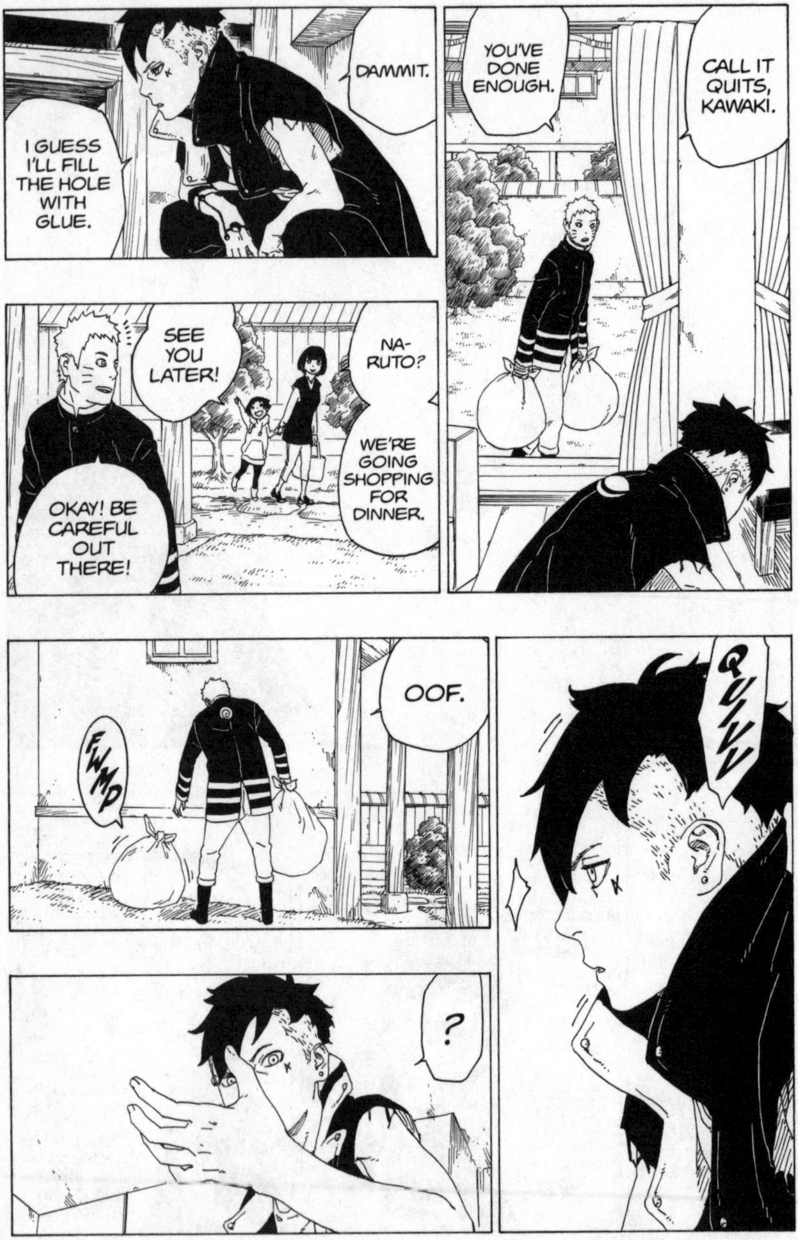
CALL IT QUITS, KAWAKI.
YOU'VE DONE ENOUGH.
DAMMIT.
I GUESS I'LL FILL THE HOLE WITH GLUE.
NA- RUTO?
WE'RE GOING SHOPPING FOR DINNER.
SEE YOU LATER!
OKAY! BE CAREFUL OUT THERE!
QUIVV
OOF.
FWMP
?

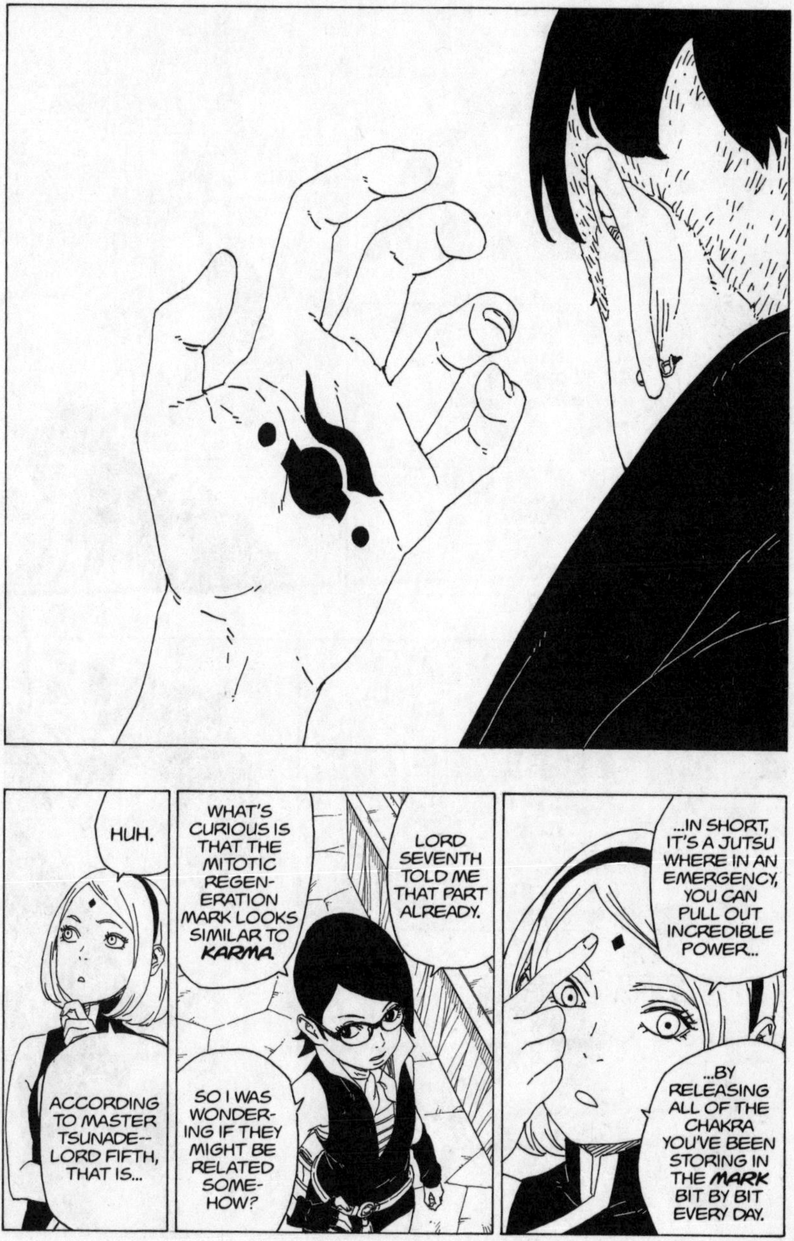
...IN SHORT, IT'S A JUTSU WHERE IN AN EMERGENCY, YOU CAN PULL OUT INCREDIBLE POWER...
...BY RELEASING ALL OF THE CHAKRA YOU'VE BEEN STORING IN THE MARK BIT BY BIT EVERY DAY.
LORD SEVENTH TOLD ME THAT PART ALREADY.
WHAT'S CURIOUS IS THAT THE MITOTIC REGENERATION MARK LOOKS SIMILAR TO KARMA.
SO I WAS WONDERING IF THEY MIGHT BE RELATED SOMEHOW?
HUH.
ACCORDING TO MASTER TSUNADE--LORD FIFTH, THAT IS...

...IT'S A JUTSU THAT'S EXISTED FOR A REALLY LONG TIME. FROM THE AGE OF THE SAGE OF SIX PATHS.
...
THE SAGE OF SIX PATHS?
OH, THAT'S RIGHT!
I HAVE TO GO GROCERY SHOPPING AFTER THIS, SO...
...DO YOU MIND TAKING THESE FLOWERS HOME WITH YOU?
FLOWERS? YOU MEAN...
...DAD'S COMING HOME?!
HEE!
GTUNK

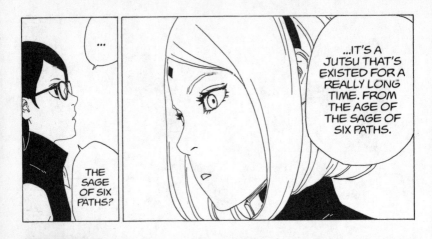

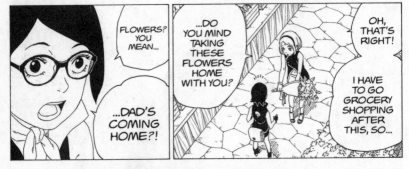

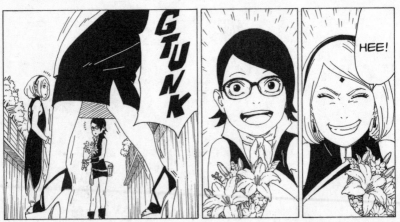

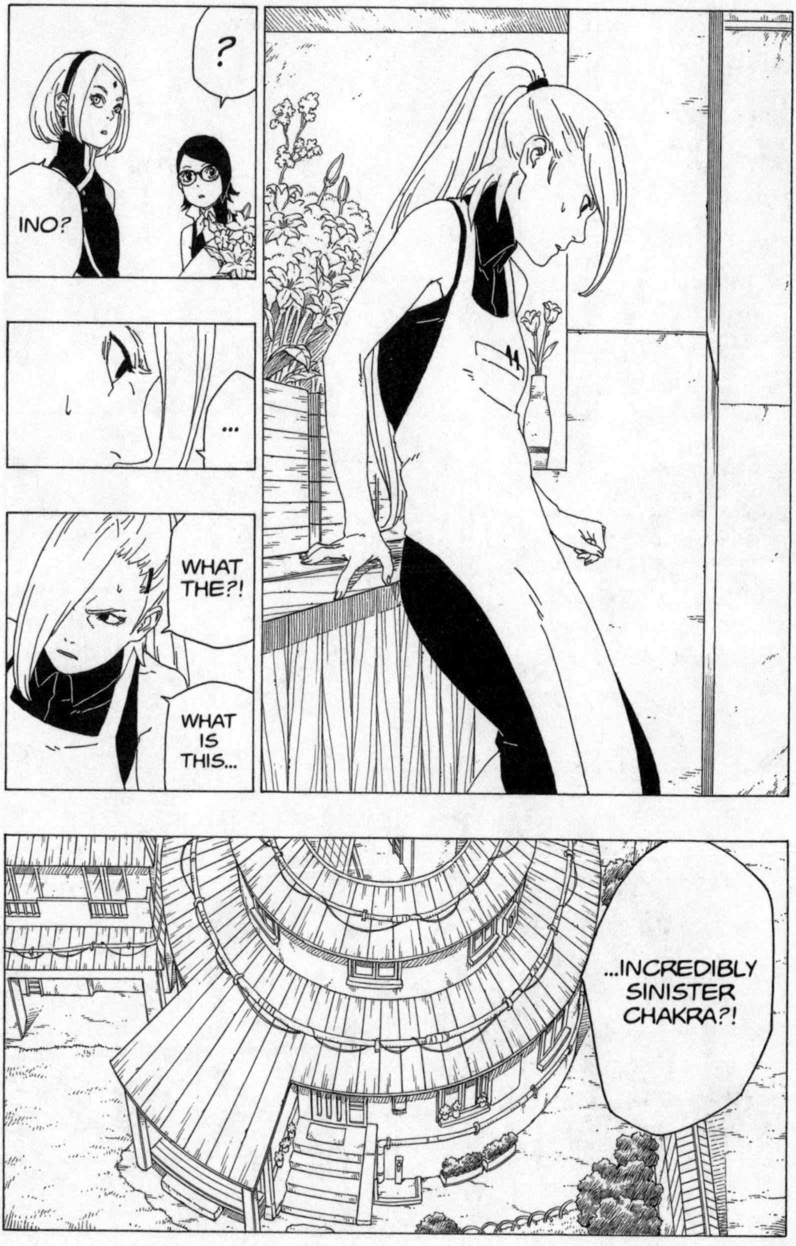
?
INO?
...
WHAT THE?!
WHAT IS THIS...
...INCREDIBLY SINISTER CHAKRA?!

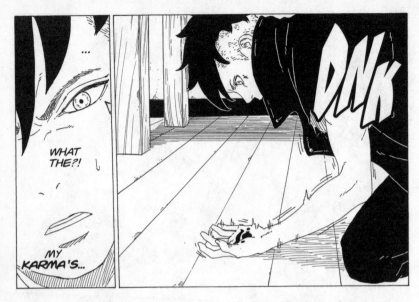

...

WHAT THE?!

MY KARMA'S...

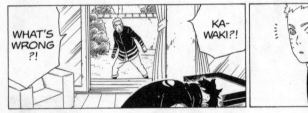

WHAT'S WRONG ?!

KA-WAKI?!

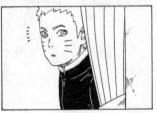

!!

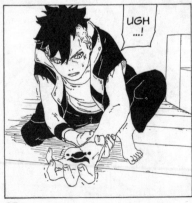

UGH ...!

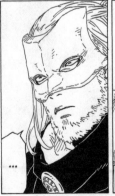

...

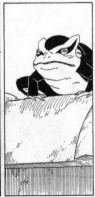

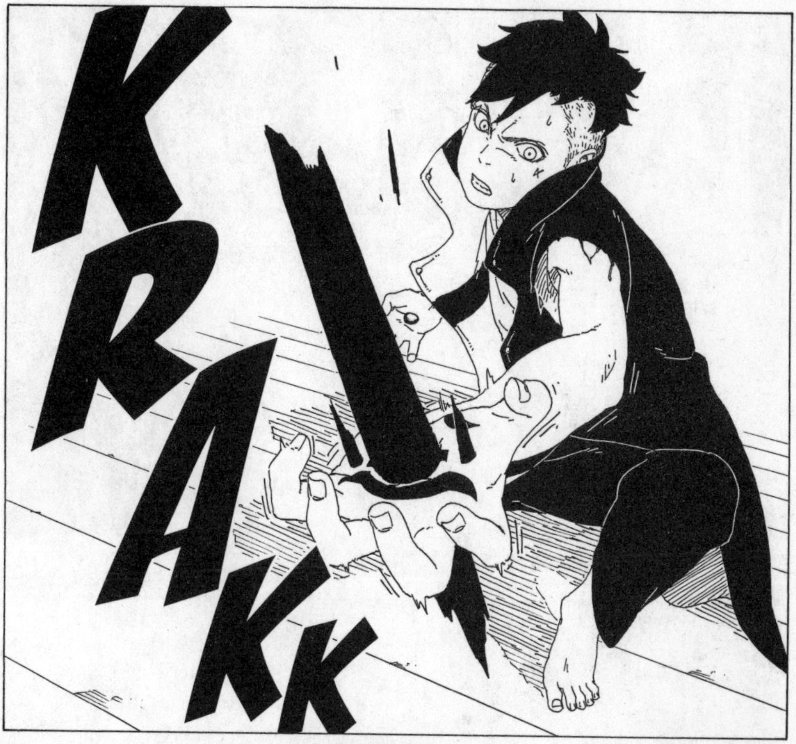
KRAKK

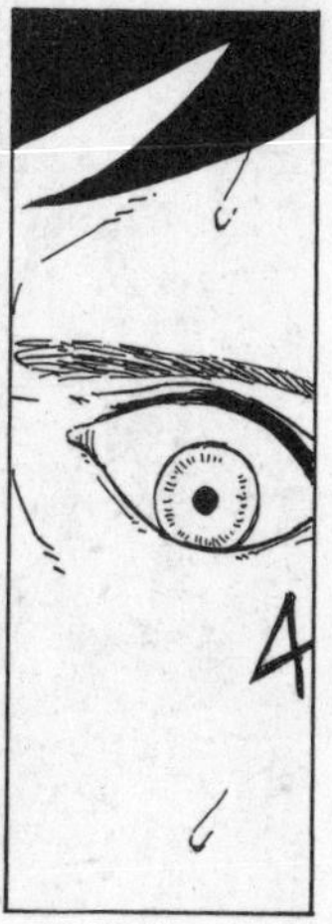

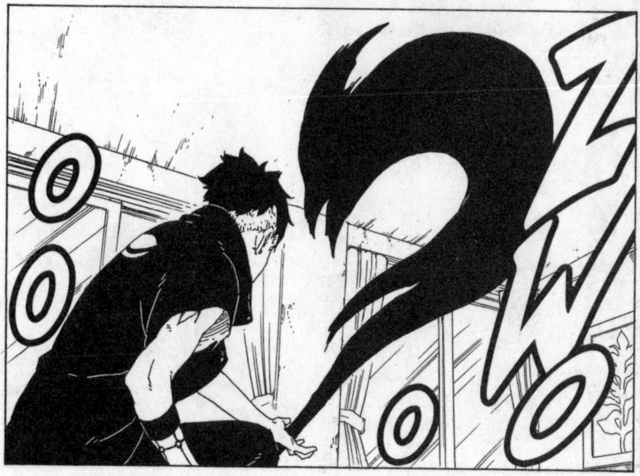
ZWOOOOO

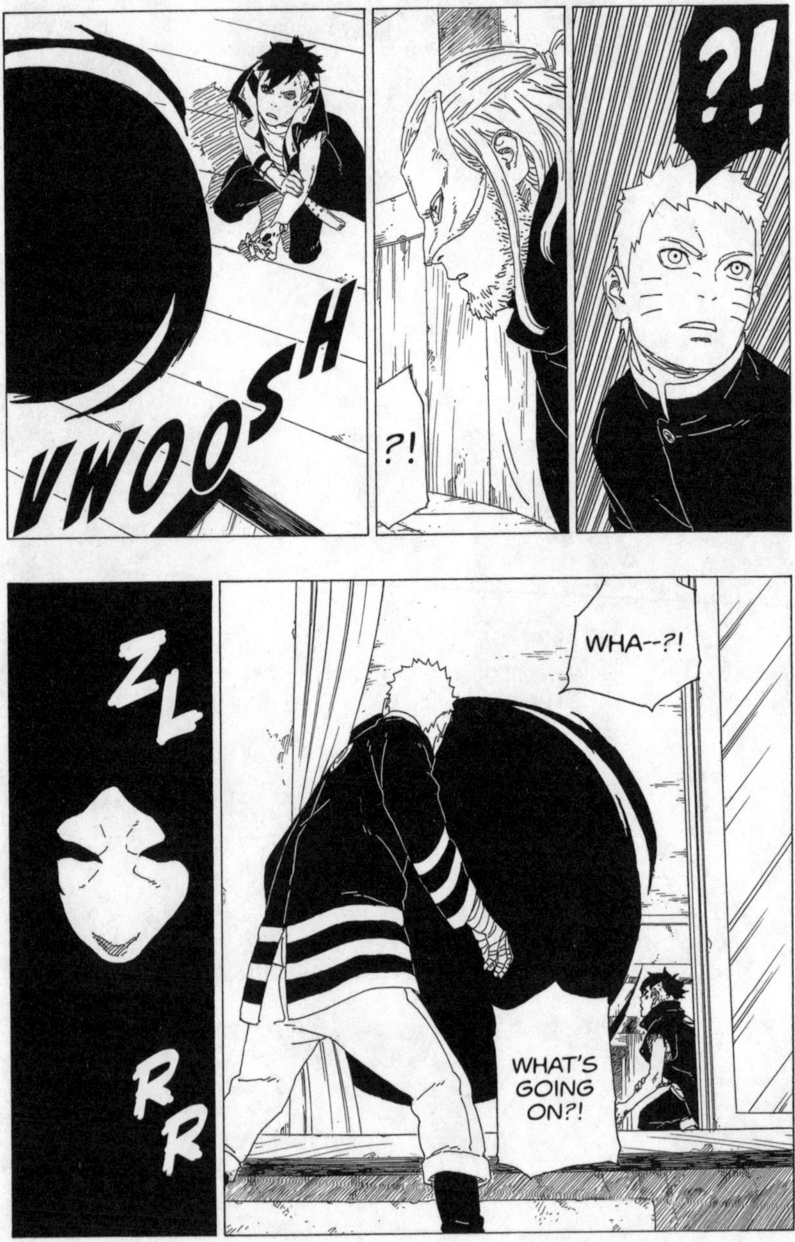
?!
?!
VWOOSH
WHA--?!
WHAT'S GOING ON?!
ZZRR

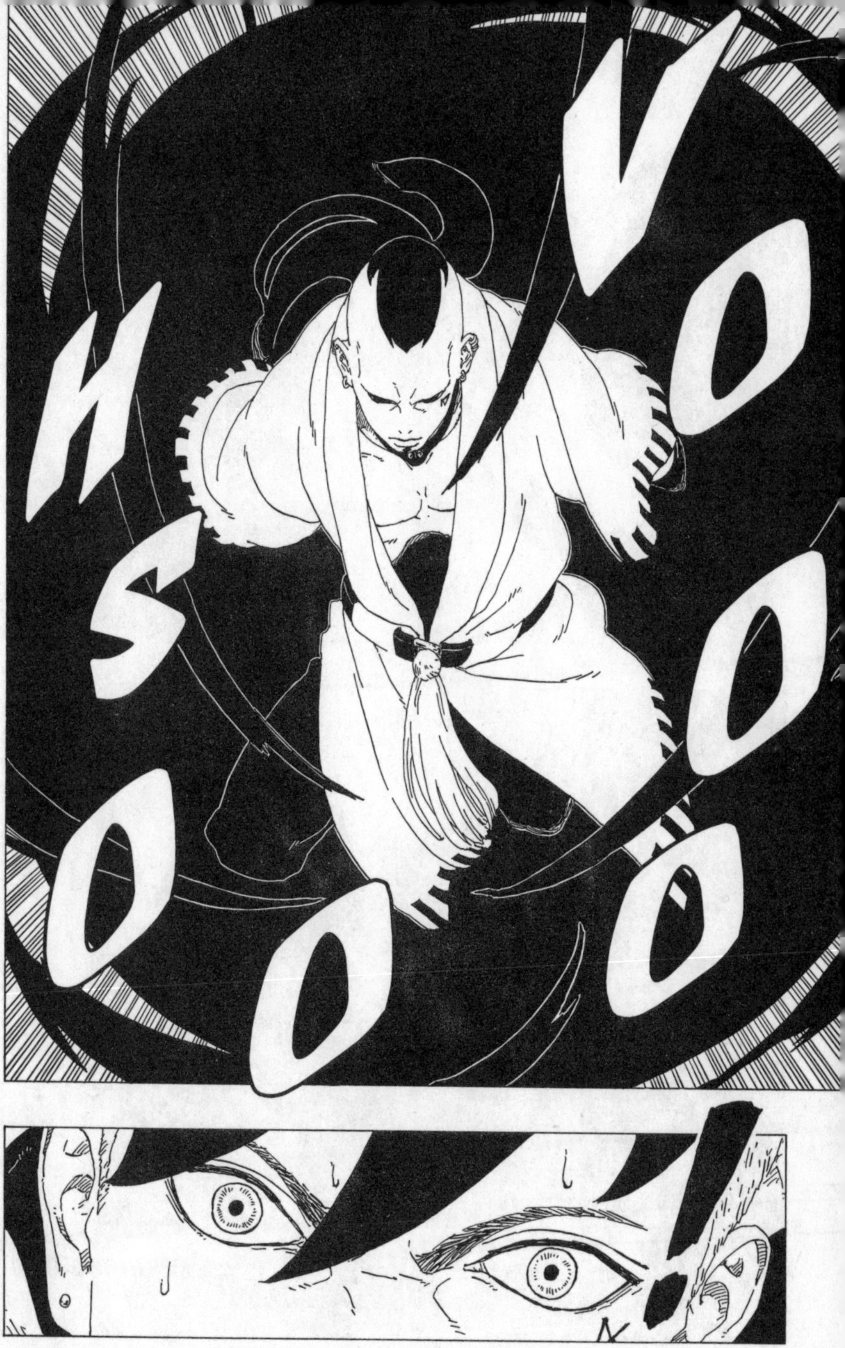
VOOOOOSH

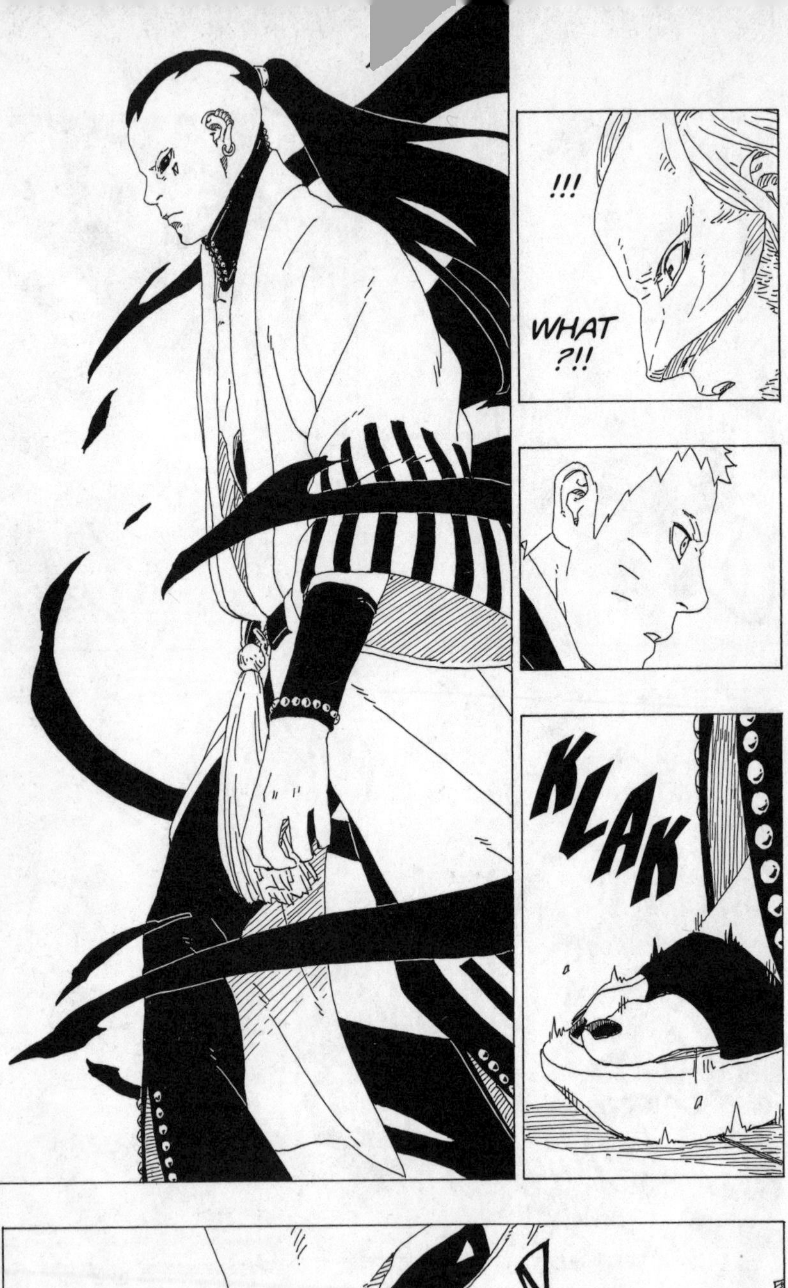
!!!
WHAT ?!!
KLAK

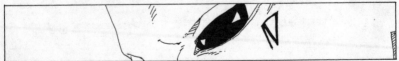

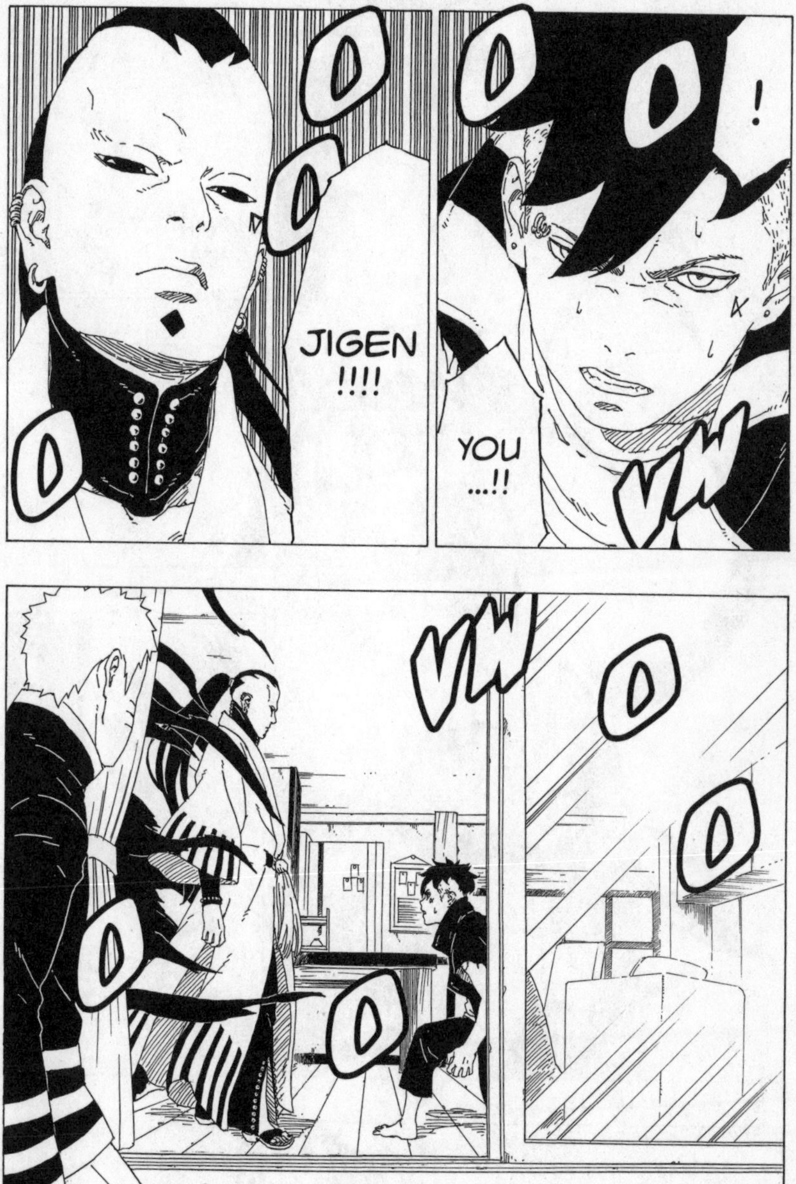
!
YOU ...!!
JIGEN !!!!

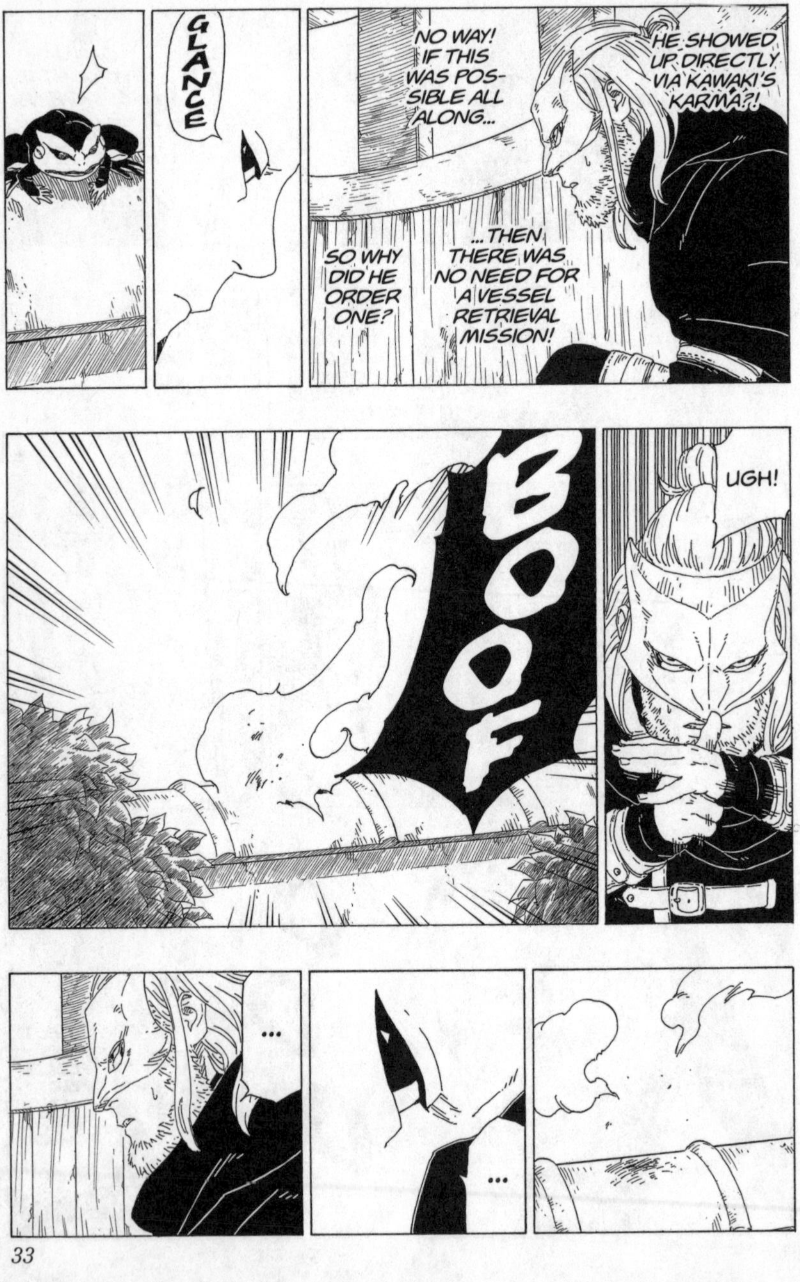
HE SHOWED UP DIRECTLY VIA KAWAKI'S KARMA?!
NO WAY! IF THIS WAS POSSIBLE ALL ALONG...
...THEN THERE WAS NO NEED FOR A VESSEL RETRIEVAL MISSION!
SO WHY DID HE ORDER ONE?
GLANCE
UGH!
BOOF
...
...

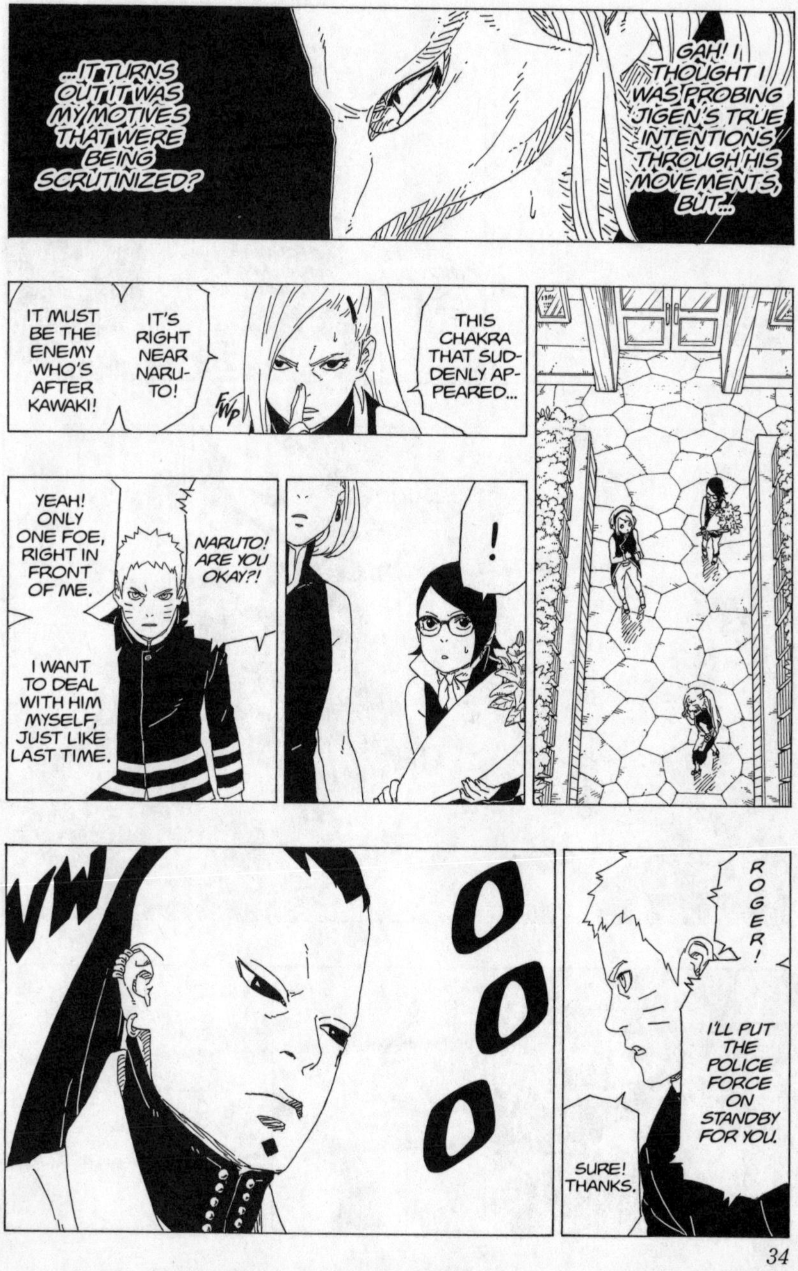
GAH! I THOUGHT I WAS PROBING JIGEN'S TRUE INTENTIONS THROUGH HIS MOVEMENTS, BUT...
...IT TURNS OUT IT WAS MY MOTIVES THAT WERE BEING SCRUTINIZED?
THIS CHAKRA THAT SUDDENLY APPEARED...
FWP
IT'S RIGHT NEAR NARUTO!
IT MUST BE THE ENEMY WHO'S AFTER KAWAKI!
!
NARUTO! ARE YOU OKAY?!
YEAH! ONLY ONE FOE, RIGHT IN FRONT OF ME.
I WANT TO DEAL WITH HIM MYSELF, JUST LIKE LAST TIME.
ROGER!
I'LL PUT THE POLICE FORCE ON STANDBY FOR YOU.
SURE! THANKS.
VWOOOO

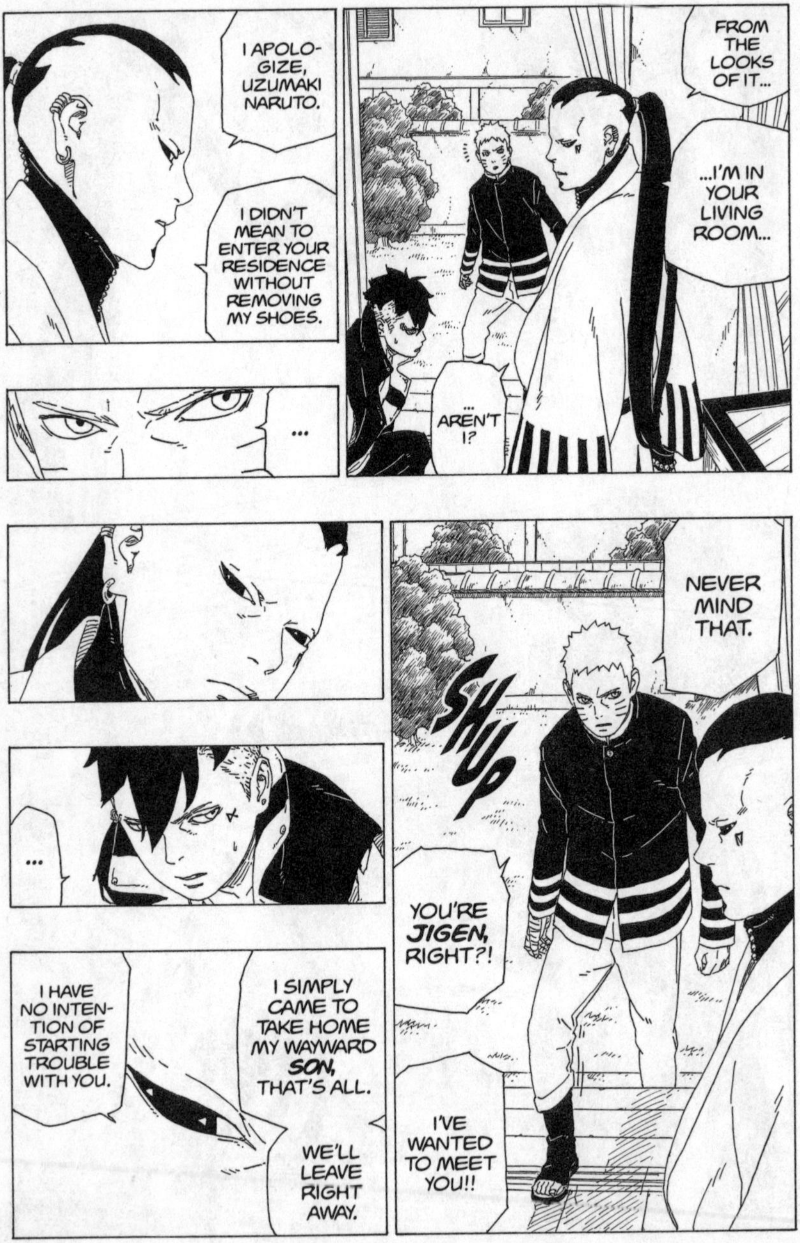
FROM THE LOOKS OF IT...
...I'M IN YOUR LIVING ROOM...
...AREN'T I?
I APOLOGIZE, UZUMAKI NARUTO.
I DIDN'T MEAN TO ENTER YOUR RESIDENCE WITHOUT REMOVING MY SHOES.
...
NEVER MIND THAT.
SHUP
YOU'RE **JIGEN**, RIGHT?!
I'VE WANTED TO MEET YOU!!
...
I SIMPLY CAME TO TAKE HOME MY WAYWARD **SON**, THAT'S ALL.
I HAVE NO INTENTION OF STARTING TROUBLE WITH YOU.
WE'LL LEAVE RIGHT AWAY.

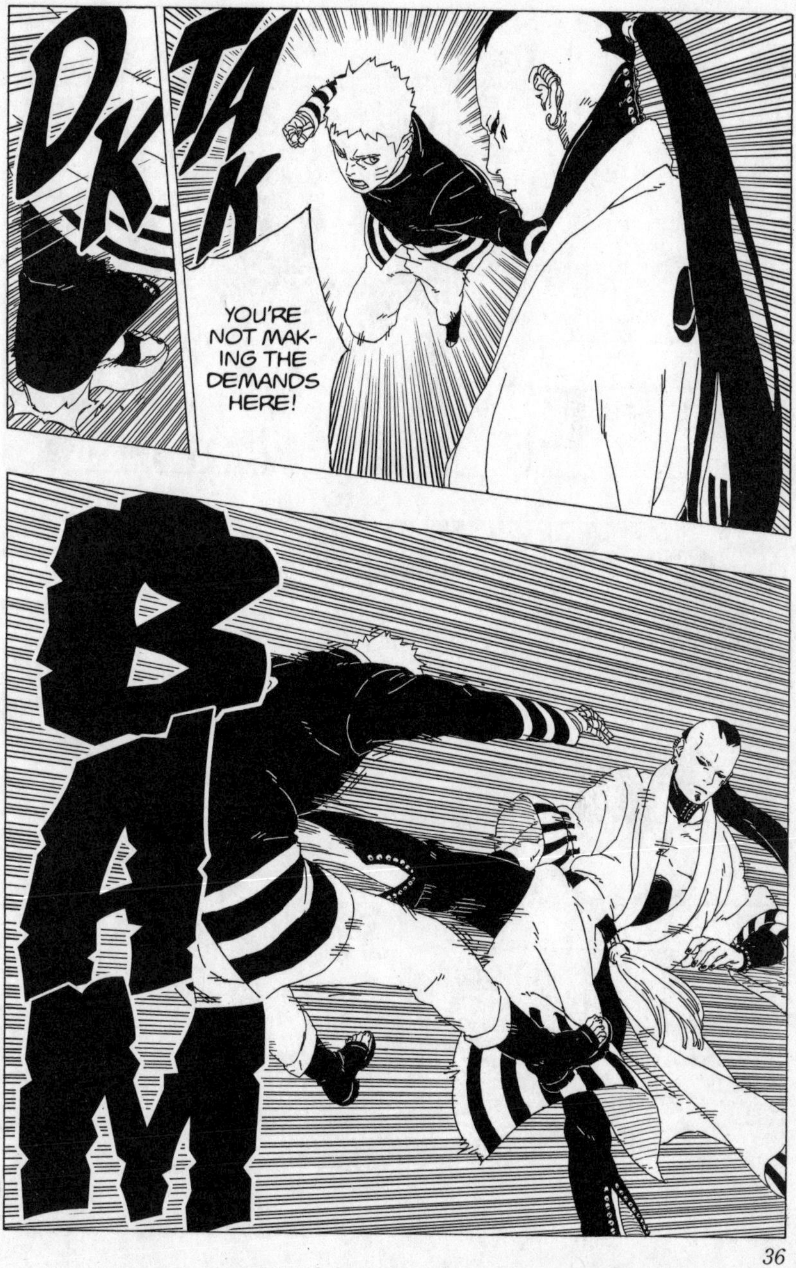
TAK
YOU'RE NOT MAKING THE DEMANDS HERE!
DK
BAM

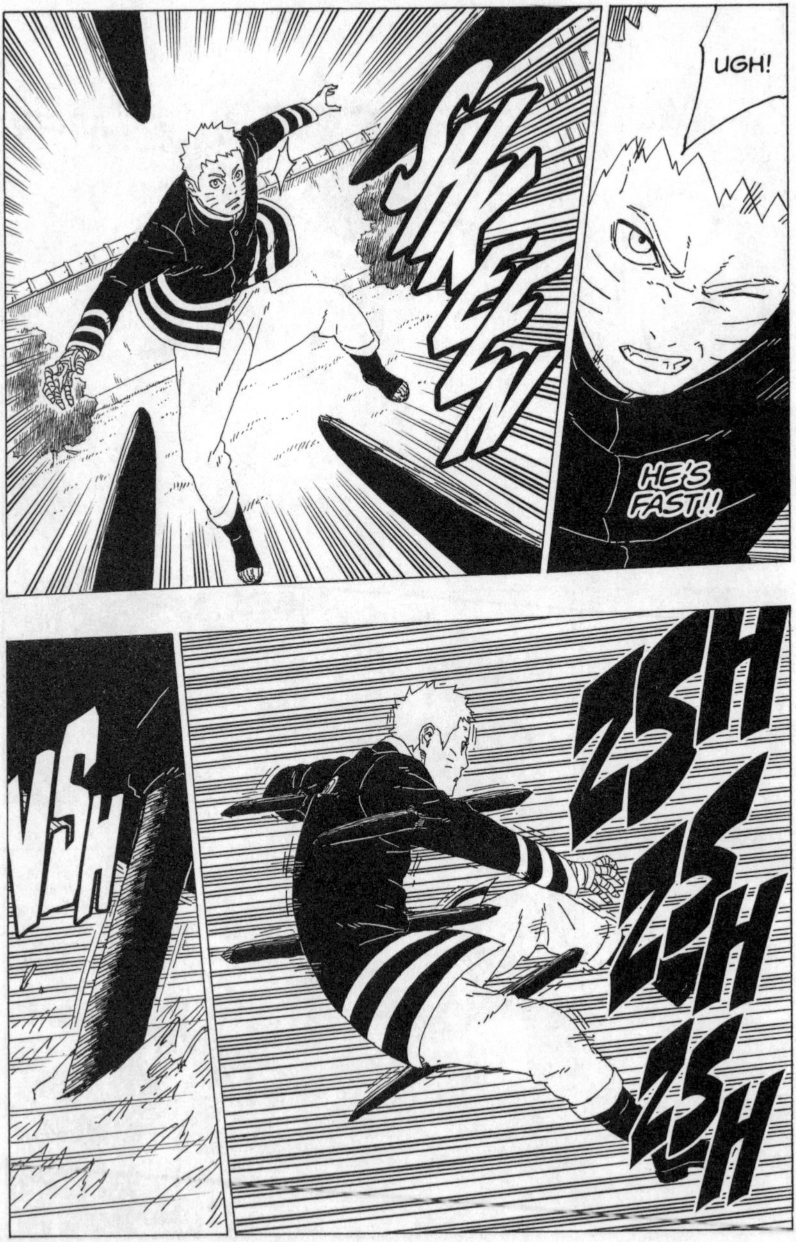
UGH!
HE'S FAST!!
SHKEEN
ZSH ZSH ZSH ZSH
VSH

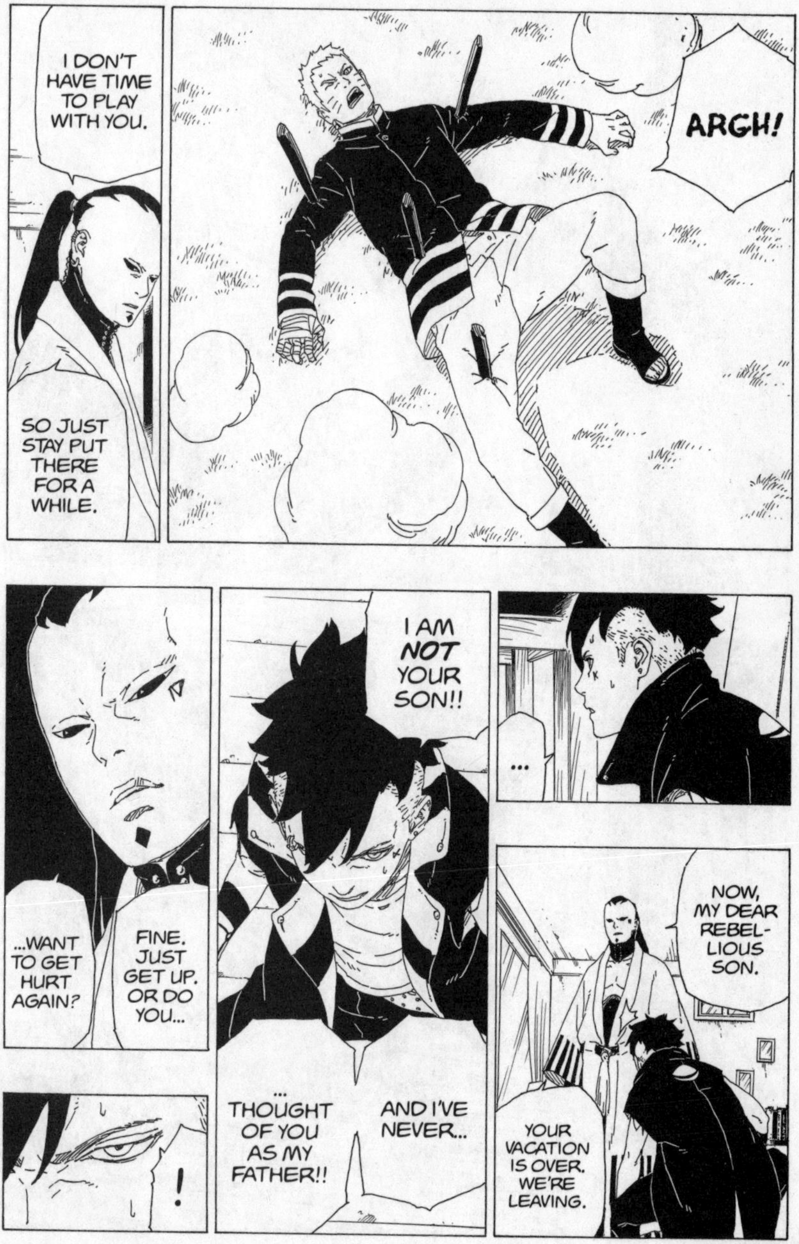
ARGH!
I DON'T HAVE TIME TO PLAY WITH YOU.
SO JUST STAY PUT THERE FOR A WHILE.
...
NOW, MY DEAR REBEL-LIOUS SON.
YOUR VACATION IS OVER. WE'RE LEAVING.
I AM *NOT* YOUR SON!!
AND I'VE NEVER...
...THOUGHT OF YOU AS MY FATHER!!
FINE. JUST GET UP. OR DO YOU...
...WANT TO GET HURT AGAIN?
!

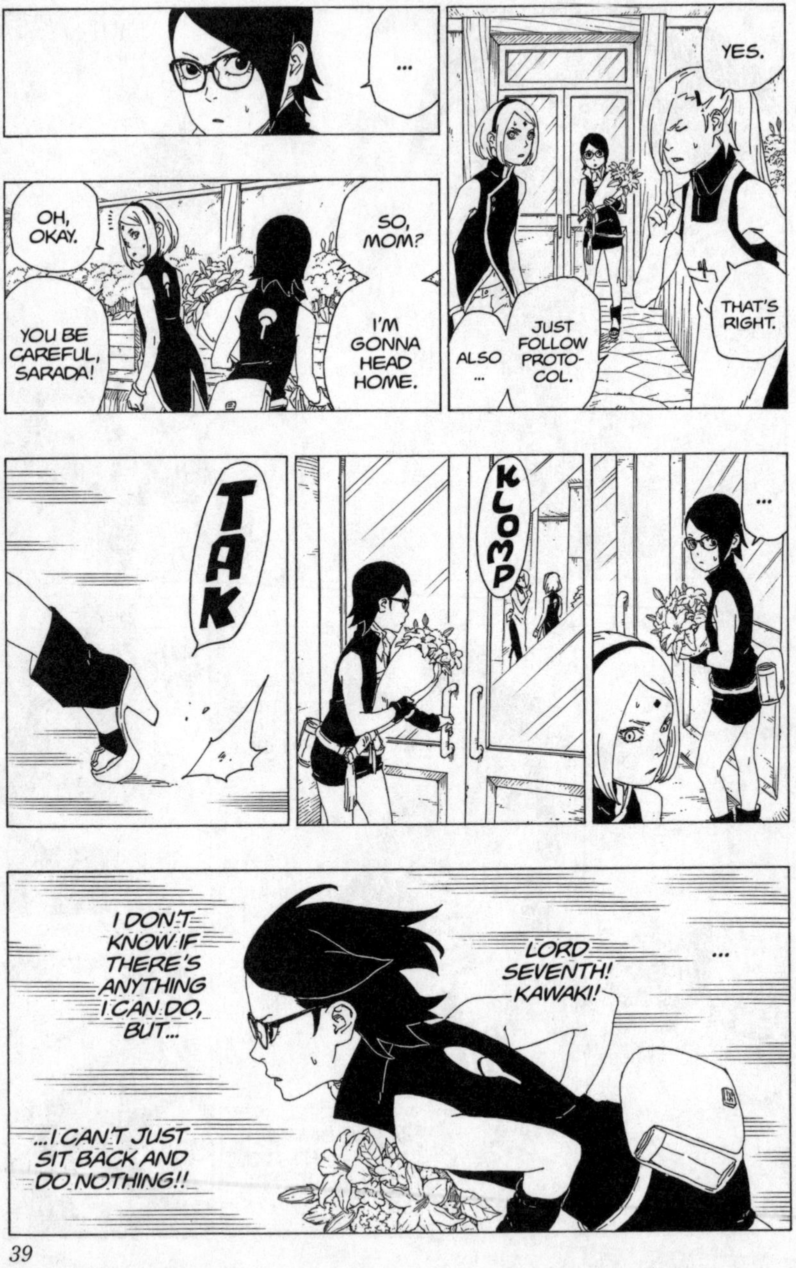
YES.
THAT'S RIGHT.
JUST FOLLOW PROTOCOL.
ALSO ...
...
SO, MOM?
I'M GONNA HEAD HOME.
OH, OKAY.
YOU BE CAREFUL, SARADA!
...
KLOMP
TAK
...
LORD SEVENTH! KAWAKI!
I DON'T KNOW IF THERE'S ANYTHING I CAN DO, BUT...
...I CAN'T JUST SIT BACK AND DO NOTHING!!

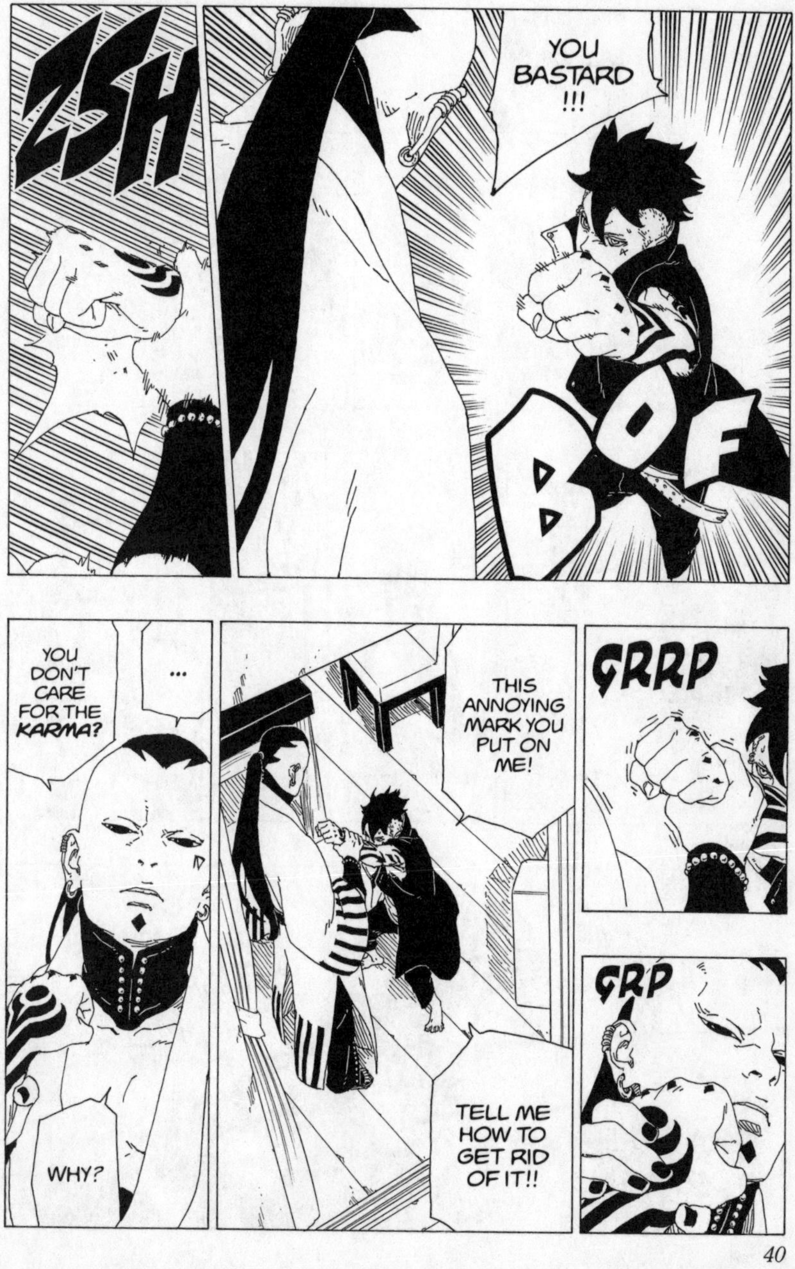
YOU BASTARD !!!
BOF
ZSH
GRRP
GRP
THIS ANNOYING MARK YOU PUT ON ME!
TELL ME HOW TO GET RID OF IT!!
...
YOU DON'T CARE FOR THE *KARMA*?
WHY?

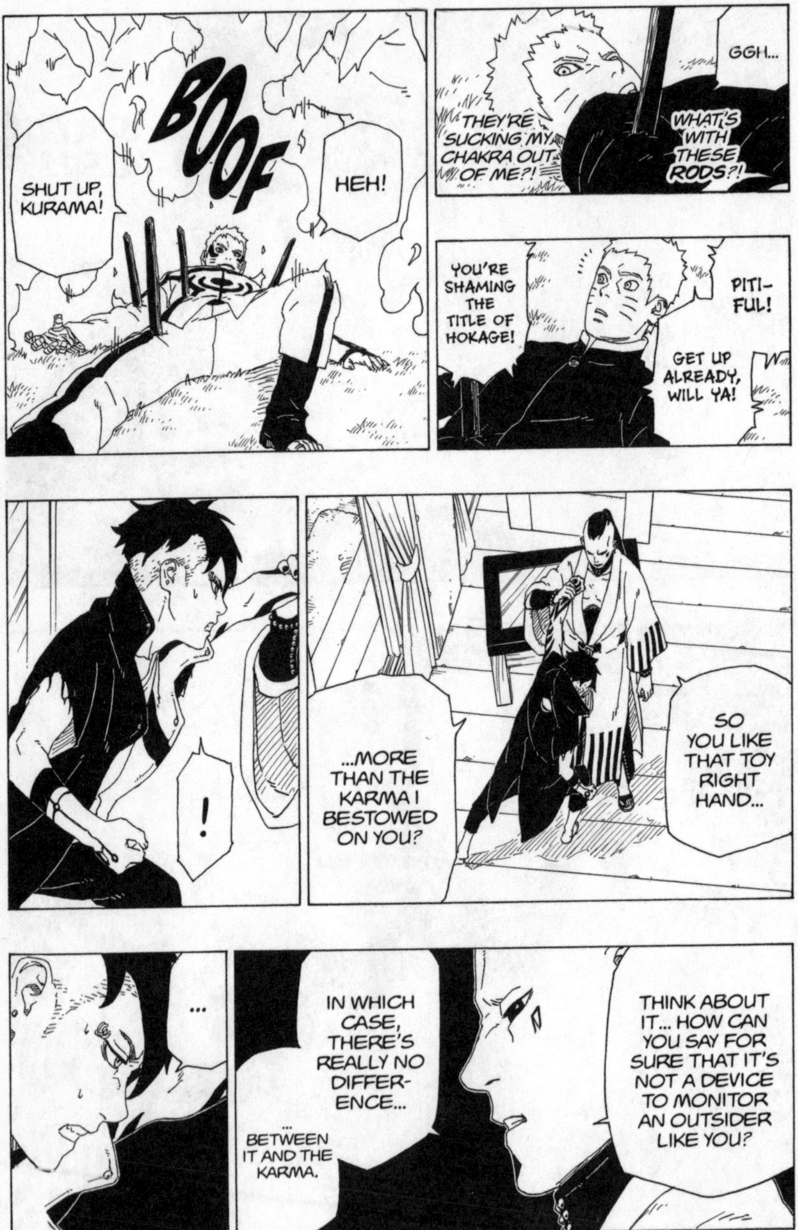
GGH...
WHAT'S WITH THESE RODS?!
THEY'RE SUCKING MY CHAKRA OUT OF ME?!
PITI-FUL!
GET UP ALREADY, WILL YA!
YOU'RE SHAMING THE TITLE OF HOKAGE!
HEH!
BOOF
SHUT UP, KURAMA!
SO YOU LIKE THAT TOY RIGHT HAND...
...MORE THAN THE KARMA I BESTOWED ON YOU?
!
THINK ABOUT IT... HOW CAN YOU SAY FOR SURE THAT IT'S NOT A DEVICE TO MONITOR AN OUTSIDER LIKE YOU?
IN WHICH CASE, THERE'S REALLY NO DIFFER-ENCE...
...BETWEEN IT AND THE KARMA.
...

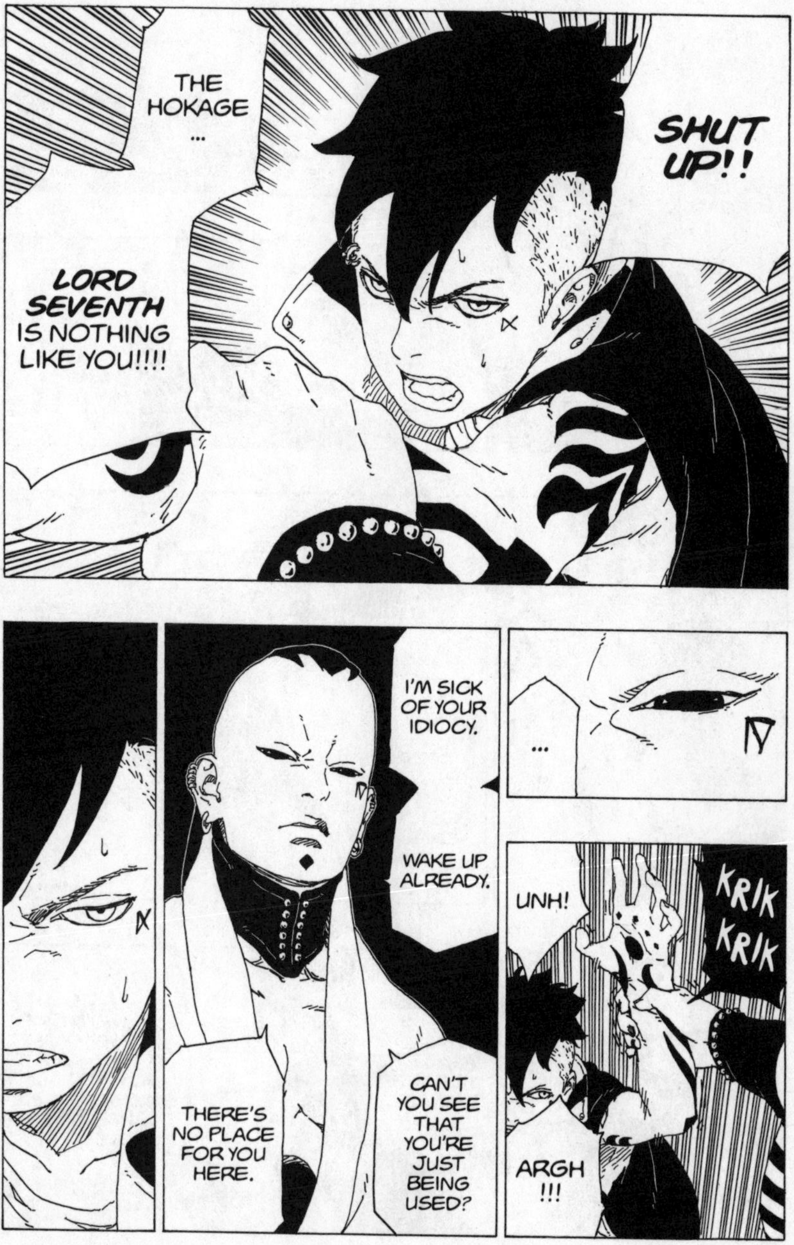
SHUT UP!!
THE HOKAGE ...
LORD SEVENTH IS NOTHING LIKE YOU!!!!
...
KRIK KRIK
UNH!
ARGH !!!
I'M SICK OF YOUR IDIOCY.
WAKE UP ALREADY.
CAN'T YOU SEE THAT YOU'RE JUST BEING USED?
THERE'S NO PLACE FOR YOU HERE.

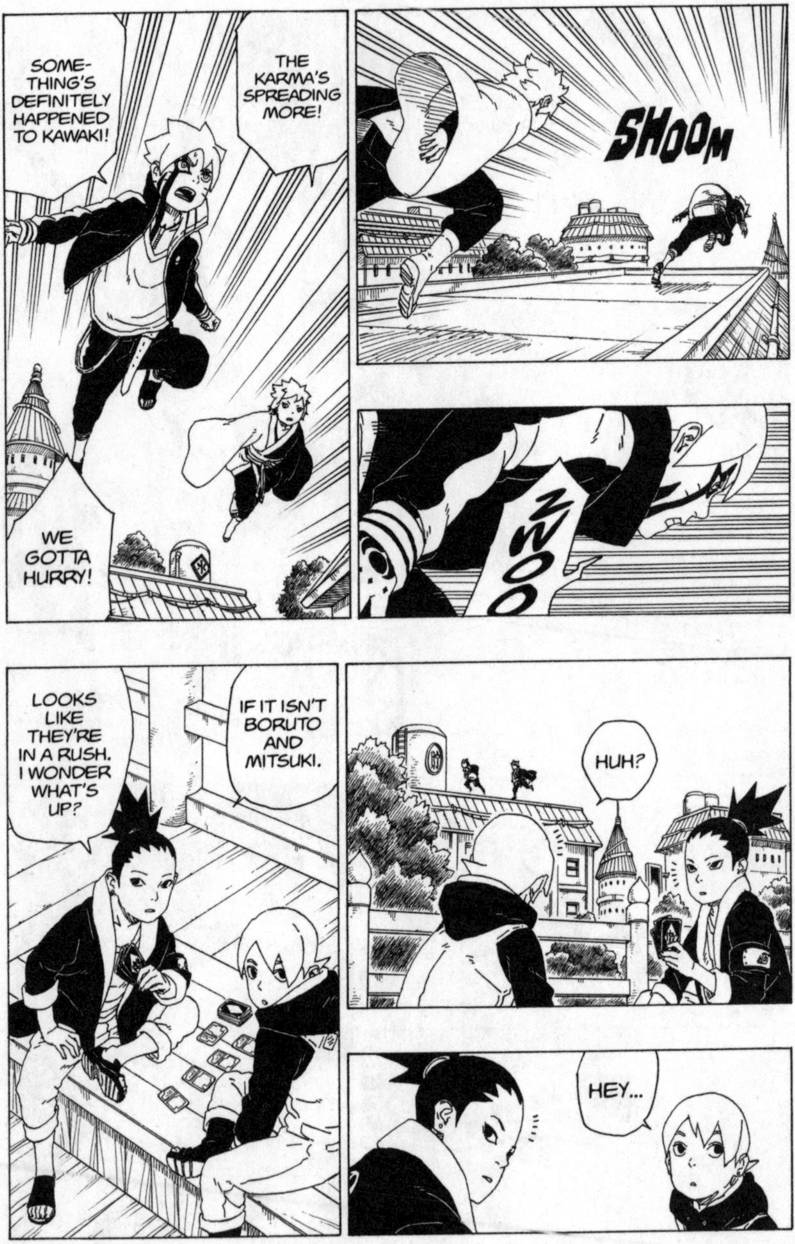
SHOOM
ZWOO
SOME-THING'S DEFINITELY HAPPENED TO KAWAKI!
THE KARMA'S SPREADING MORE!
WE GOTTA HURRY!
HUH?
HEY...
IF IT ISN'T BORUTO AND MITSUKI.
LOOKS LIKE THEY'RE IN A RUSH. I WONDER WHAT'S UP?

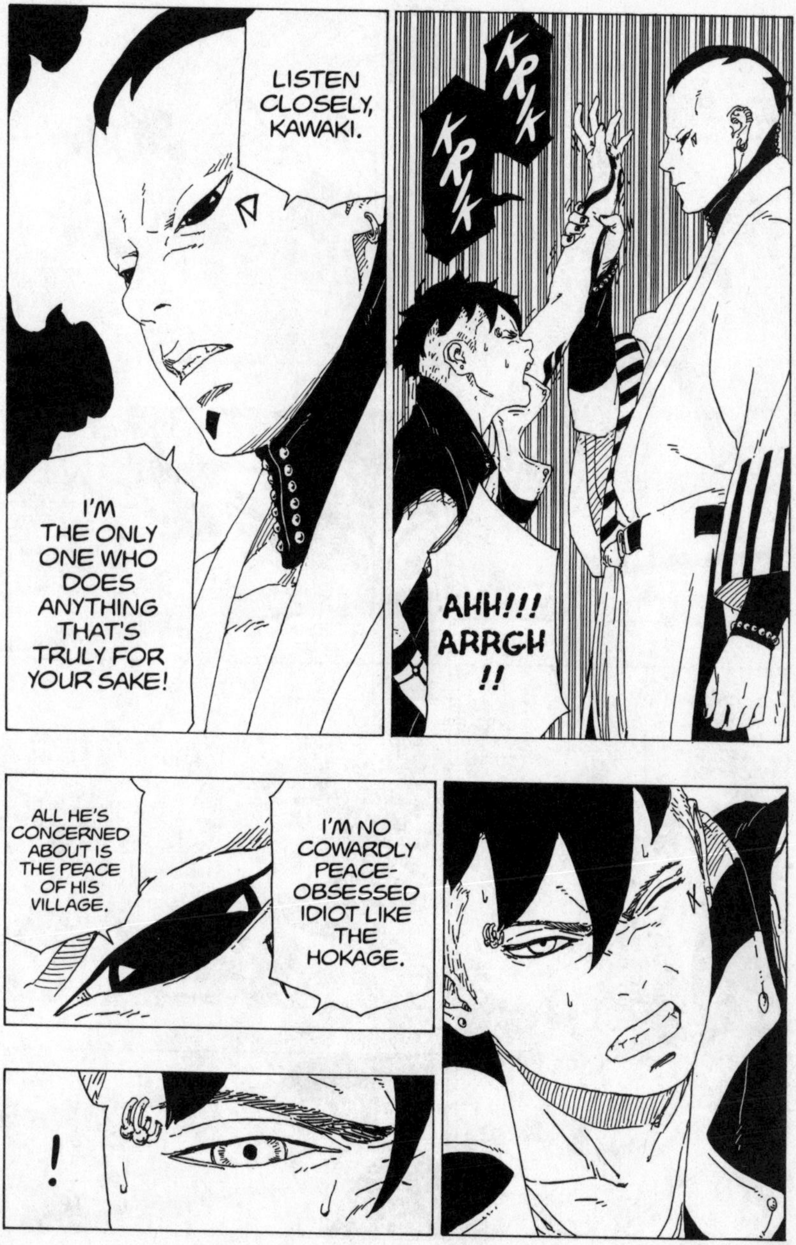
KRIK
KRIK
KRIK
AHH!!! ARRGH !!
LISTEN CLOSELY, KAWAKI.
I'M THE ONLY ONE WHO DOES ANYTHING THAT'S TRULY FOR YOUR SAKE!
I'M NO COWARDLY PEACE-OBSESSED IDIOT LIKE THE HOKAGE.
ALL HE'S CONCERNED ABOUT IS THE PEACE OF HIS VILLAGE.
!

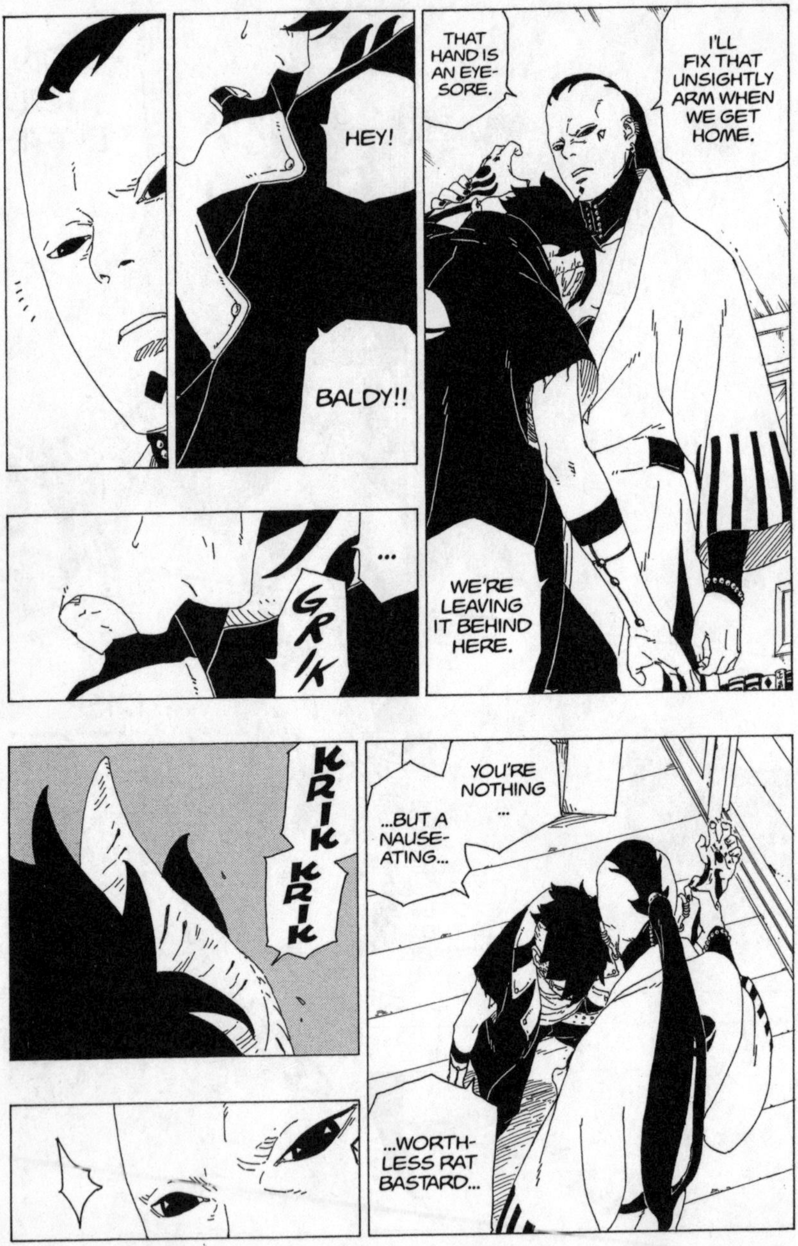
I'LL FIX THAT UNSIGHTLY ARM WHEN WE GET HOME.
THAT HAND IS AN EYE-SORE.
WE'RE LEAVING IT BEHIND HERE.
HEY!
BALDY!!
...
GRIK
YOU'RE NOTHING ...
...BUT A NAUSE-ATING...
...WORTH-LESS RAT BASTARD...
KRIK KRIK KRIK

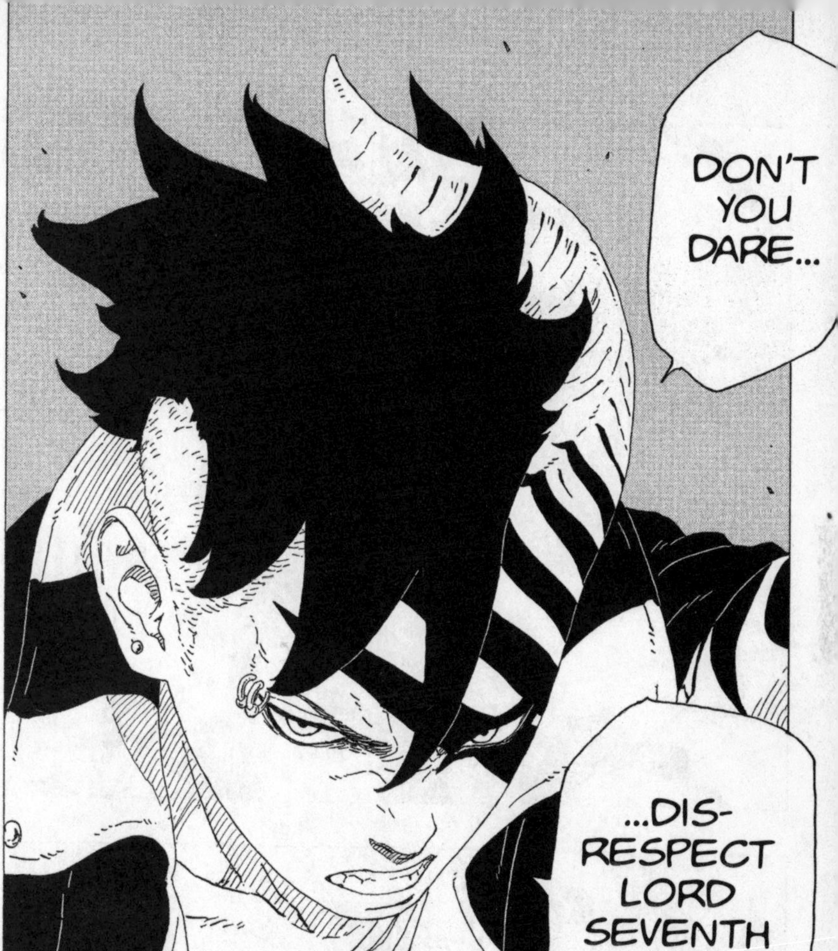
DON'T YOU DARE...
...DIS-RESPECT LORD SEVENTH !!!!!

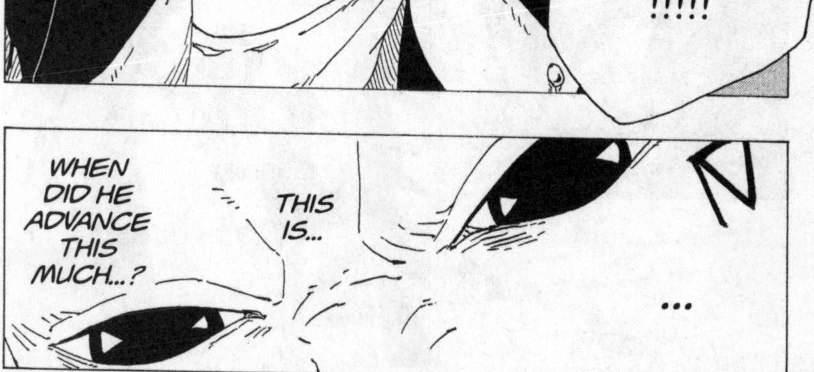
...
THIS IS...
WHEN DID HE ADVANCE THIS MUCH...?

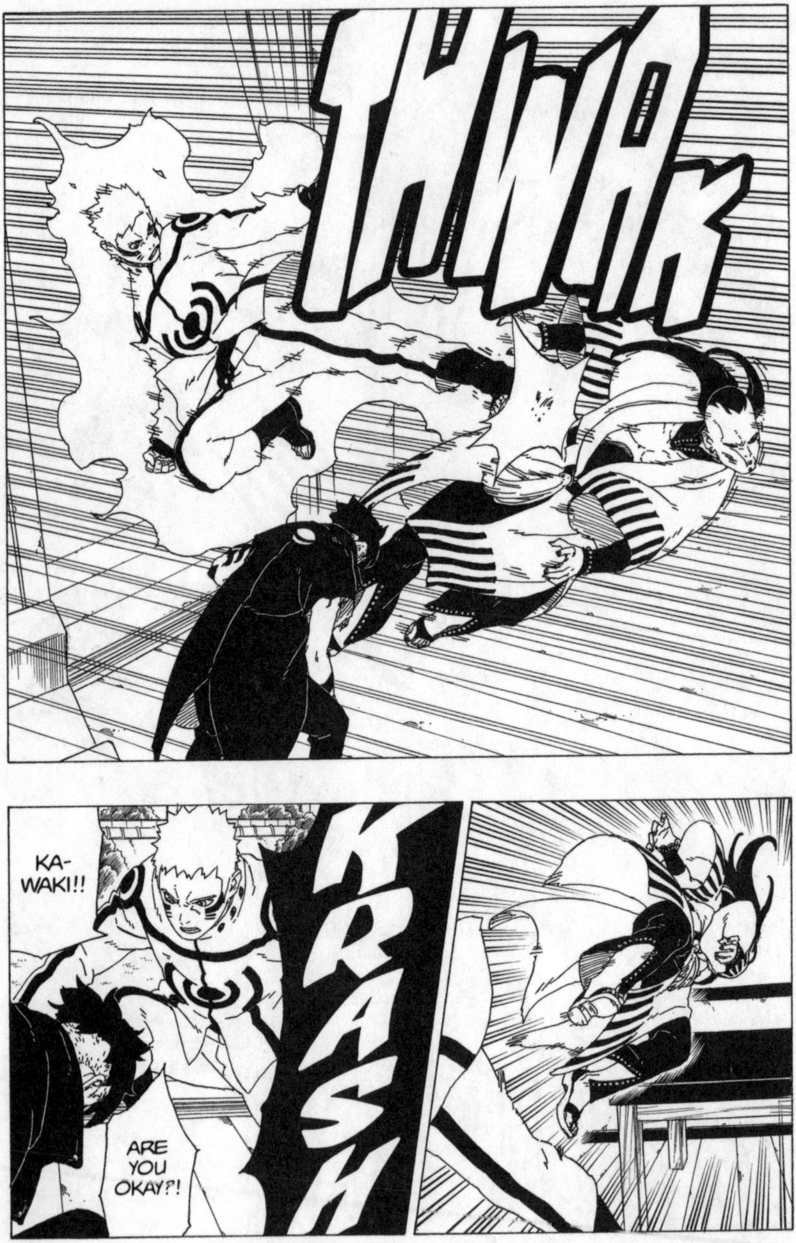
THWAK
KRASH
KA-WAKI!!
ARE YOU OKAY?!

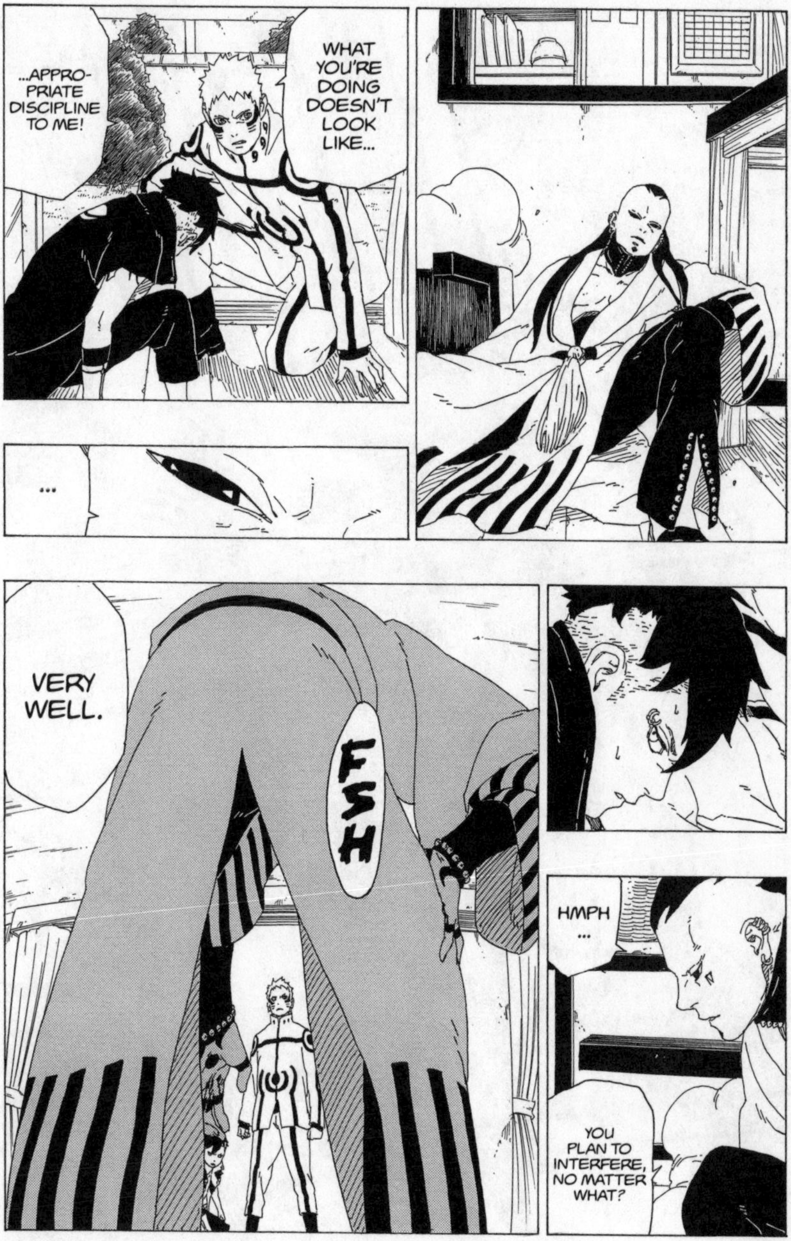
WHAT YOU'RE DOING DOESN'T LOOK LIKE...
...APPROPRIATE DISCIPLINE TO ME!
...
HMPH ...
YOU PLAN TO INTERFERE, NO MATTER WHAT?
VERY WELL.
FSH

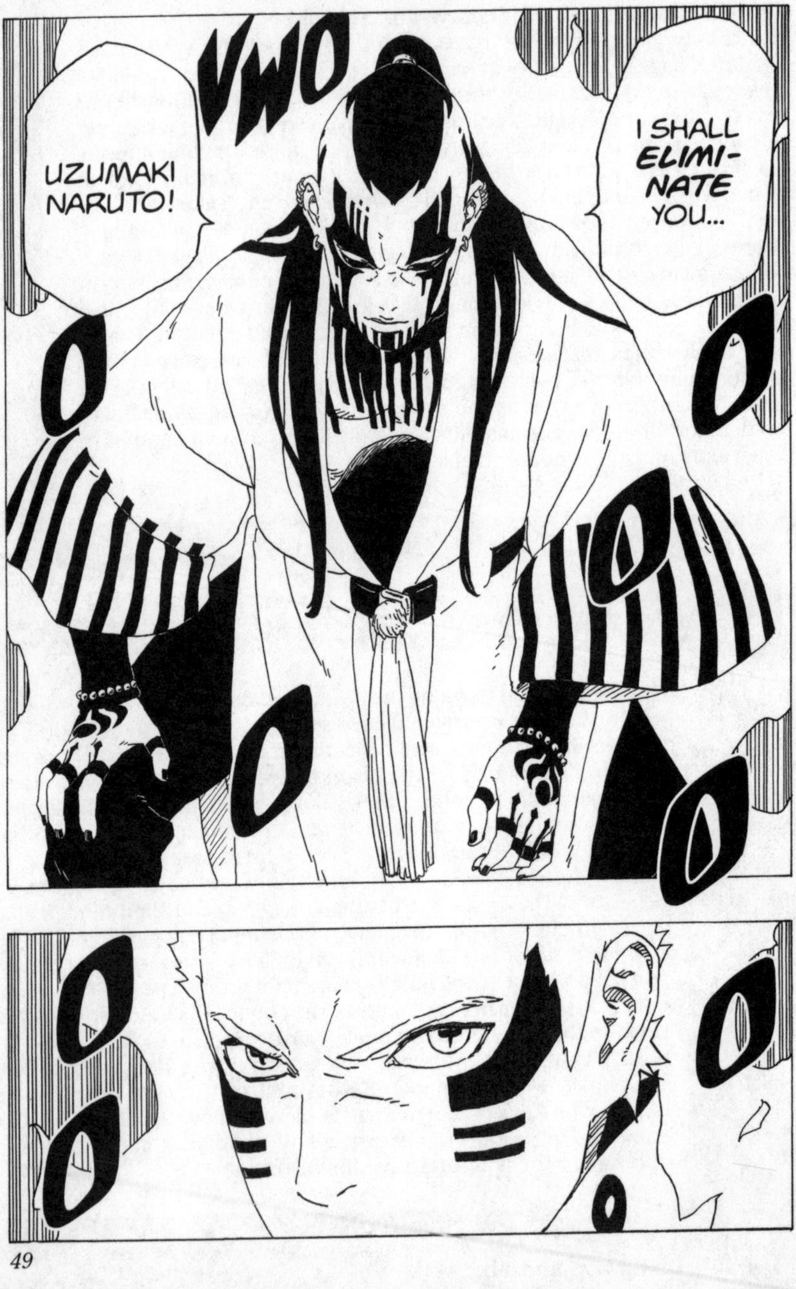
I SHALL ELIMI-NATE YOU...
VWO
UZUMAKI NARUTO!

Shinobi Hiden Column 5: Daimyo and Shinobi

Shinobi are in contractual relationships with nations. While each Hidden Village is, in theory at least, a vassal of the daimyo who is its sovereign ruler, in actuality they are in a contractual relationship of equals, where the Village executes the daimyo's will through accepting missions. Each Hidden Village is its nation's largest military force. However, it is not its only military force. In actuality, ordinary soldiers armed with spears, katana, bows and so forth, carry out "safer" missions such as border patrol and maintaining public order. Not all daimyo possess enough funds to continuously contract with a Village. Military actions involving ninja cost an immense amount of money. Short-term subversive activities are one thing, but a lengthy war where only ninja are employed would incur a sum huge enough to ruin a nation. That is why small states that do not contain Hidden Villages, such as the former Land of Waves (which is currently making great advances as an economic superpower), must hold to a policy of relying on ordinary soldiers for day-to-day armaments, and only hiring shinobi in times of need. Only ninja can counter ninja.

However, during this long peace, every daimyo has started wanting to reduce their massive military spending. This is only natural, as they are in the business of collecting taxes from their citizens and then (re)distributing it. The chain of events that led to Operation: Demolish Konoha, where Sunagakure (Hidden Sand) Village felt forced into demonstrating the threat of Konoha in reaction to the Land of Wind's disarmament, is still a fresh memory. That's right; daimyo do not consider the perpetual existence of shinobi to be necessary. The cases of Ohtsutsuki Kaguya, and then Momoshiki, were sufficient to remind daimyo of the importance of shinobi. The current Land of Fire daimyo, Ikkyu, holds Naruto in high esteem, and supports him in all possible ways, but his own political power is not rock-solid either. Members of the council of elders who wish to remove the too-heroic Uzumaki Naruto appear to be seeking to oust Ikkyu along with Naruto. Among them are quite a few individuals who are under **Kara**'s control through **Outers**. The reason why **Kara** is able to not-so-secretly move squads inside the Land of Fire is due to the actions of politicians and merchants opposed to the Ikkyu-Naruto administration.

Text: Ukyo Kodachi

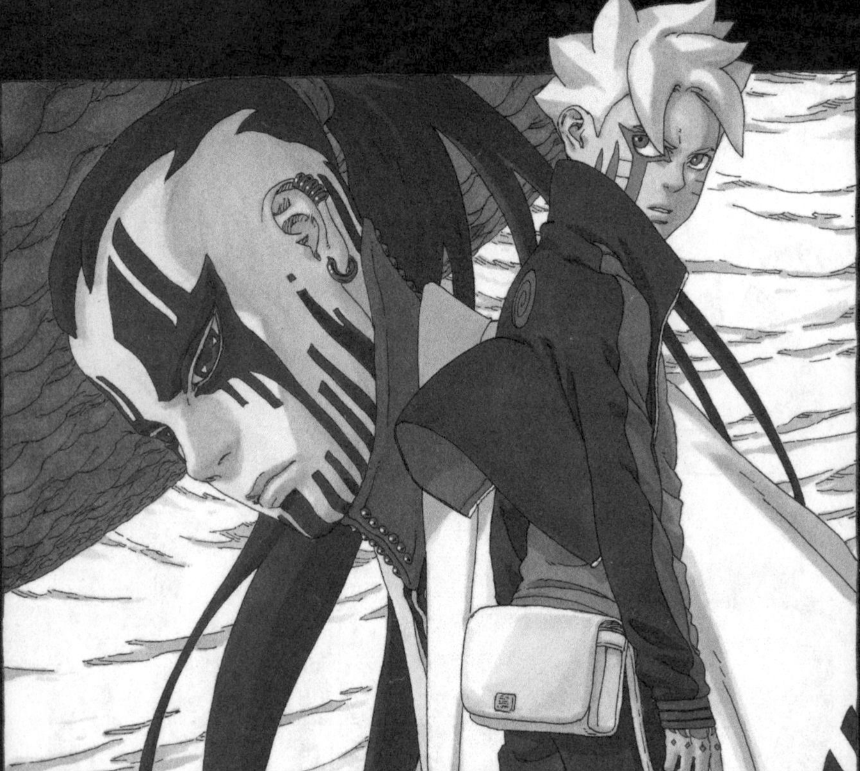

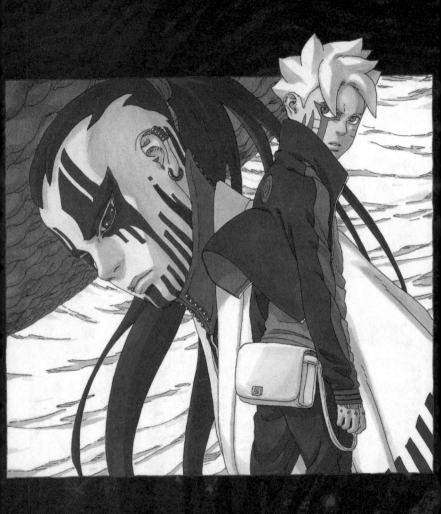

Number 37: United Front!!

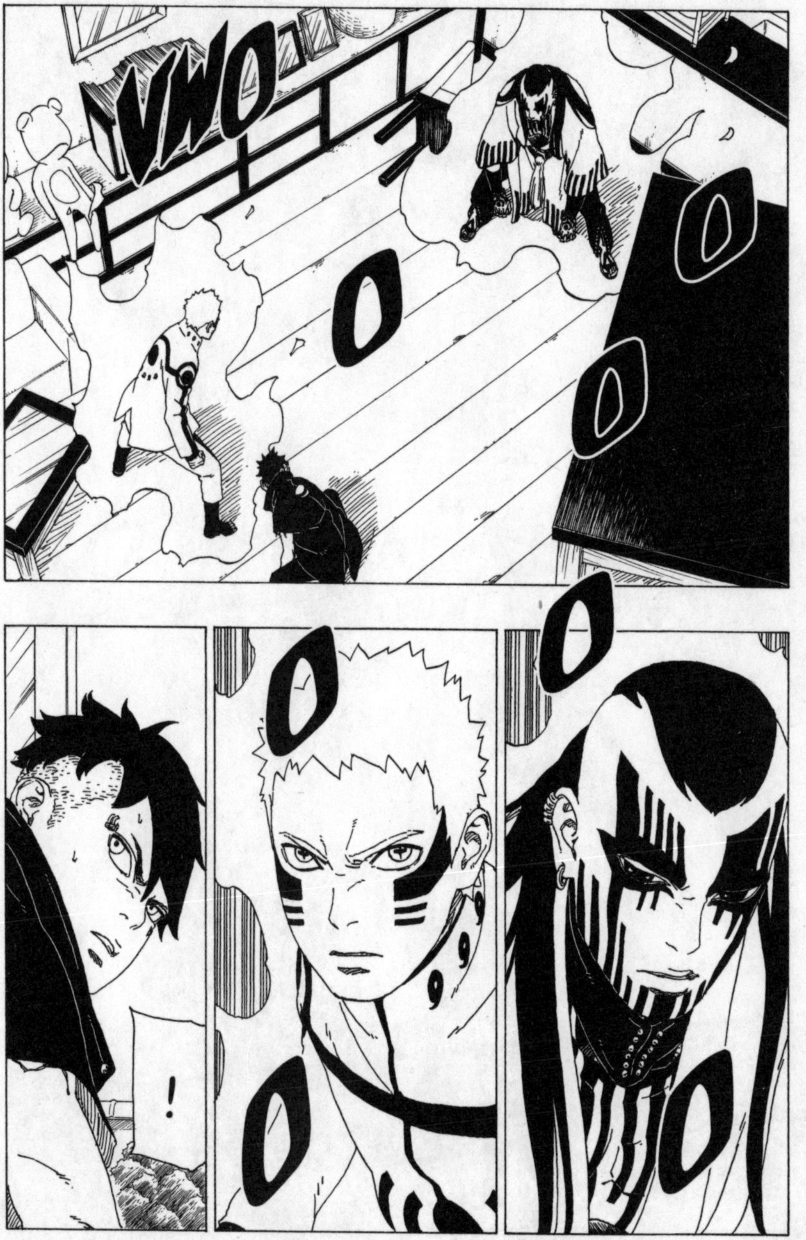
VWO
!

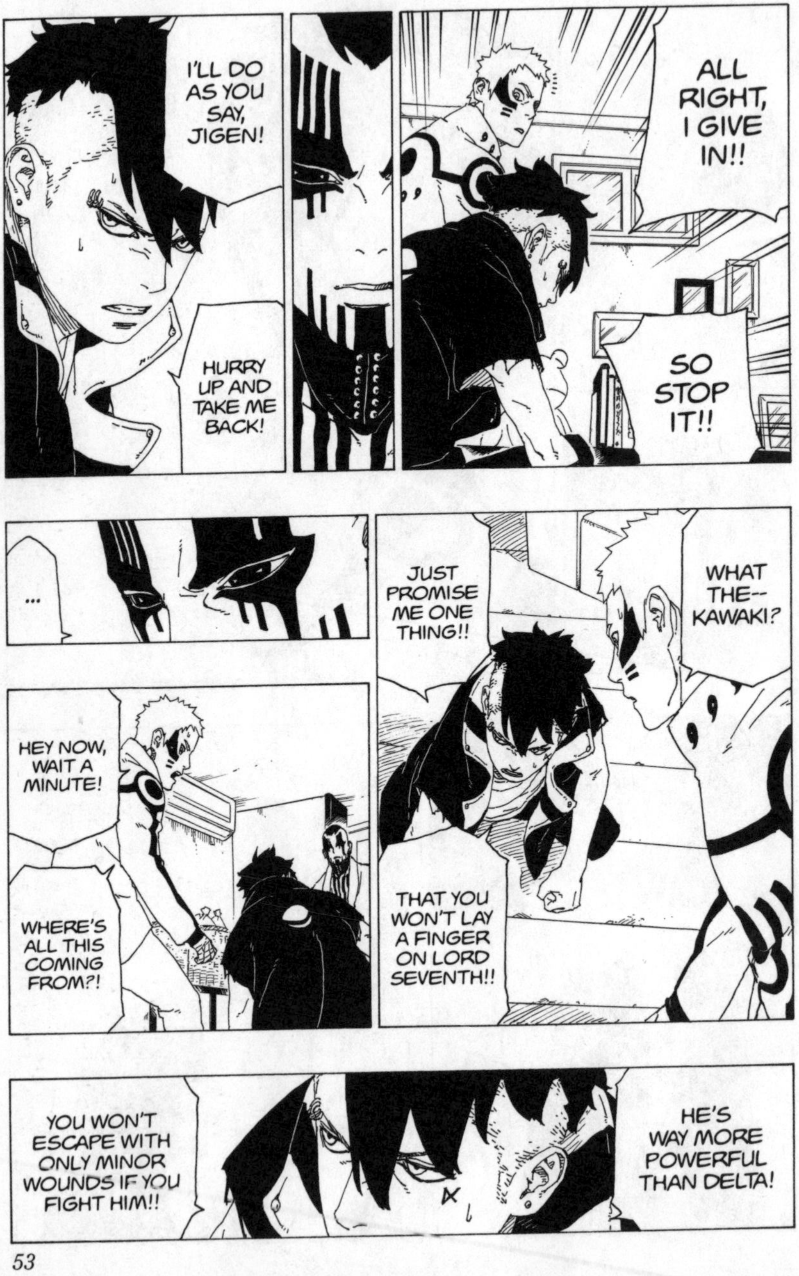
ALL RIGHT, I GIVE IN!!
SO STOP IT!!
I'LL DO AS YOU SAY, JIGEN!
HURRY UP AND TAKE ME BACK!
WHAT THE-- KAWAKI?
JUST PROMISE ME ONE THING!!
THAT YOU WON'T LAY A FINGER ON LORD SEVENTH!!
...
HEY NOW, WAIT A MINUTE!
WHERE'S ALL THIS COMING FROM?!
HE'S WAY MORE POWERFUL THAN DELTA!
YOU WON'T ESCAPE WITH ONLY MINOR WOUNDS IF YOU FIGHT HIM!!

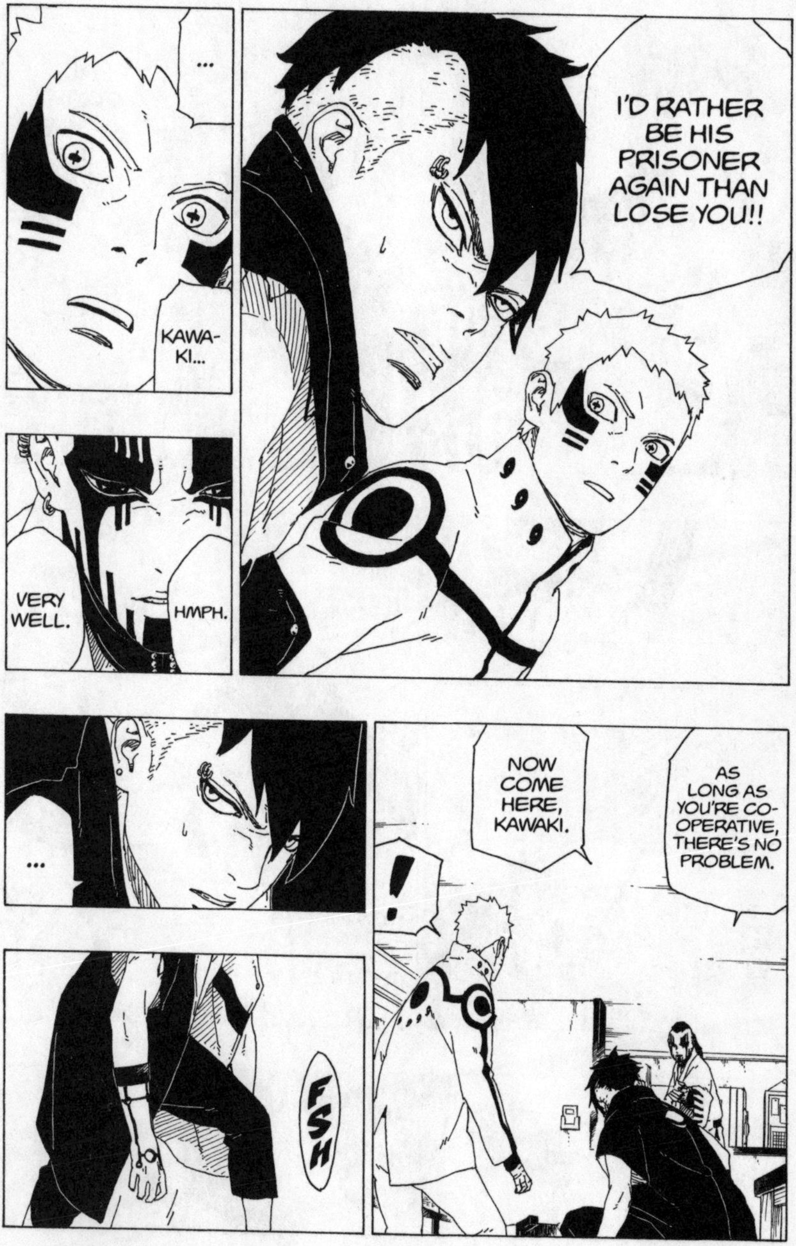
I'D RATHER BE HIS PRISONER AGAIN THAN LOSE YOU!!
...
KAWAKI...
HMPH.
VERY WELL.
AS LONG AS YOU'RE CO-OPERATIVE, THERE'S NO PROBLEM.
NOW COME HERE, KAWAKI.
!
...
FSH

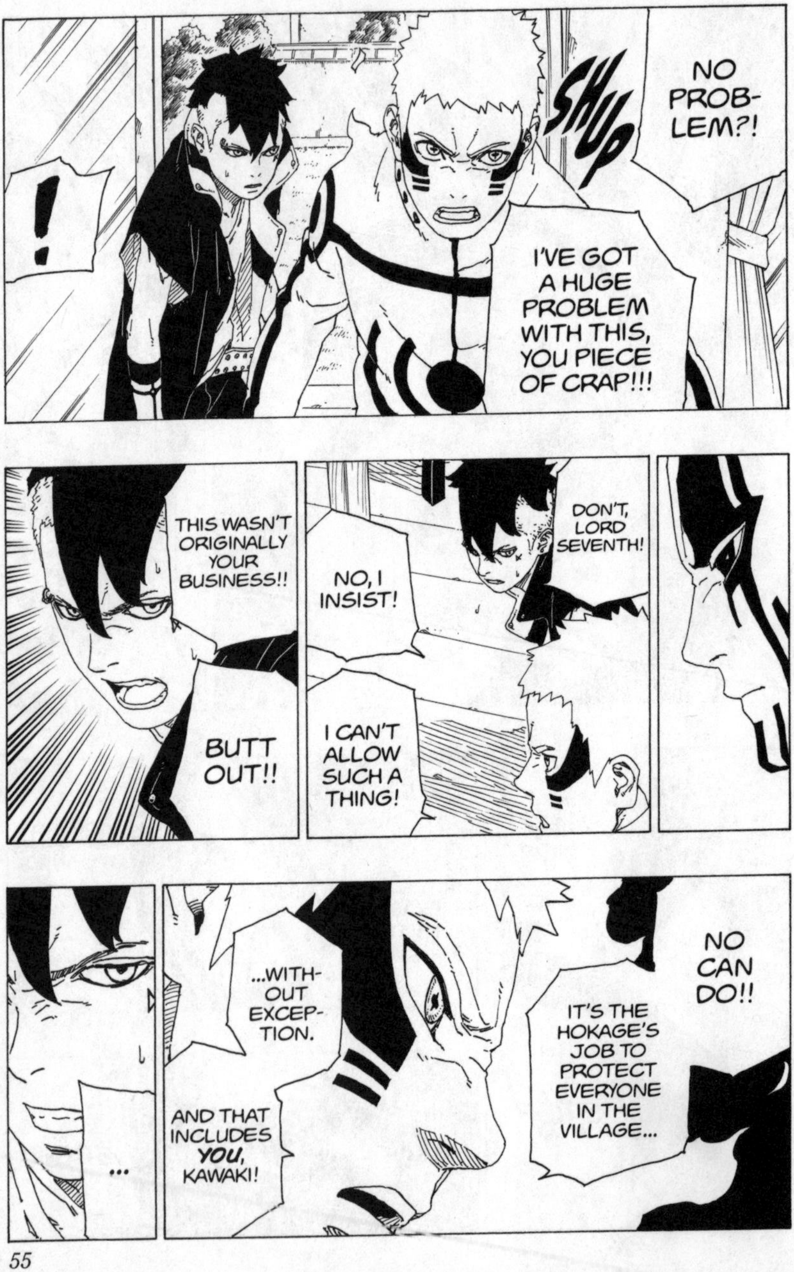
NO PROB-LEM?!
SHUP
I'VE GOT A HUGE PROBLEM WITH THIS, YOU PIECE OF CRAP!!!
!
DON'T, LORD SEVENTH!
NO, I INSIST!
I CAN'T ALLOW SUCH A THING!
THIS WASN'T ORIGINALLY YOUR BUSINESS!!
BUTT OUT!!
NO CAN DO!!
IT'S THE HOKAGE'S JOB TO PROTECT EVERYONE IN THE VILLAGE...
...WITH-OUT EXCEP-TION.
AND THAT INCLUDES *YOU*, KAWAKI!
...

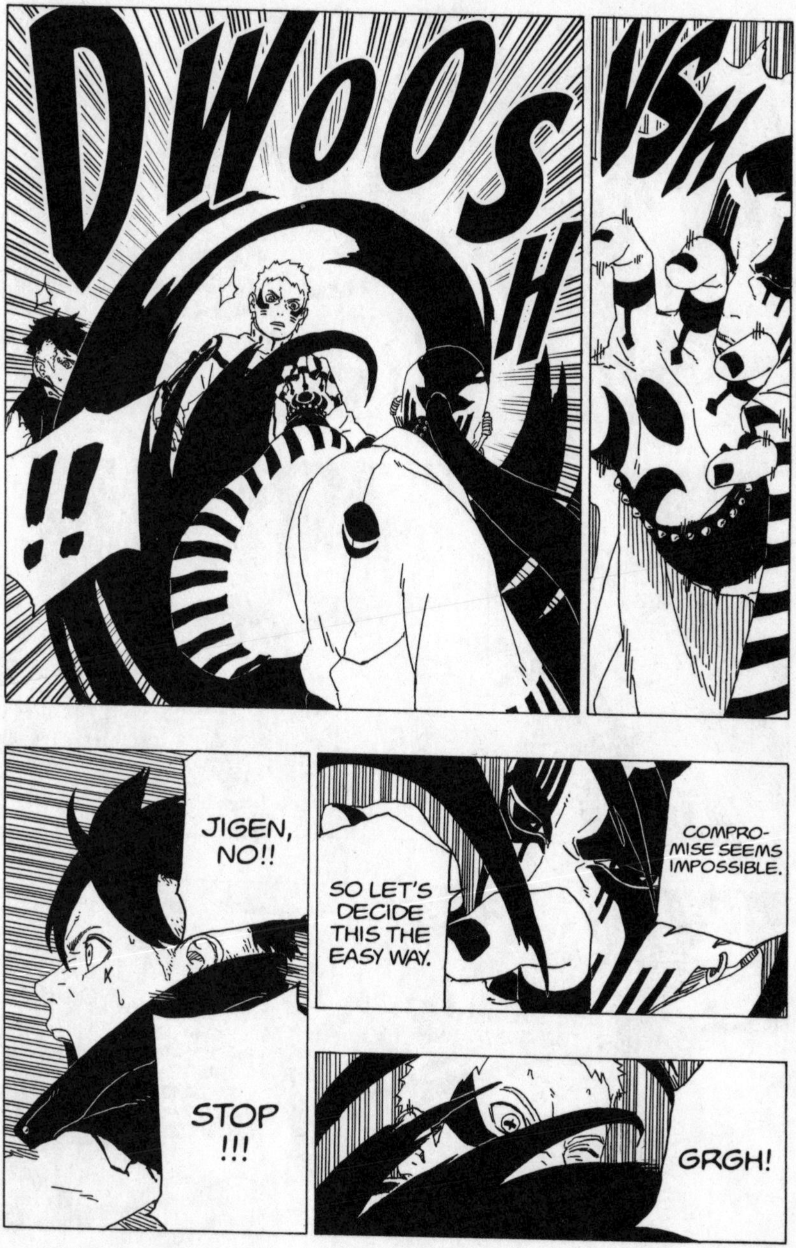
VSH
DWOOSH
!!
COMPRO-MISE SEEMS IMPOSSIBLE.
SO LET'S DECIDE THIS THE EASY WAY.
GRGH!
JIGEN, NO!!
STOP !!!

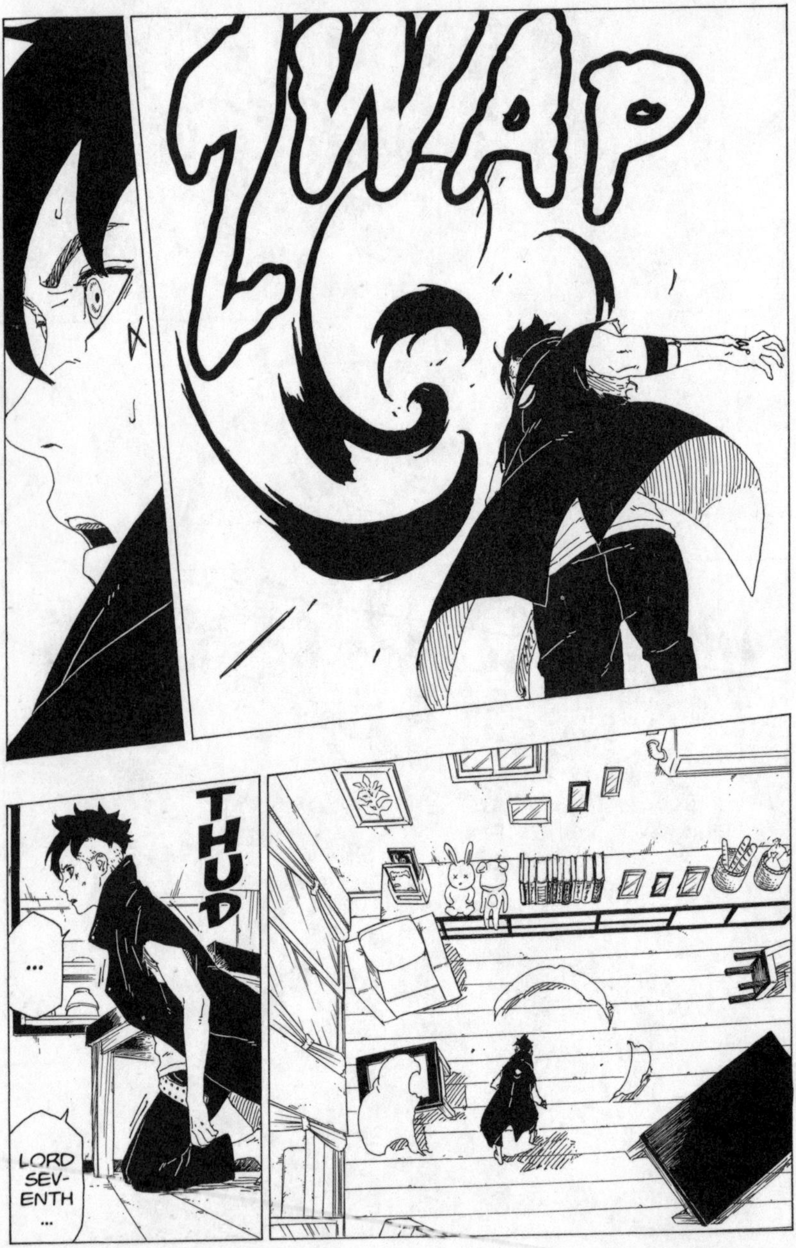

WAP
THUD
...
LORD SEV-
ENTH
...

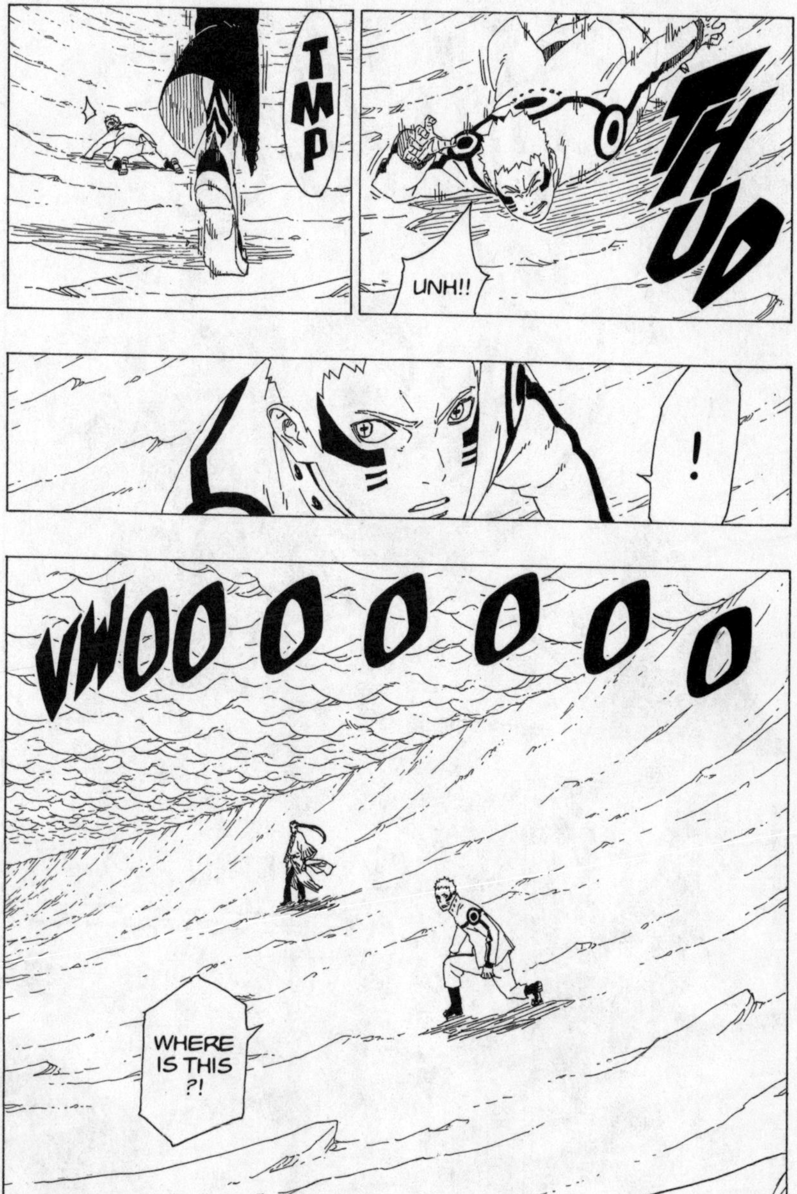
THUD
UNH!!
TMP
!
VWOOOOOOOO
WHERE IS THIS ?!

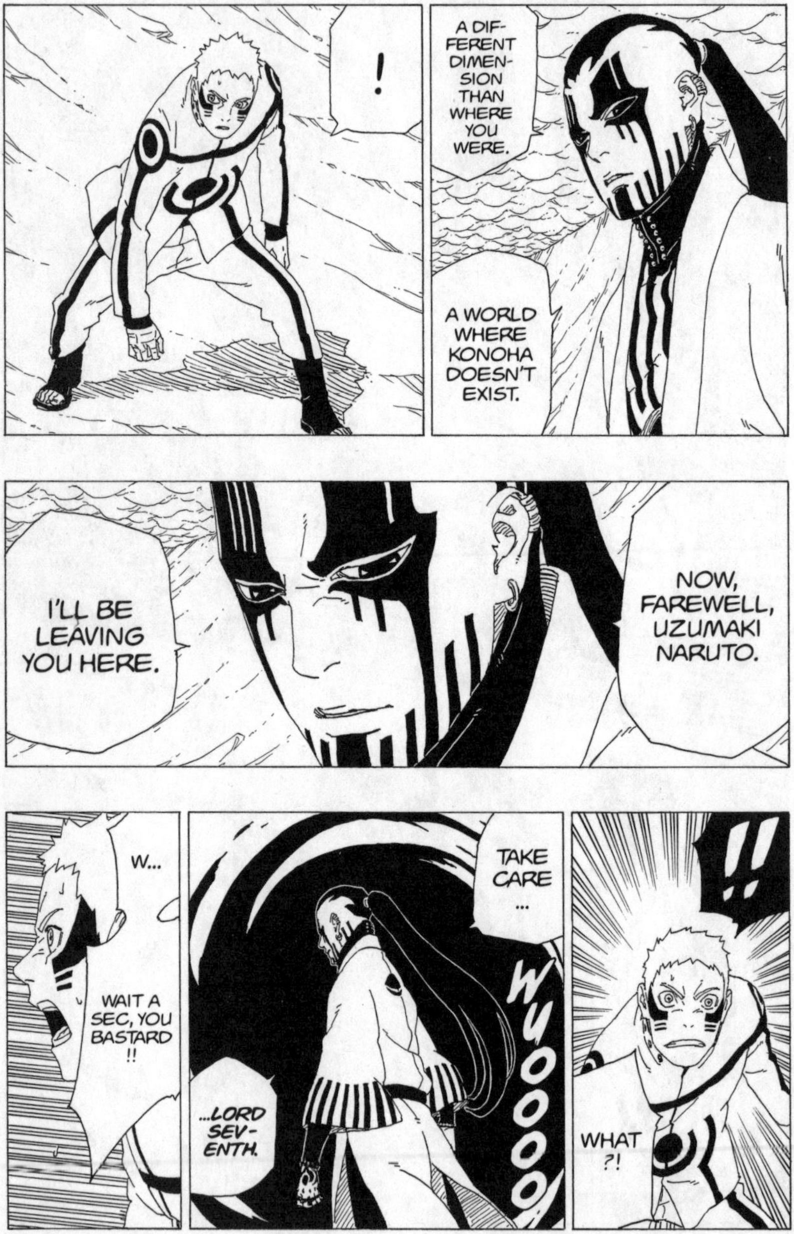
A DIF-FERENT DIMEN-SION THAN WHERE YOU WERE.
A WORLD WHERE KONOHA DOESN'T EXIST.
!
NOW, FAREWELL, UZUMAKI NARUTO.
I'LL BE LEAVING YOU HERE.
!!
WHAT ?!
TAKE CARE ...
WUOOOOO
...LORD SEV-ENTH.
W...
WAIT A SEC, YOU BASTARD !!

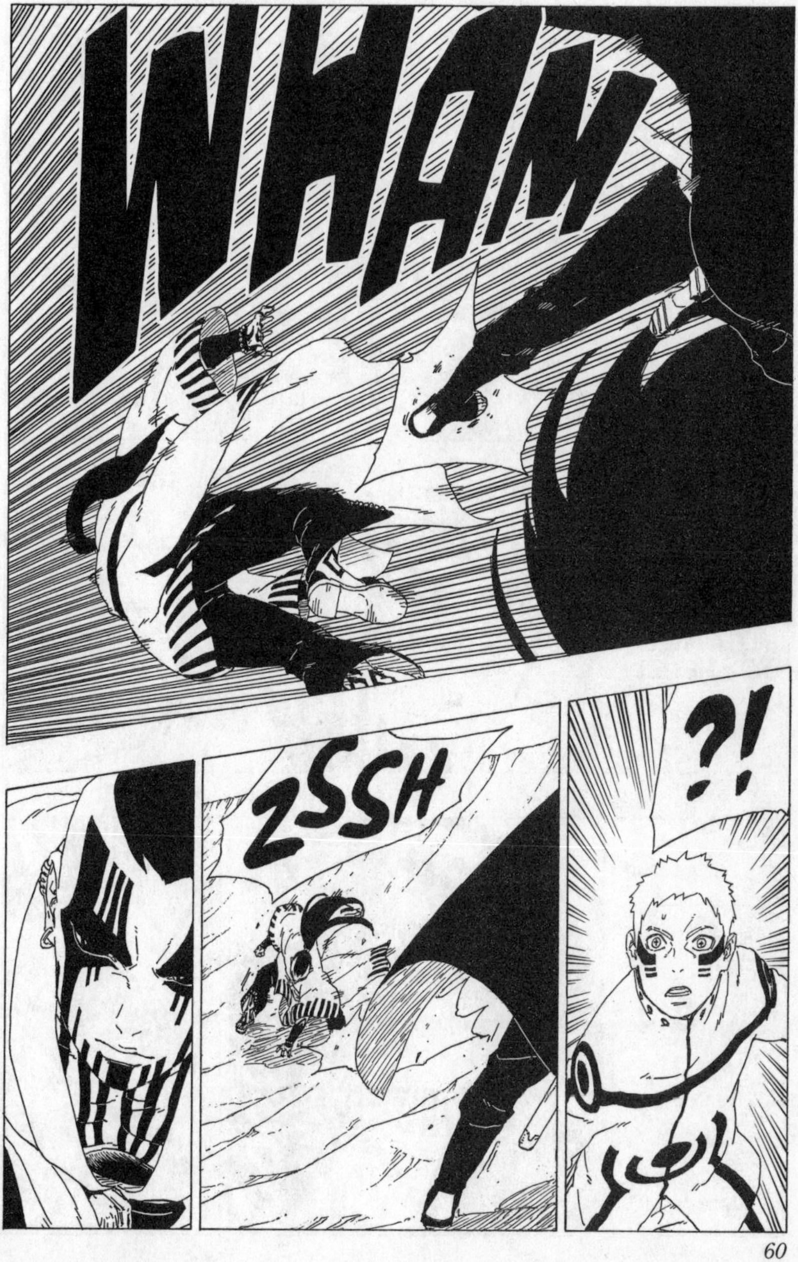
WHAM
?!
ZSSH

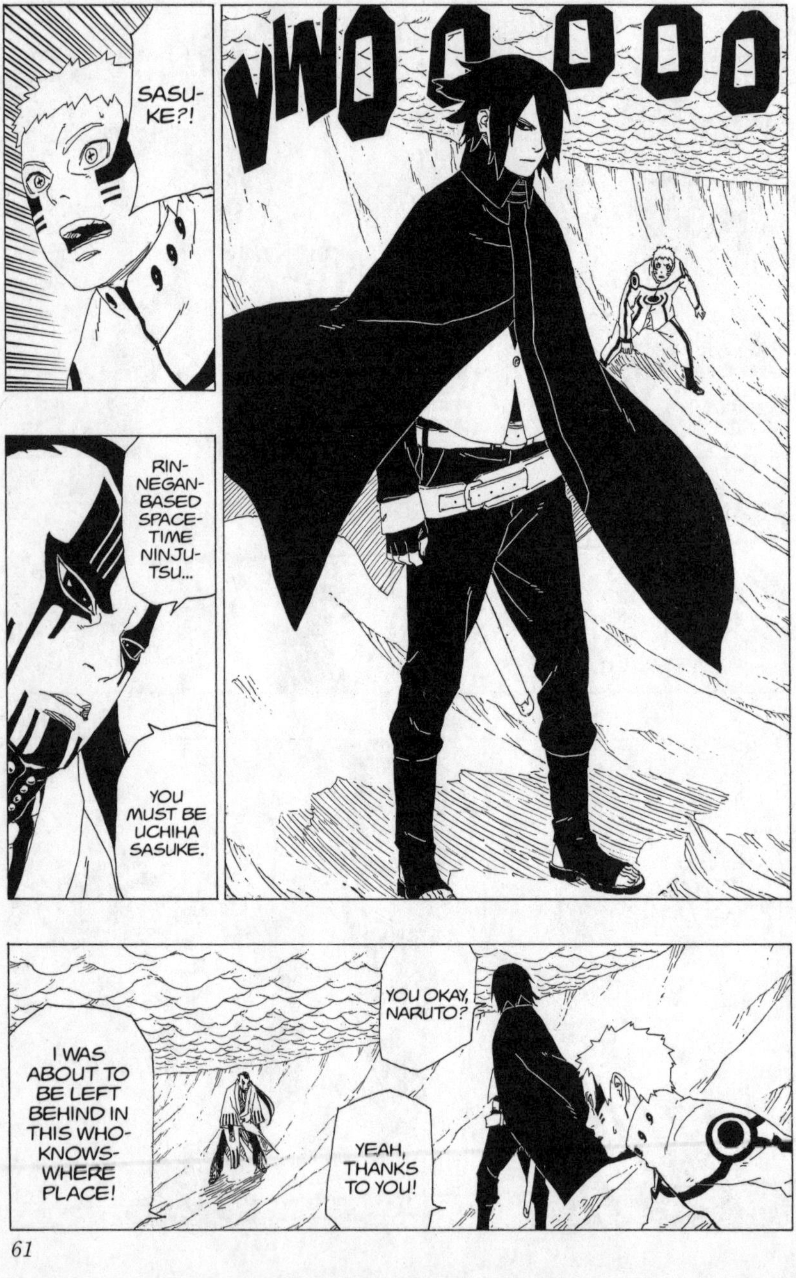
VWOOOOOO
SASUKE?!
RINNEGAN-BASED SPACE-TIME NINJUTSU...
YOU MUST BE UCHIHA SASUKE.
YOU OKAY, NARUTO?
YEAH, THANKS TO YOU!
I WAS ABOUT TO BE LEFT BEHIND IN THIS WHO-KNOWS-WHERE PLACE!

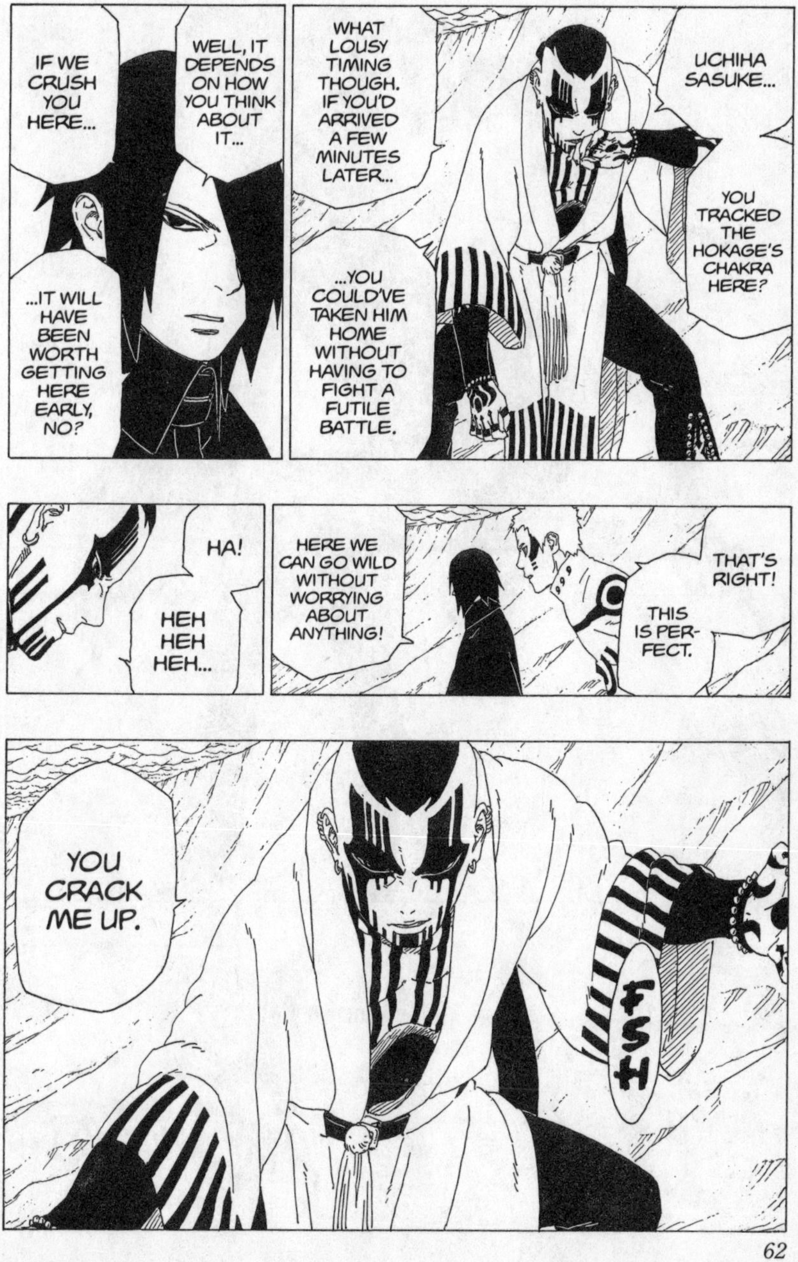
UCHIHA SASUKE...
YOU TRACKED THE HOKAGE'S CHAKRA HERE?
WHAT LOUSY TIMING THOUGH. IF YOU'D ARRIVED A FEW MINUTES LATER...
...YOU COULD'VE TAKEN HIM HOME WITHOUT HAVING TO FIGHT A FUTILE BATTLE.
WELL, IT DEPENDS ON HOW YOU THINK ABOUT IT...
IF WE CRUSH YOU HERE...
...IT WILL HAVE BEEN WORTH GETTING HERE EARLY, NO?
THAT'S RIGHT!
THIS IS PERFECT.
HERE WE CAN GO WILD WITHOUT WORRYING ABOUT ANYTHING!
HA!
HEH HEH HEH...
FSH
YOU CRACK ME UP.

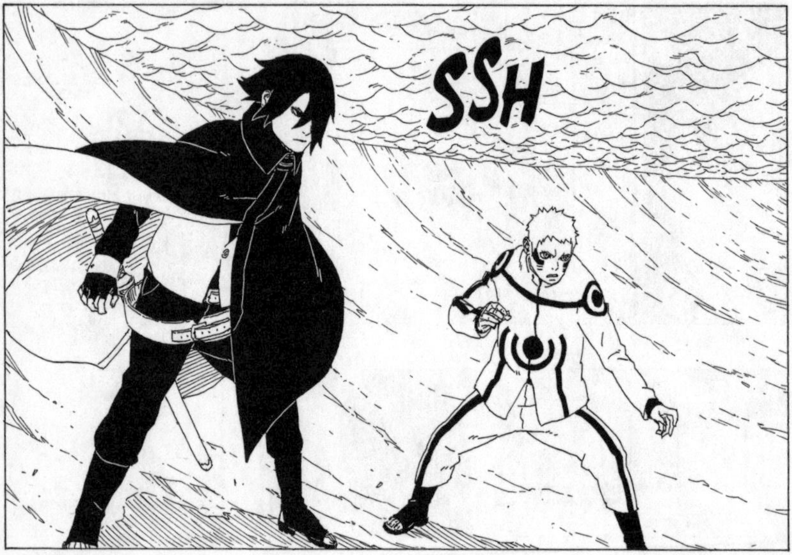
SSH

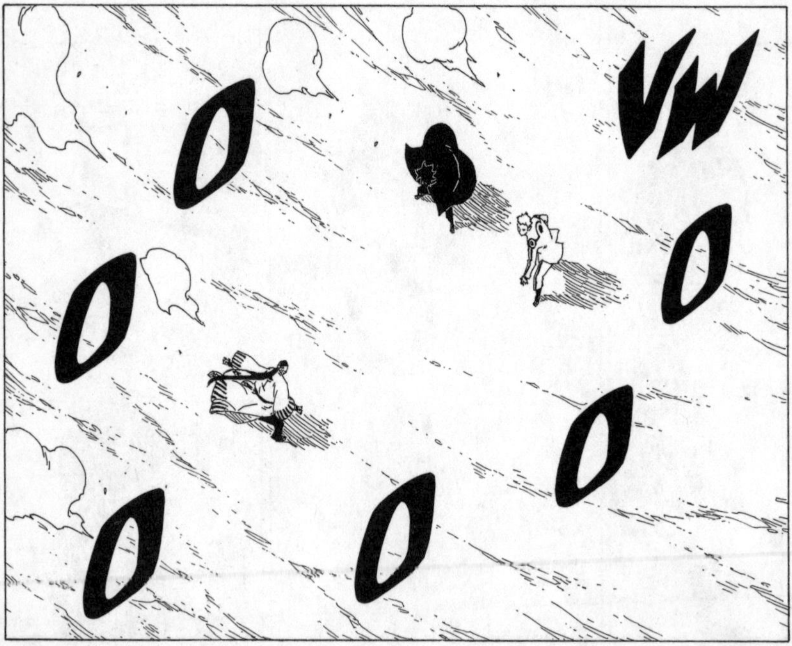
VWOOOOOO

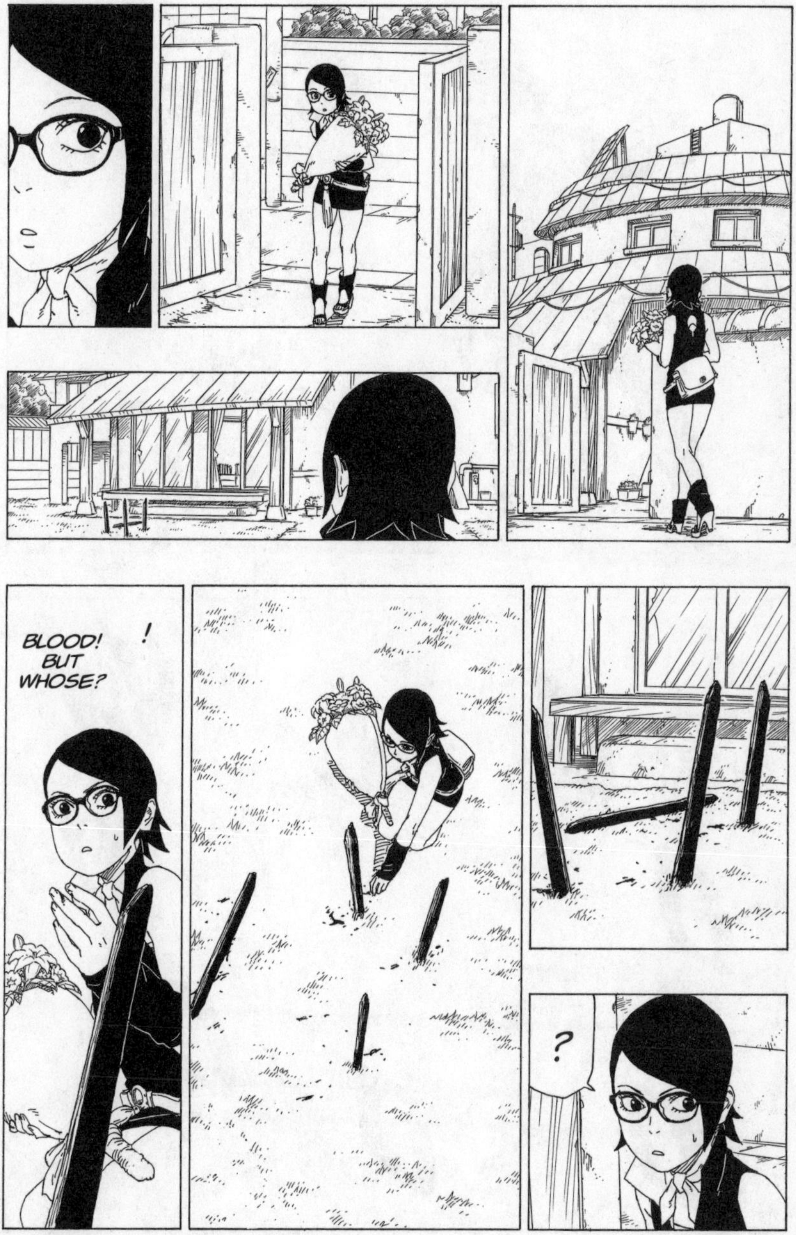
?
!
BLOOD! BUT WHOSE?

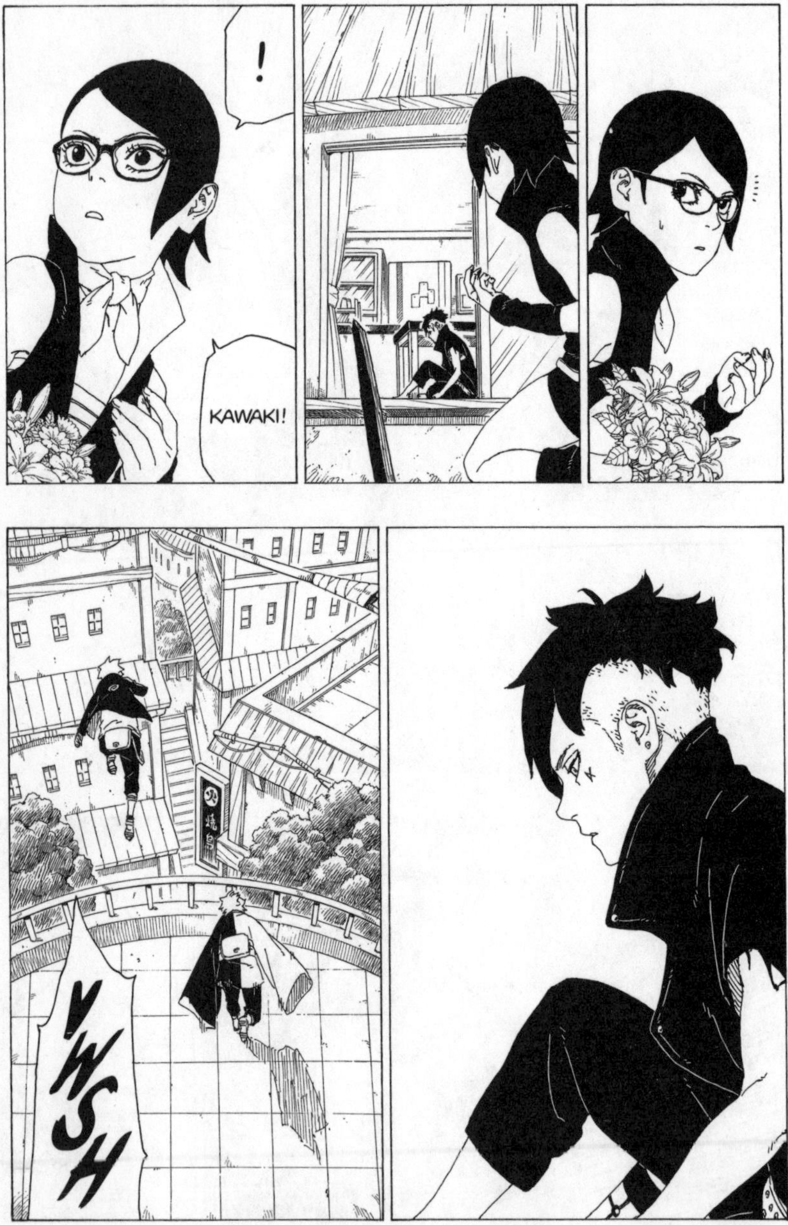
!
KAWAKI!
VWSH

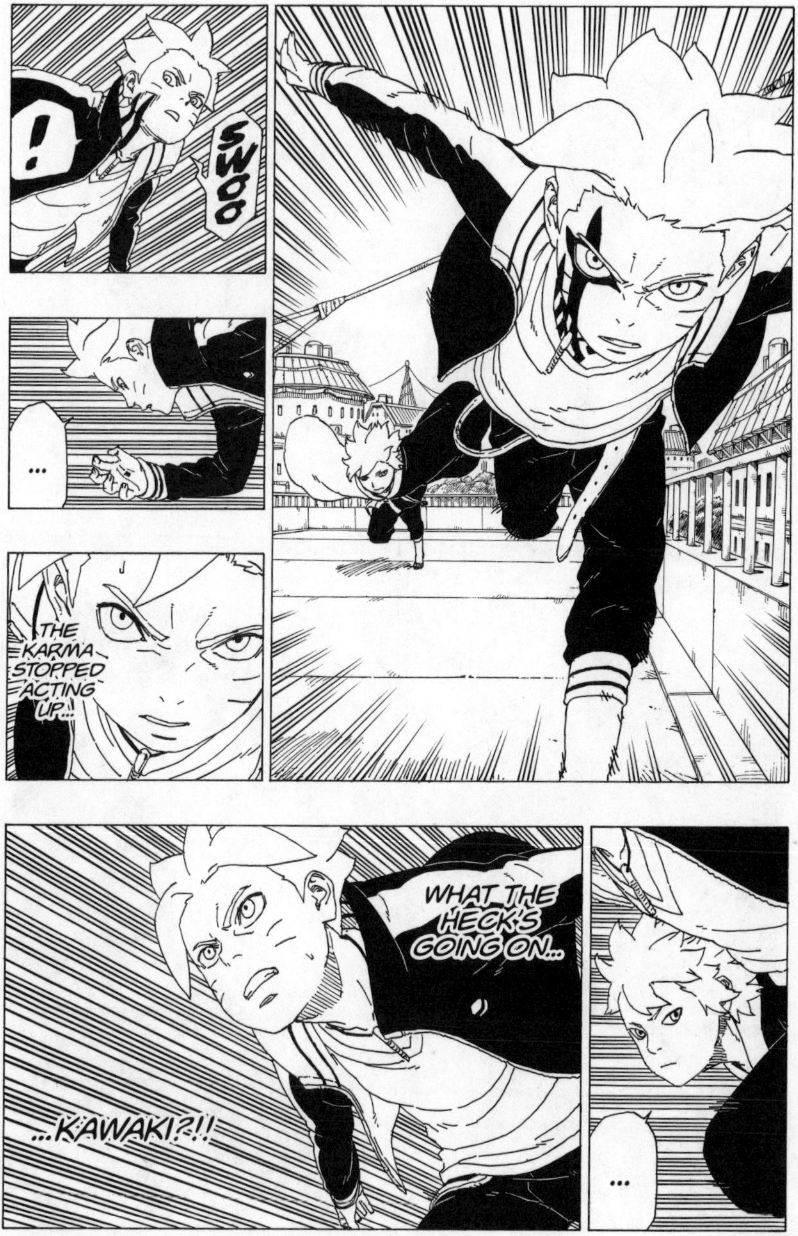
!
SWOO
...
THE KARMA STOPPED ACTING UP...
...
WHAT THE HECK'S GOING ON...
...KAWAKI?!!

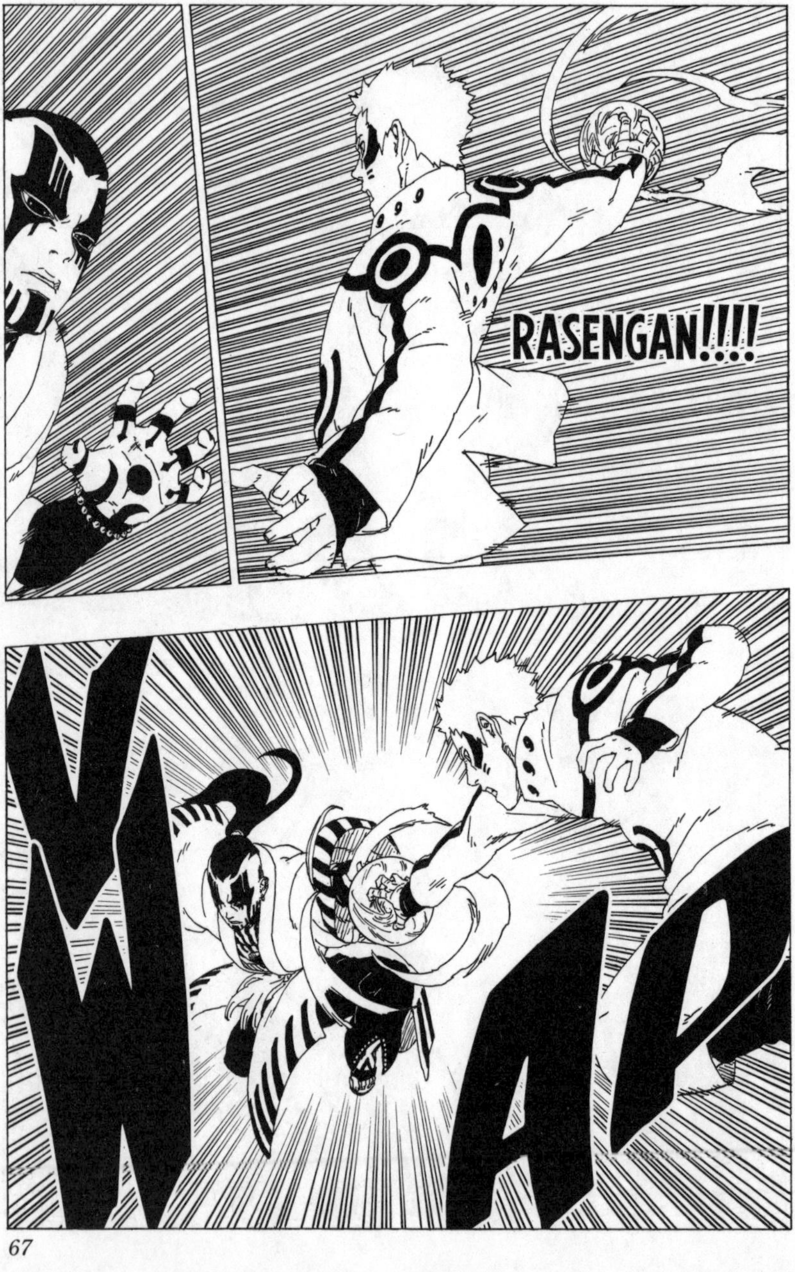
RASENGAN!!!!
WAP

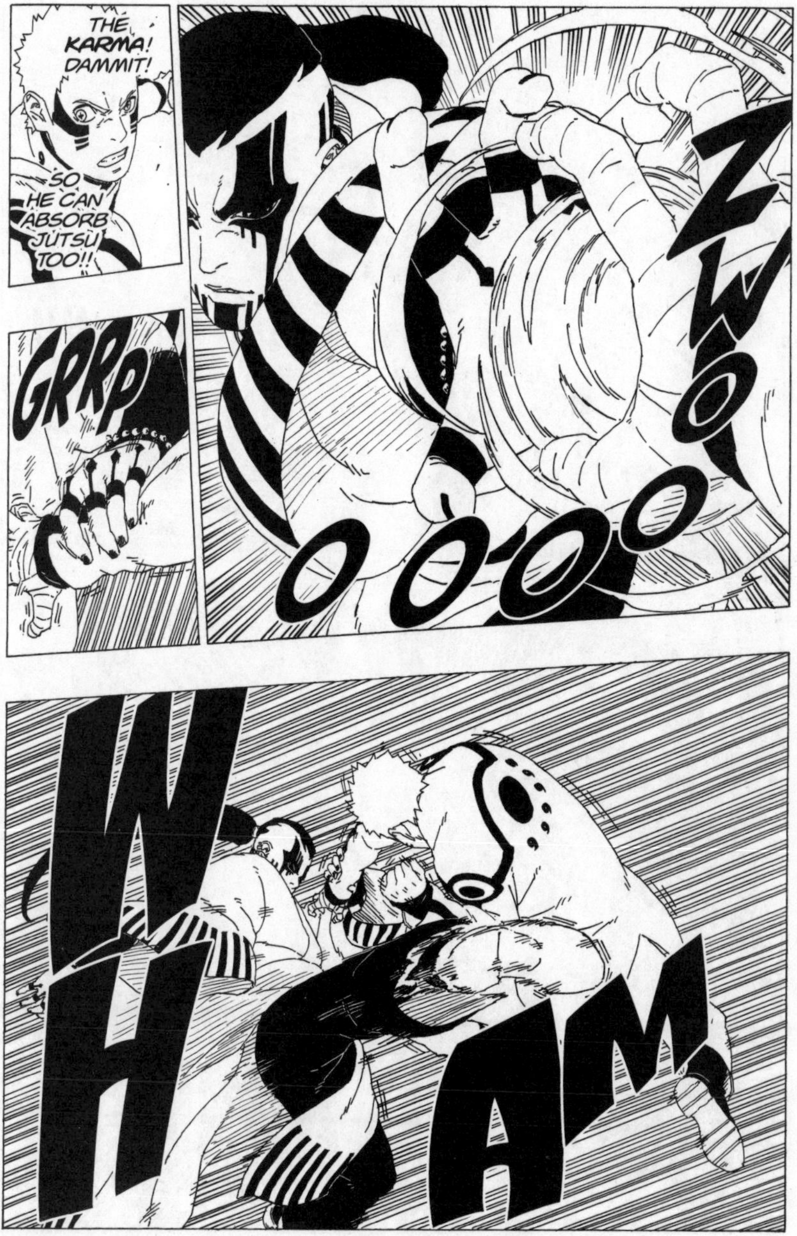
ZWOOOOOO
THE KARMA! DAMMIT!
SO HE CAN ABSORB JUTSU TOO!!
GRRP
WHAM

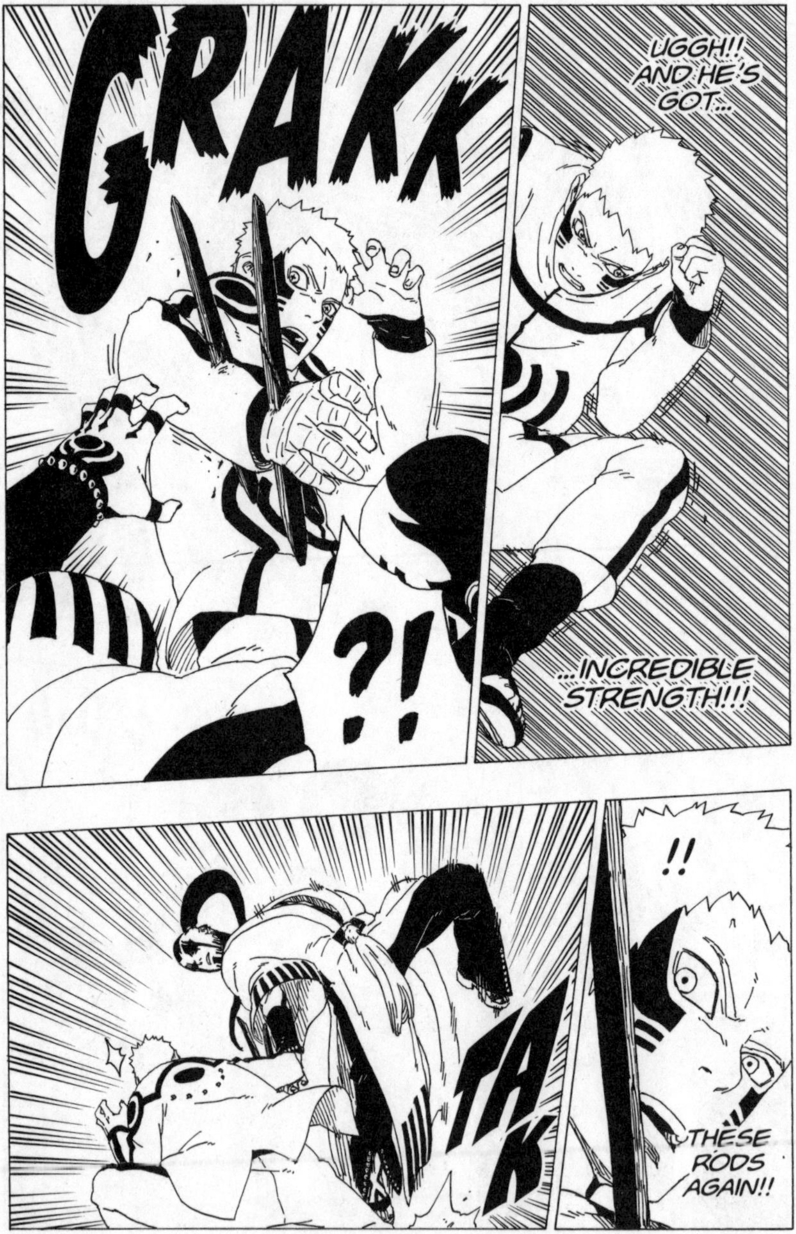
UGGH!! AND HE'S GOT...
...INCREDIBLE STRENGTH!!!
GRAKK
?!
!!
THESE RODS AGAIN!!
TAK

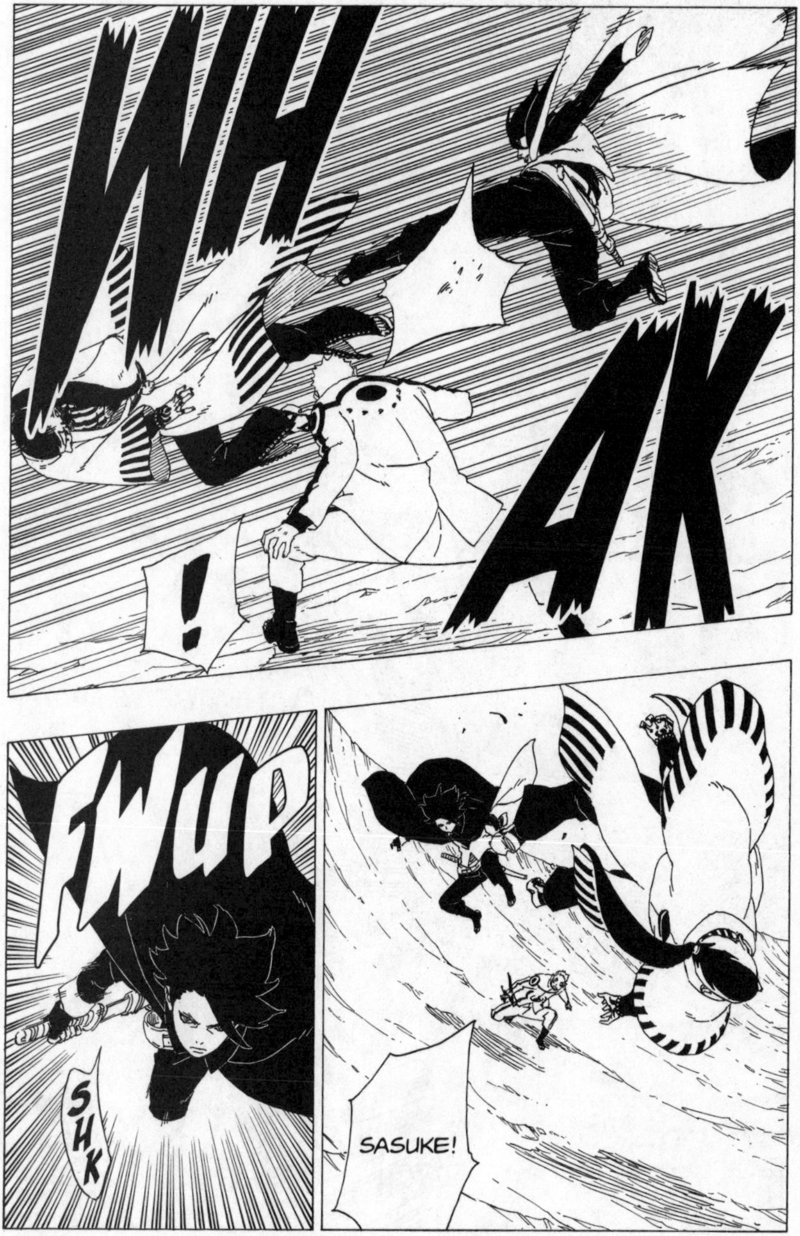
WHAK
!
SASUKE!
FWUP
SHK

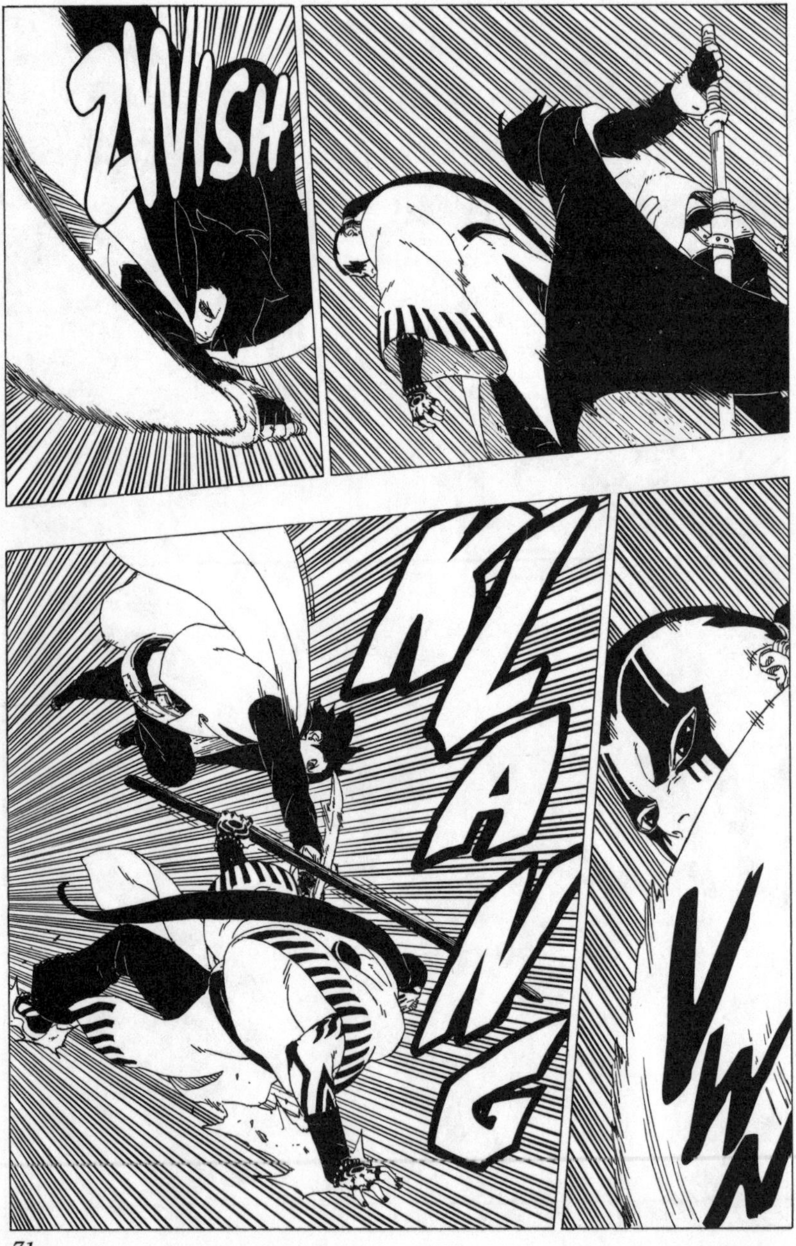
ZWISH
VWN
KLANG

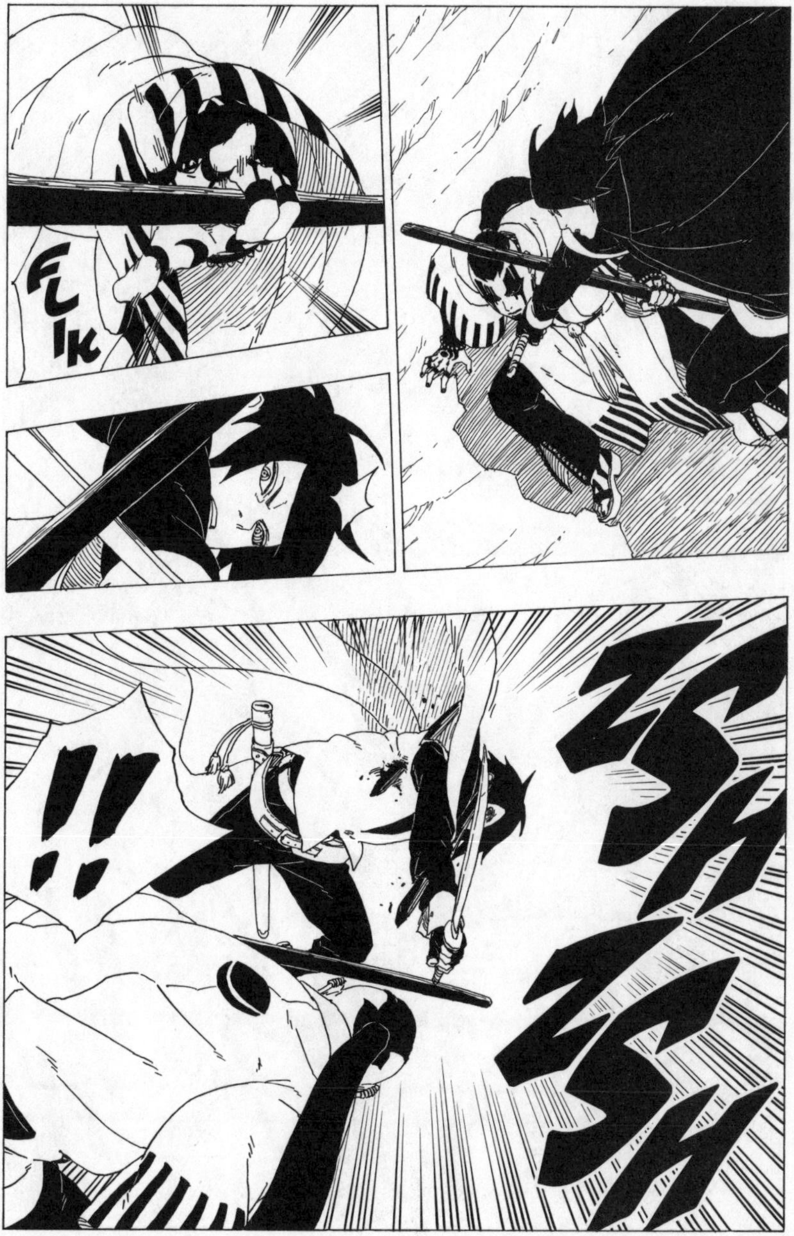
FLIK
!!
ZSHHH

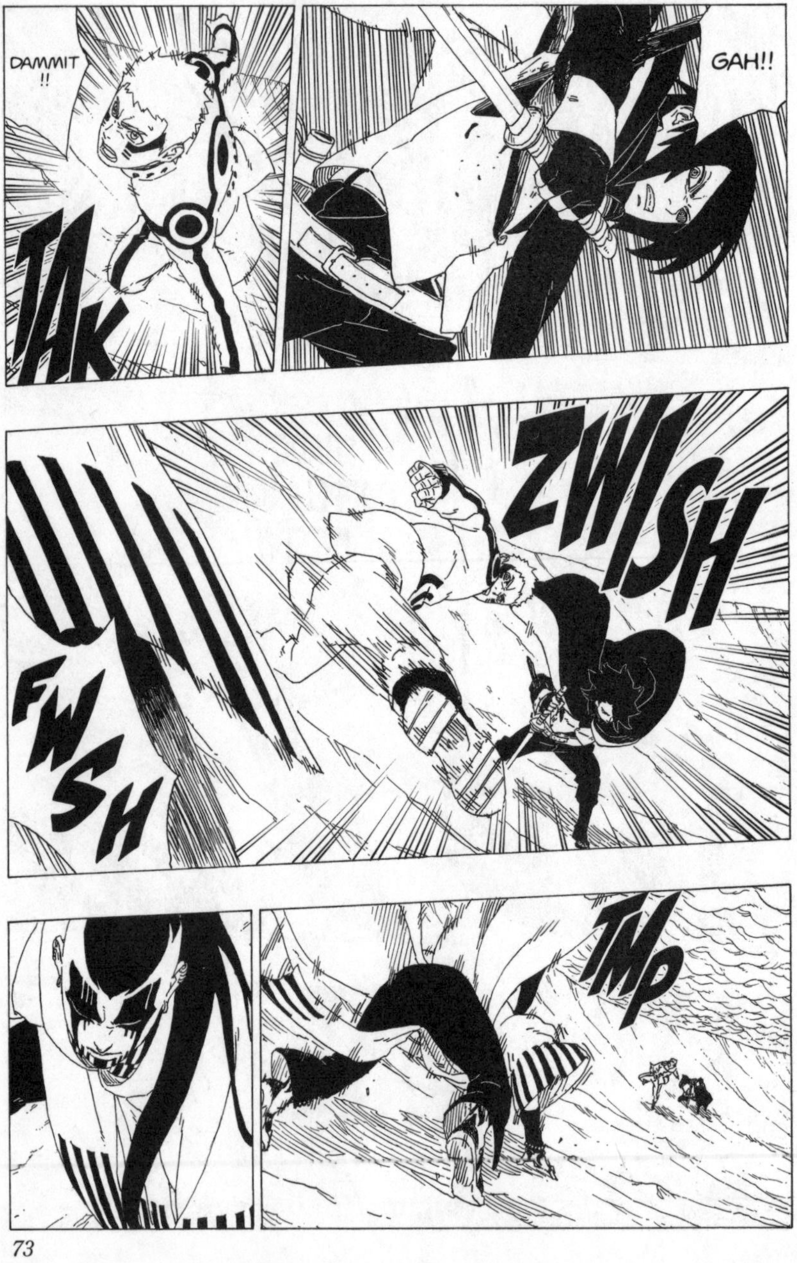
GAH!!
DAMMIT!!
TAK
ZWISH
FWSH
TMP

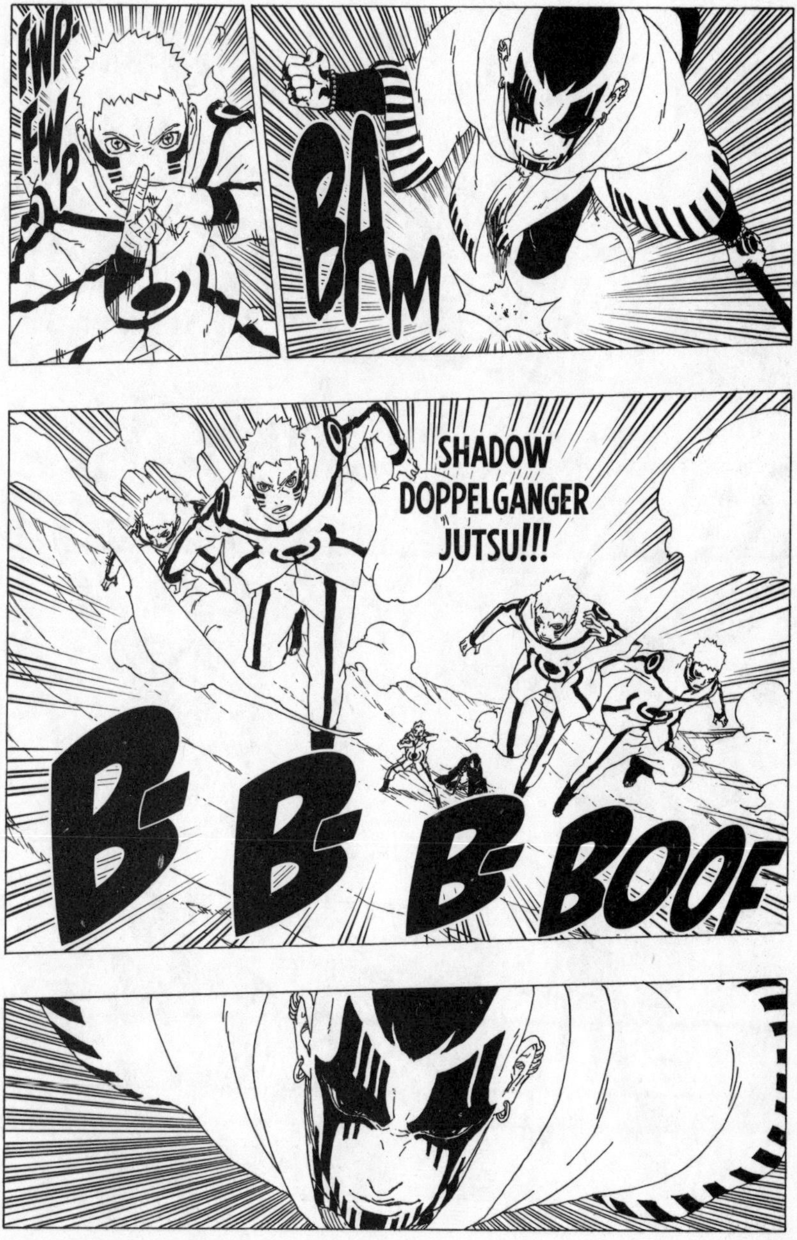
BAM
FWP-FWP
SHADOW DOPPELGANGER JUTSU!!!
B-B-B-BOOF

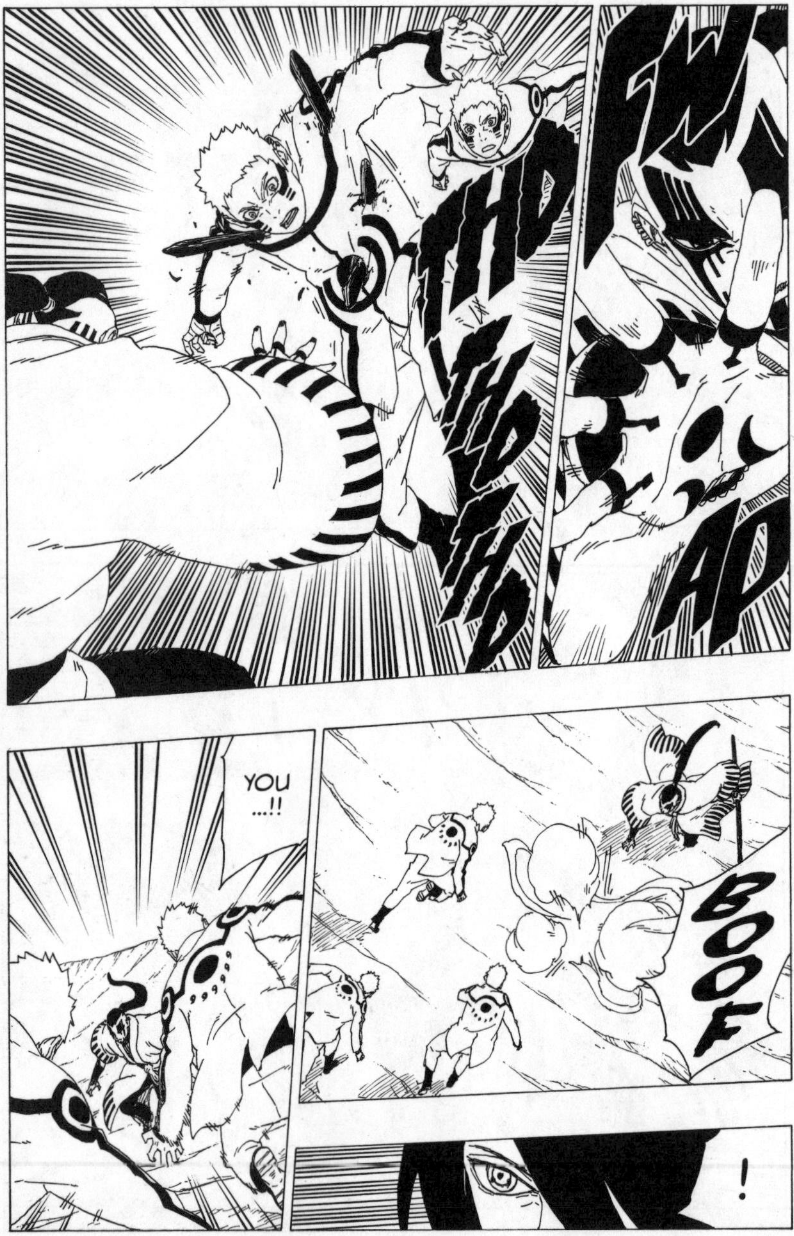
THD THD THD THD
BOOF
!
YOU ...!!

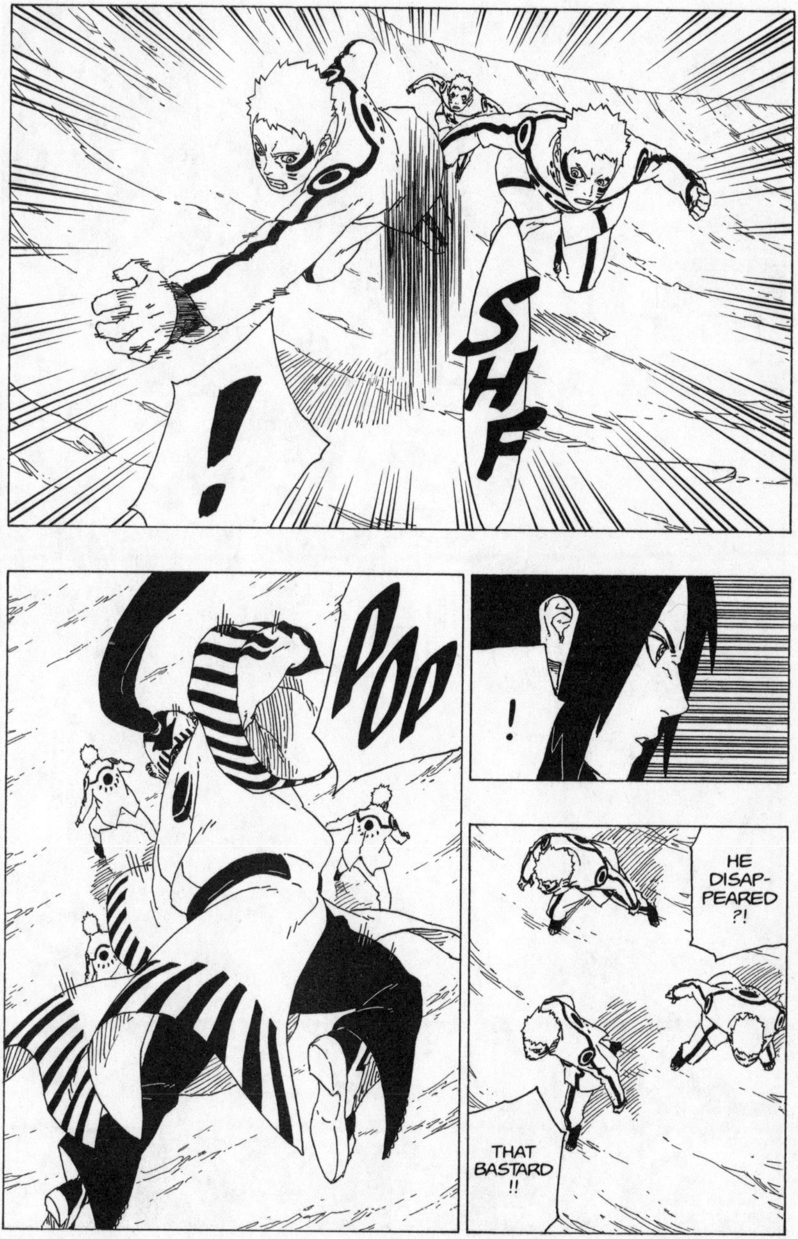
SHF
!
!
HE DISAP-PEARED ?!
THAT BASTARD !!
POP

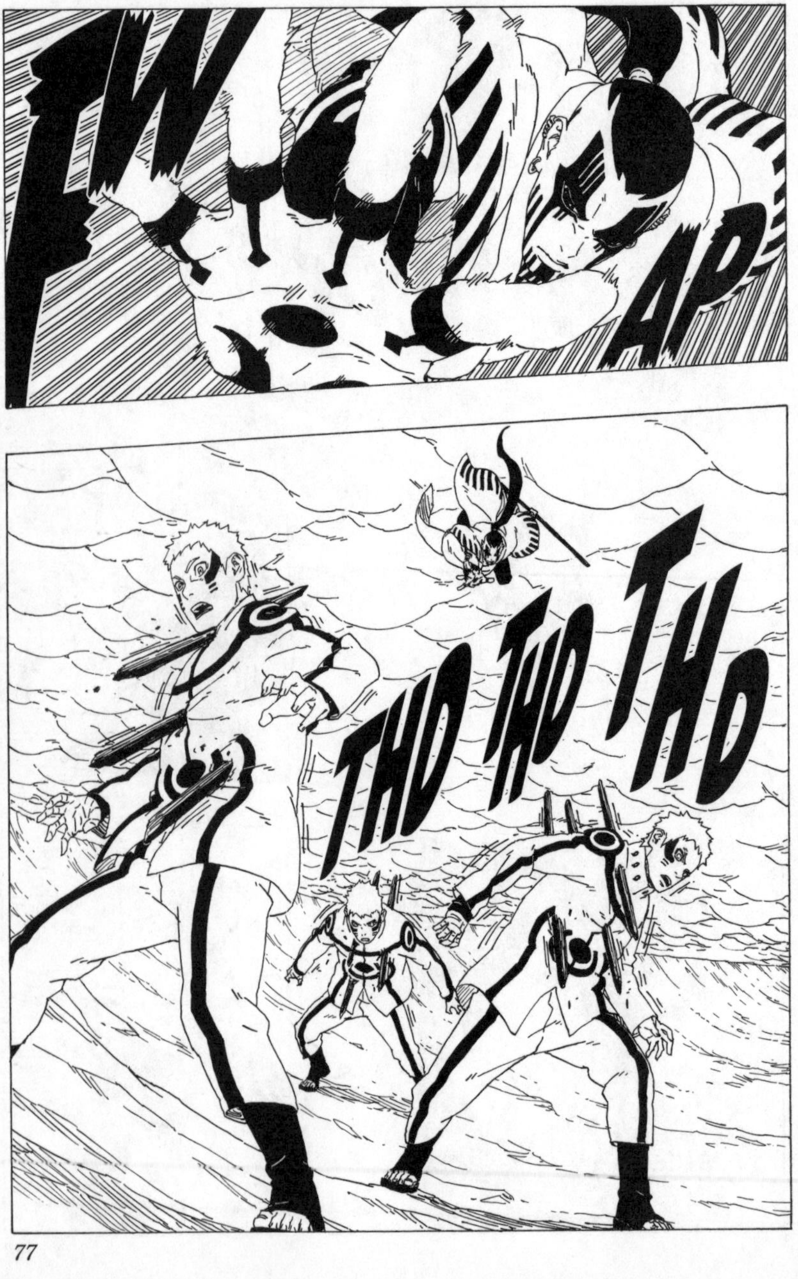
TW AP
THD THD THD

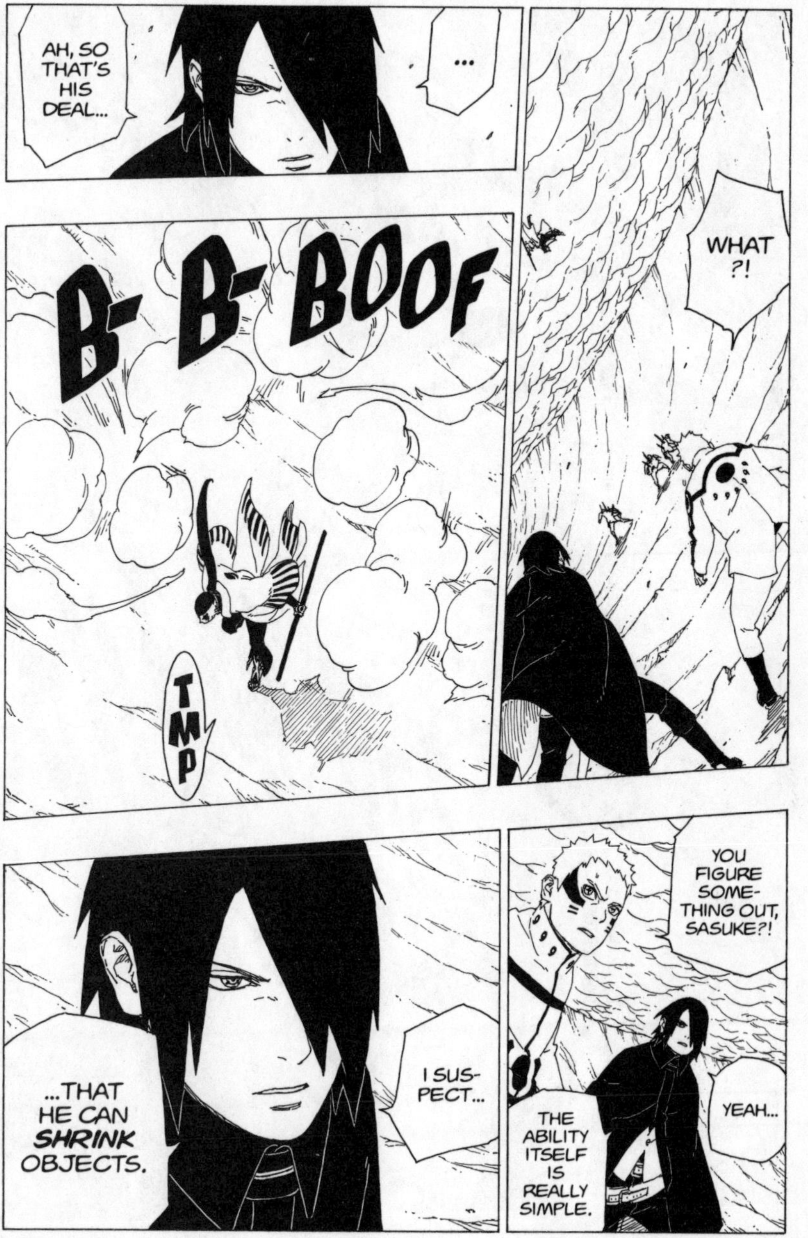
WHAT?!
...
AH, SO THAT'S HIS DEAL...
B-B-BOOF
TMP
YOU FIGURE SOME-THING OUT, SASUKE?!
YEAH...
THE ABILITY ITSELF IS REALLY SIMPLE.
I SUS-PECT...
...THAT HE CAN **SHRINK** OBJECTS.

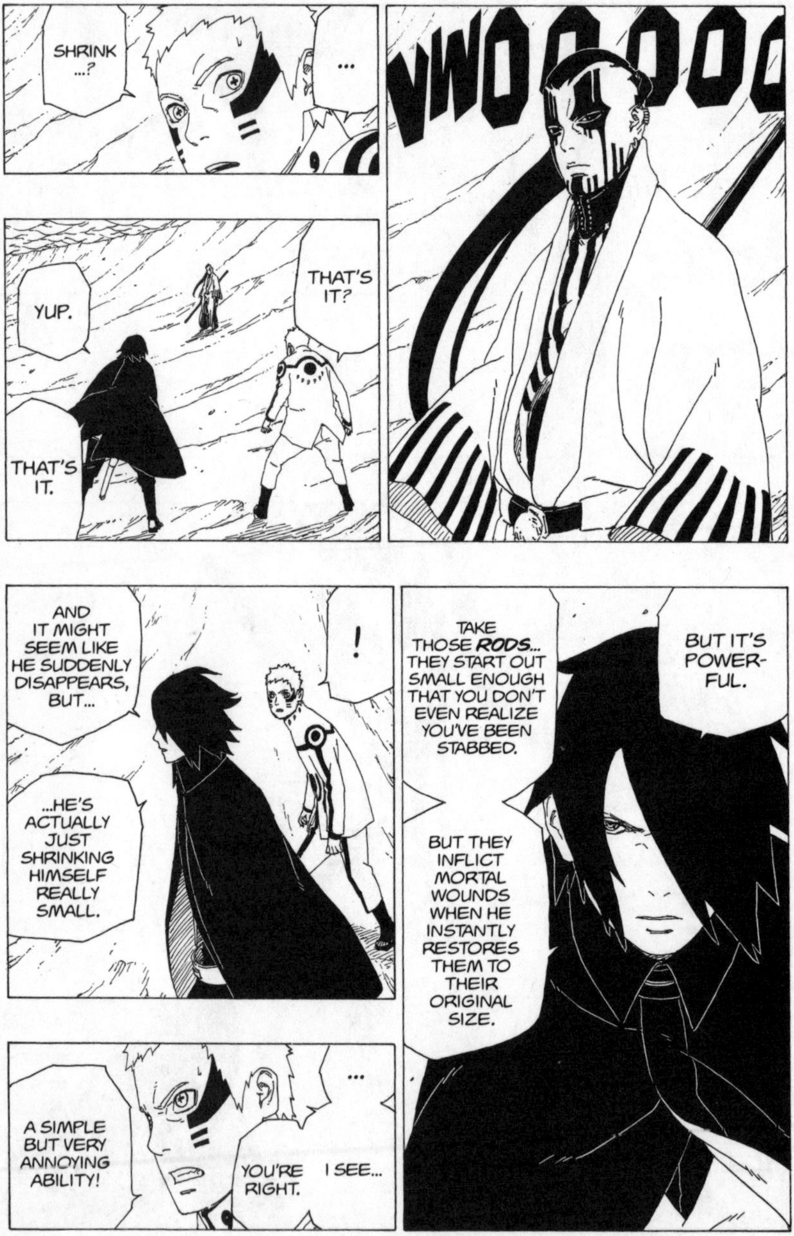
VWOOOOO
...
SHRINK ...?
THAT'S IT?
YUP.
THAT'S IT.
BUT IT'S POWERFUL.
TAKE THOSE **RODS**... THEY START OUT SMALL ENOUGH THAT YOU DON'T EVEN REALIZE YOU'VE BEEN STABBED.
BUT THEY INFLICT MORTAL WOUNDS WHEN HE INSTANTLY RESTORES THEM TO THEIR ORIGINAL SIZE.
!
AND IT MIGHT SEEM LIKE HE SUDDENLY DISAPPEARS, BUT...
...HE'S ACTUALLY JUST SHRINKING HIMSELF REALLY SMALL.
...
I SEE...
YOU'RE RIGHT.
A SIMPLE BUT VERY ANNOYING ABILITY!

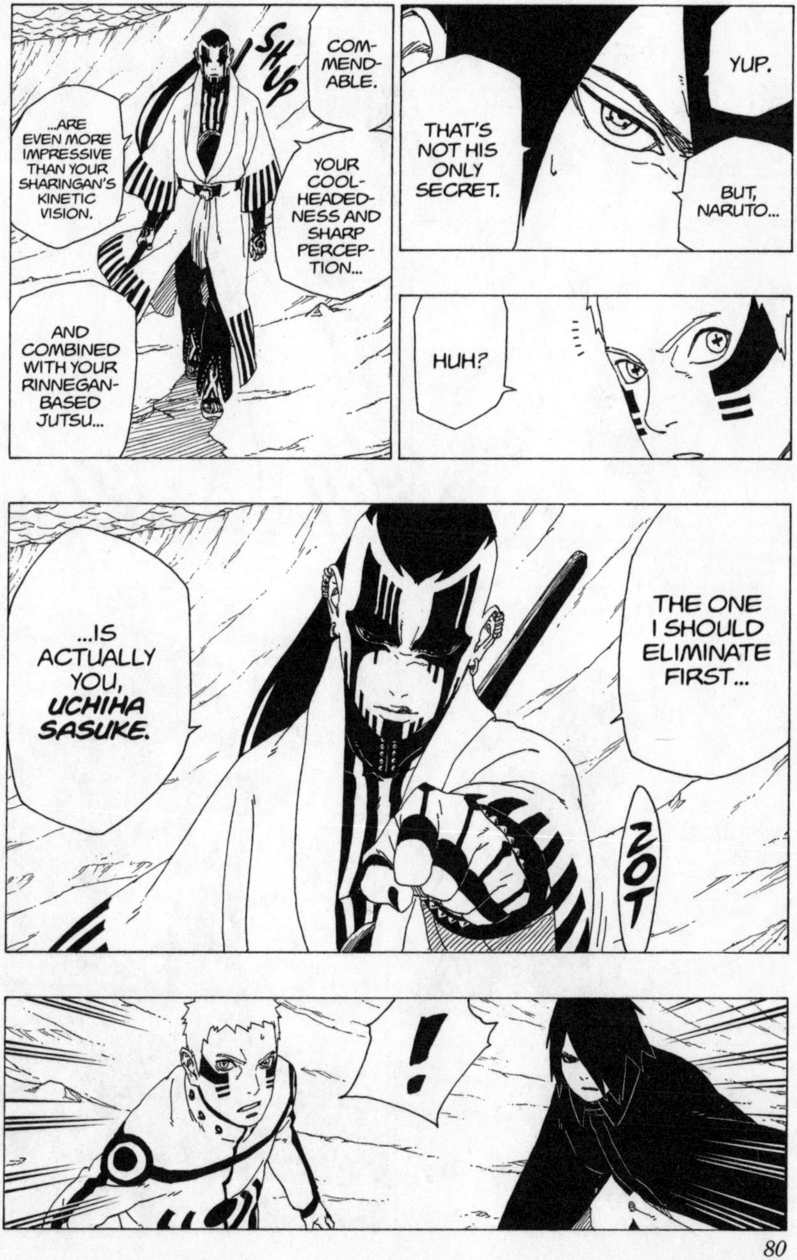
YUP.
BUT, NARUTO...
THAT'S NOT HIS ONLY SECRET.
HUH?
COMMENDABLE.
SHUP
YOUR COOL-HEADEDNESS AND SHARP PERCEPTION...
...ARE EVEN MORE IMPRESSIVE THAN YOUR SHARINGAN'S KINETIC VISION.
AND COMBINED WITH YOUR RINNEGAN-BASED JUTSU...
THE ONE I SHOULD ELIMINATE FIRST...
ZOT
...IS ACTUALLY YOU, UCHIHA SASUKE.
!

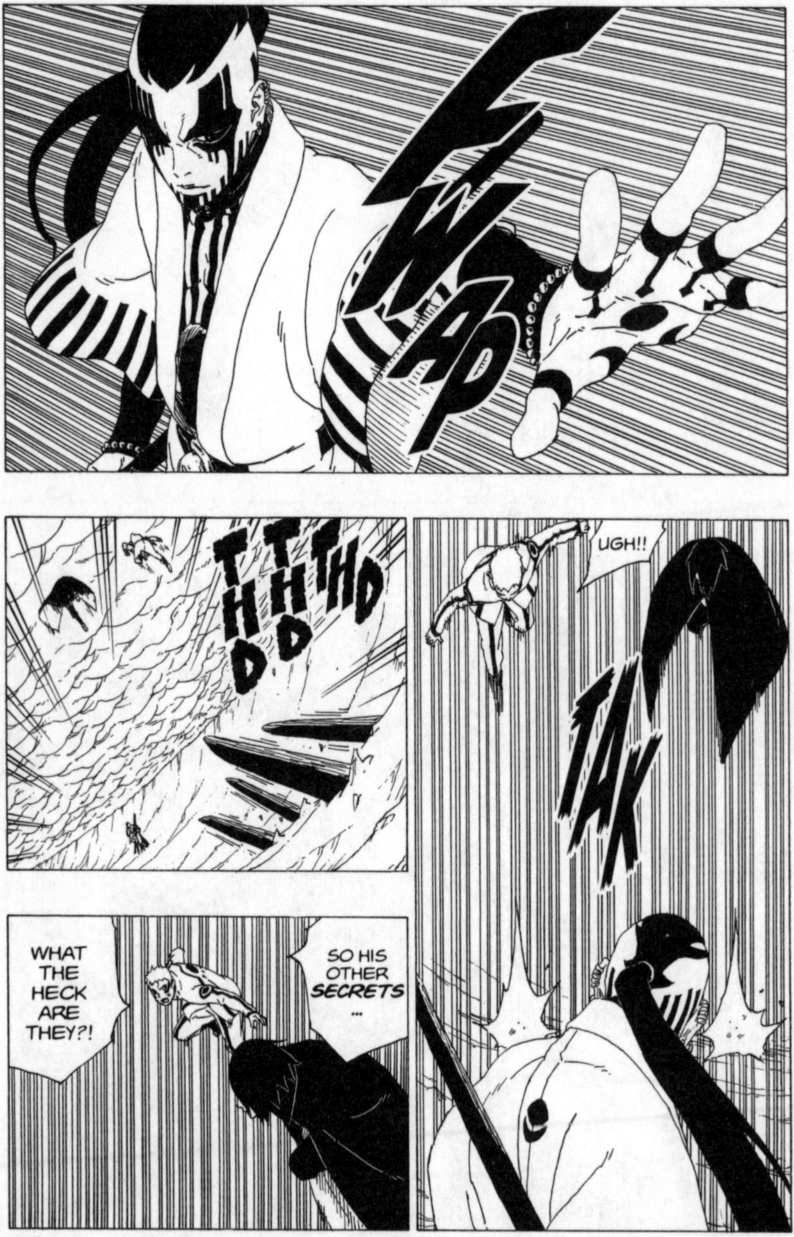
WHAP
UGH!!
TAK
THHD
SO HIS OTHER SECRETS...
WHAT THE HECK ARE THEY?!

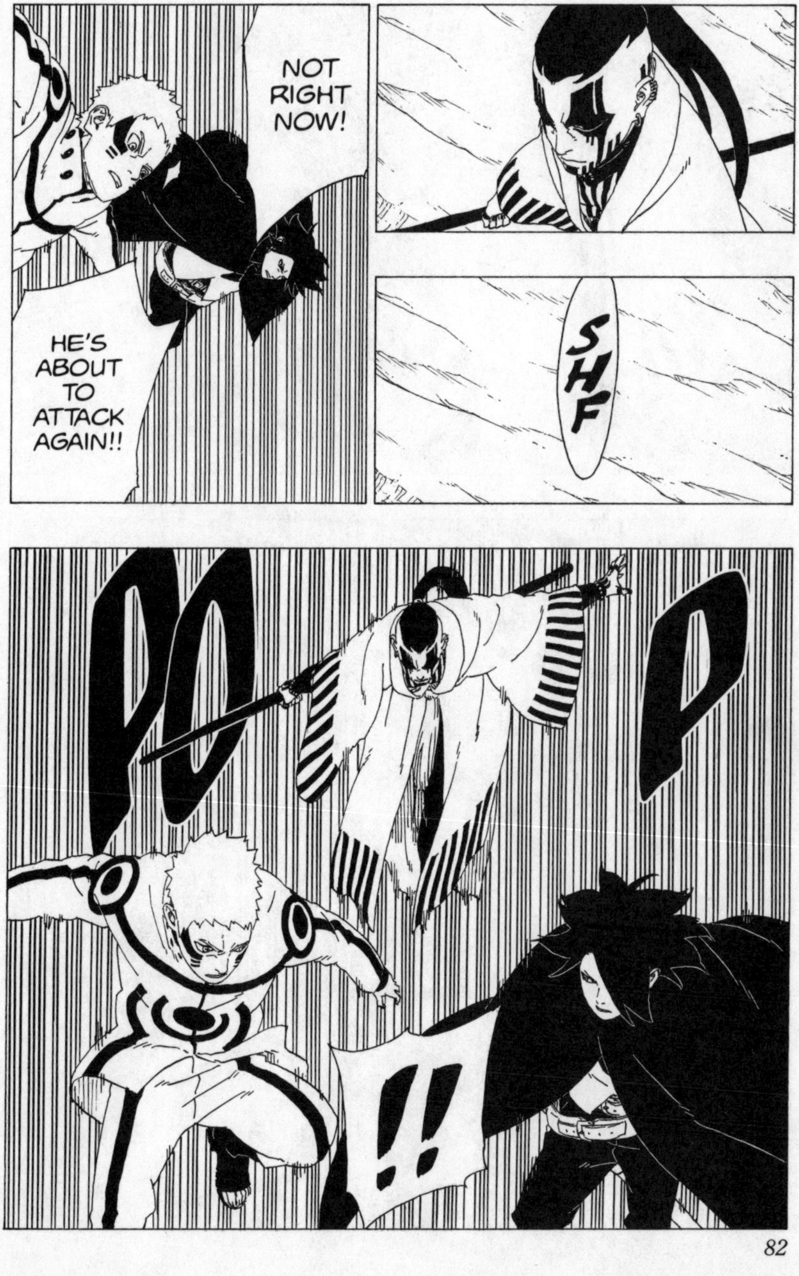
SHF
NOT RIGHT NOW!
HE'S ABOUT TO ATTACK AGAIN!!
POP
!!

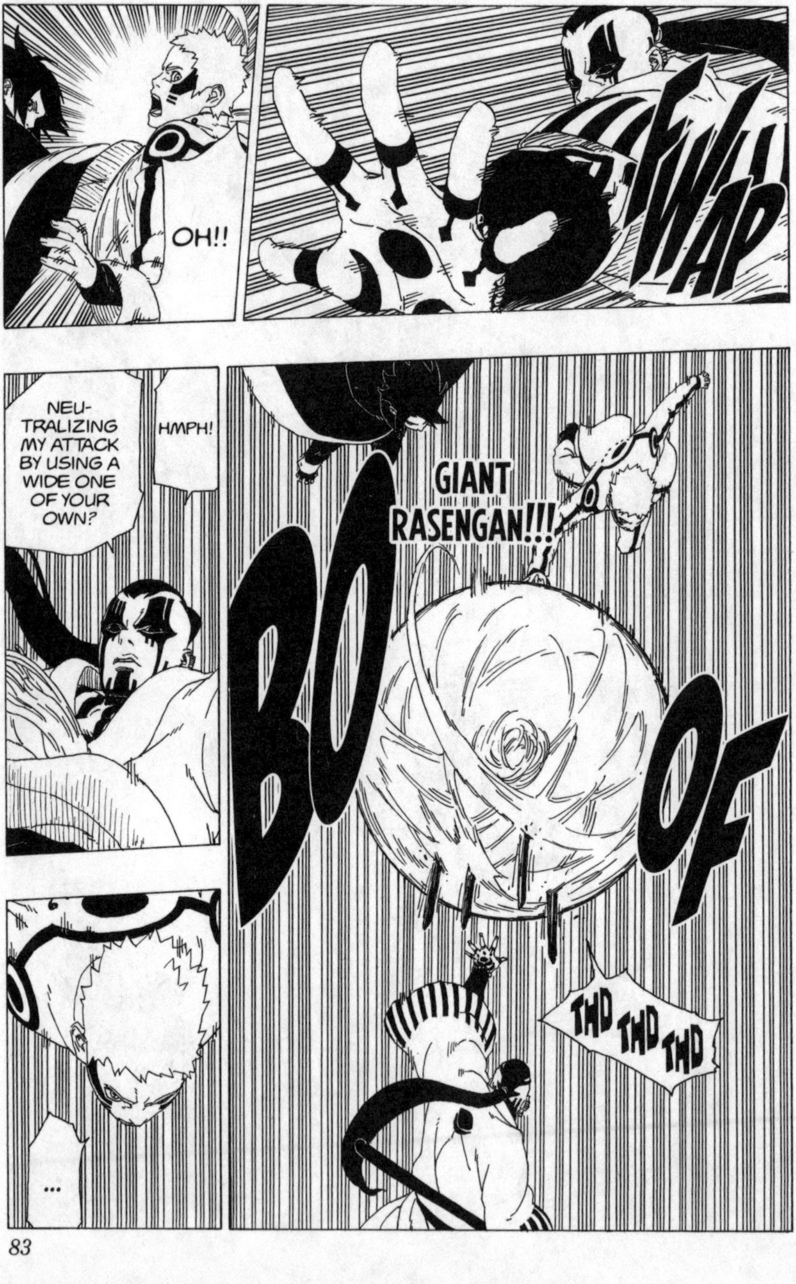
FWAP
OH!!
GIANT RASENGAN!!!
BOOF
THD THD THD
HMPH!
NEU-TRALIZING MY ATTACK BY USING A WIDE ONE OF YOUR OWN?
...

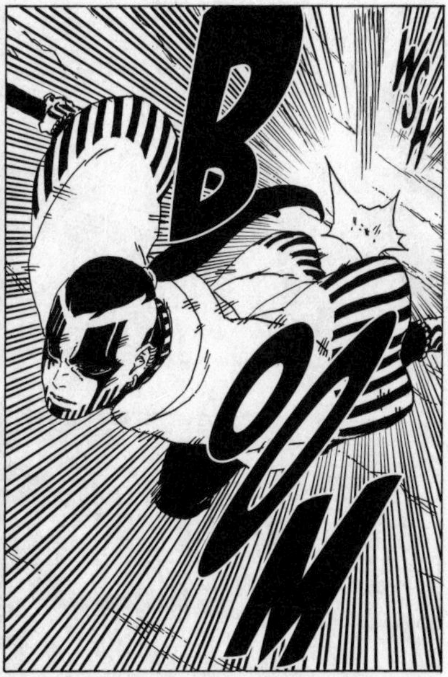
WSH
BOOM
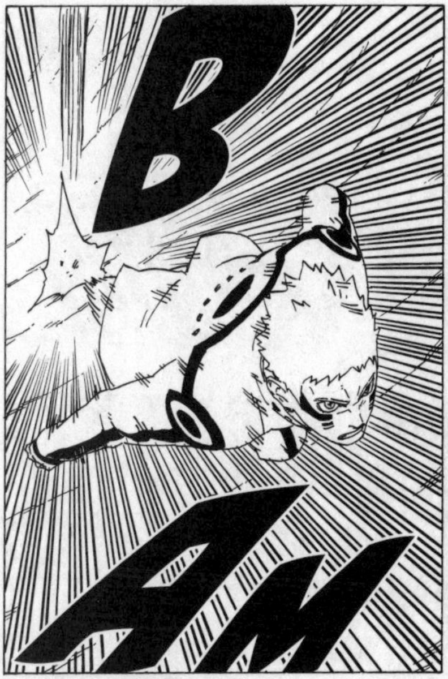
BAM
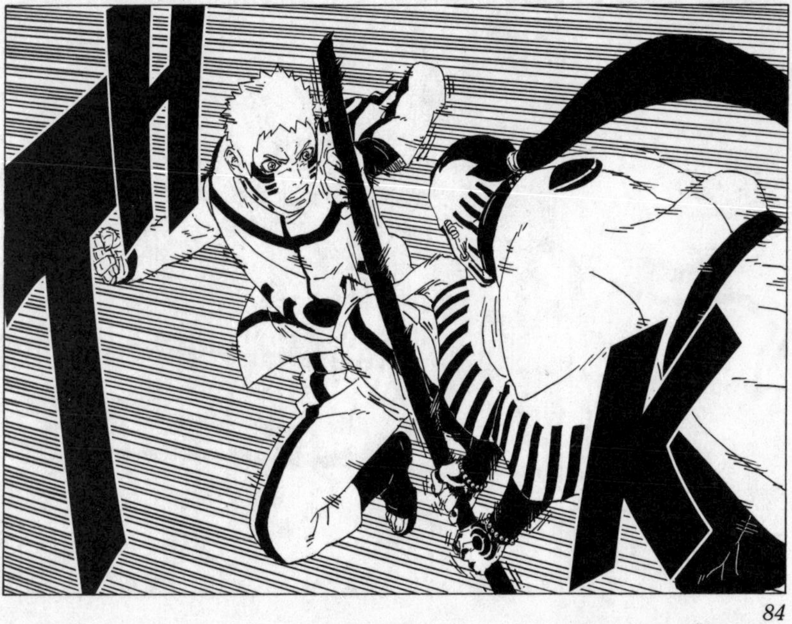
THK

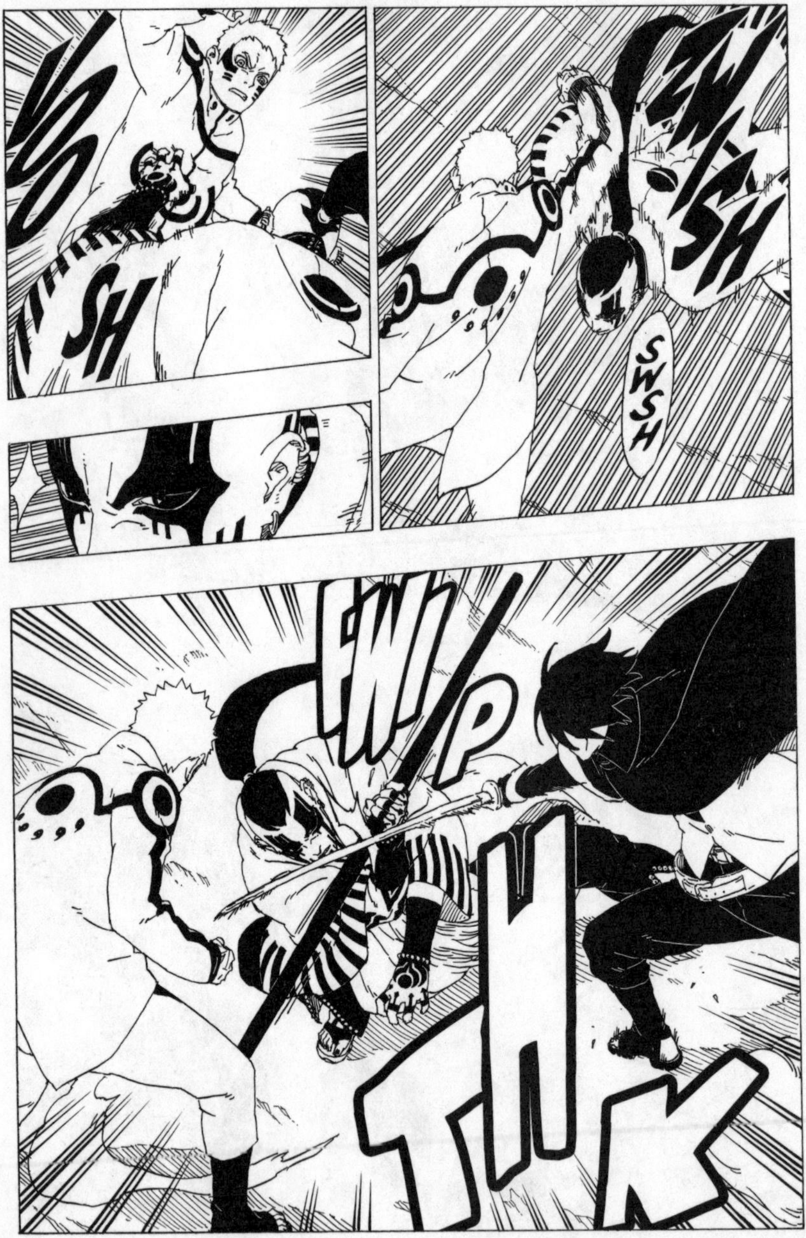
SWSH
SWSH
VOOSH
FWIP
THK

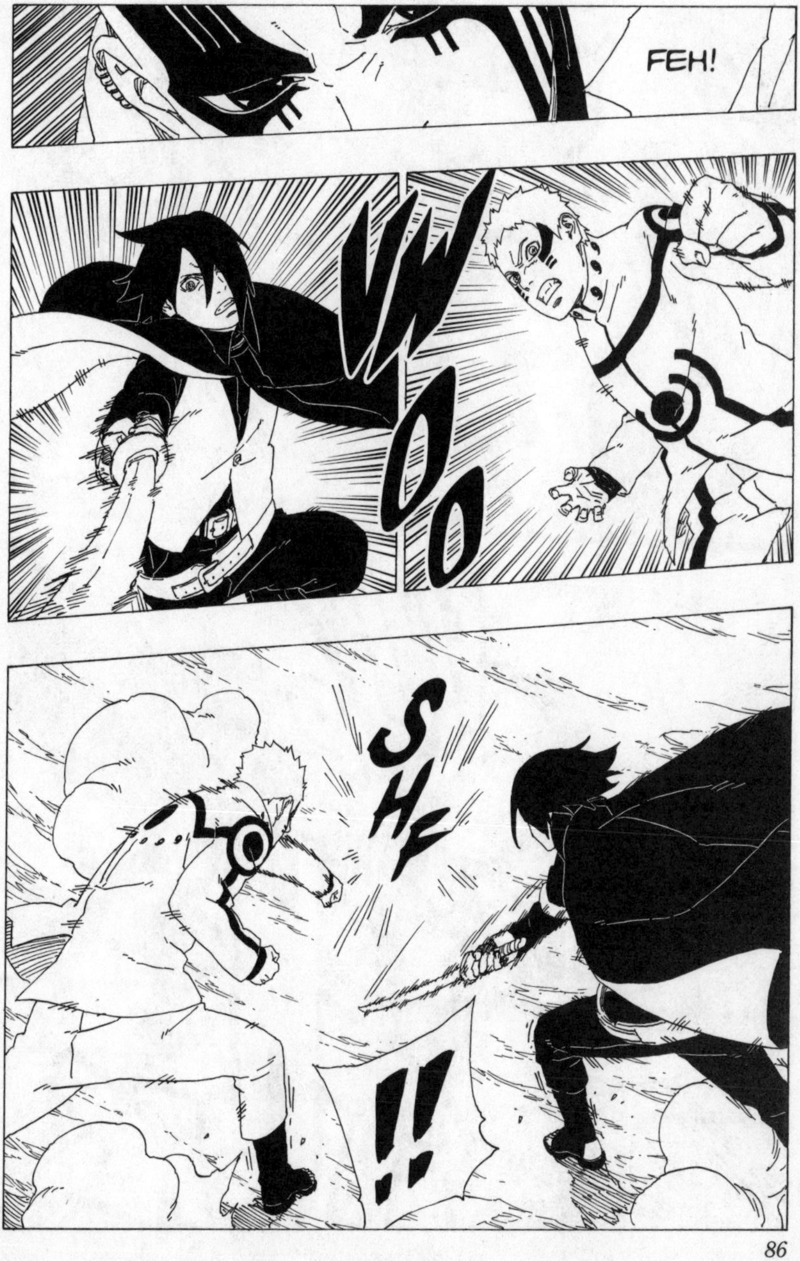
FEH!
VWOOO
SHF
!!

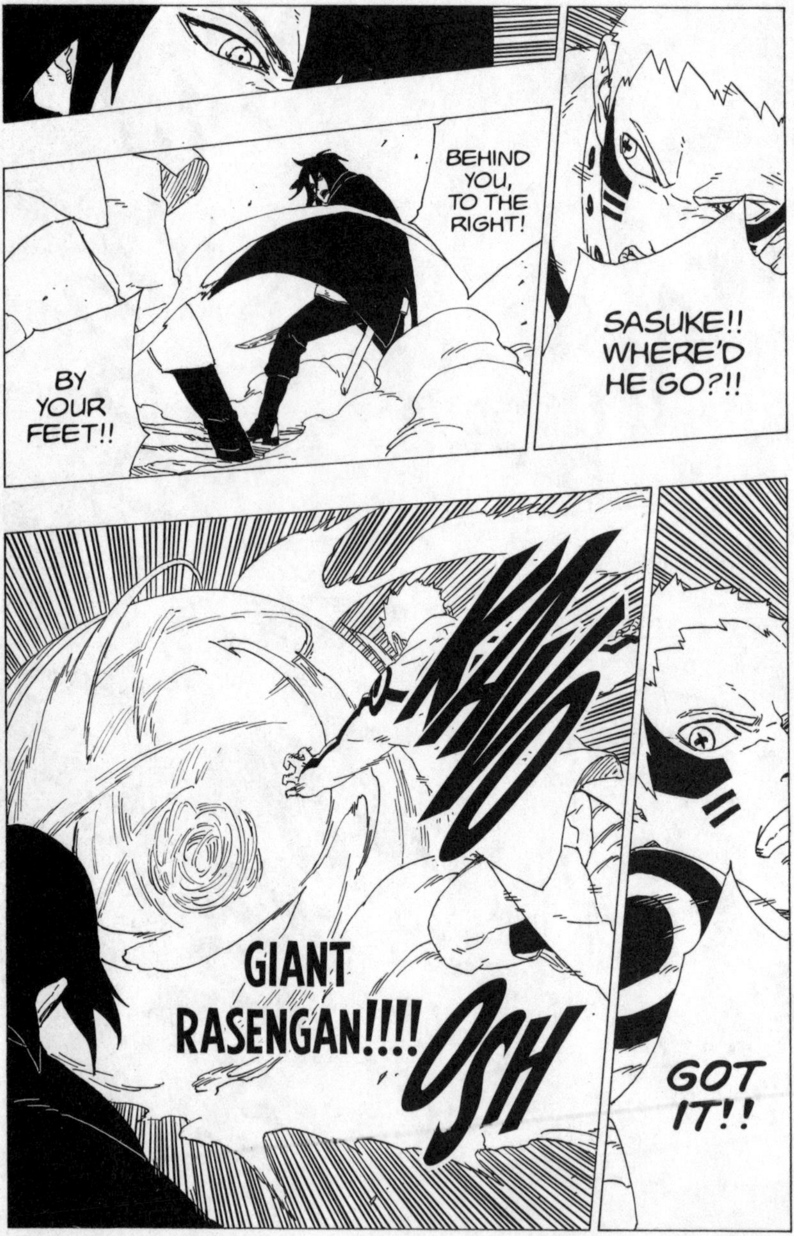
SASUKE!! WHERE'D HE GO?!!
BEHIND YOU, TO THE RIGHT!
BY YOUR FEET!!
GOT IT!!
WHOOSH
GIANT RASENGAN!!!!

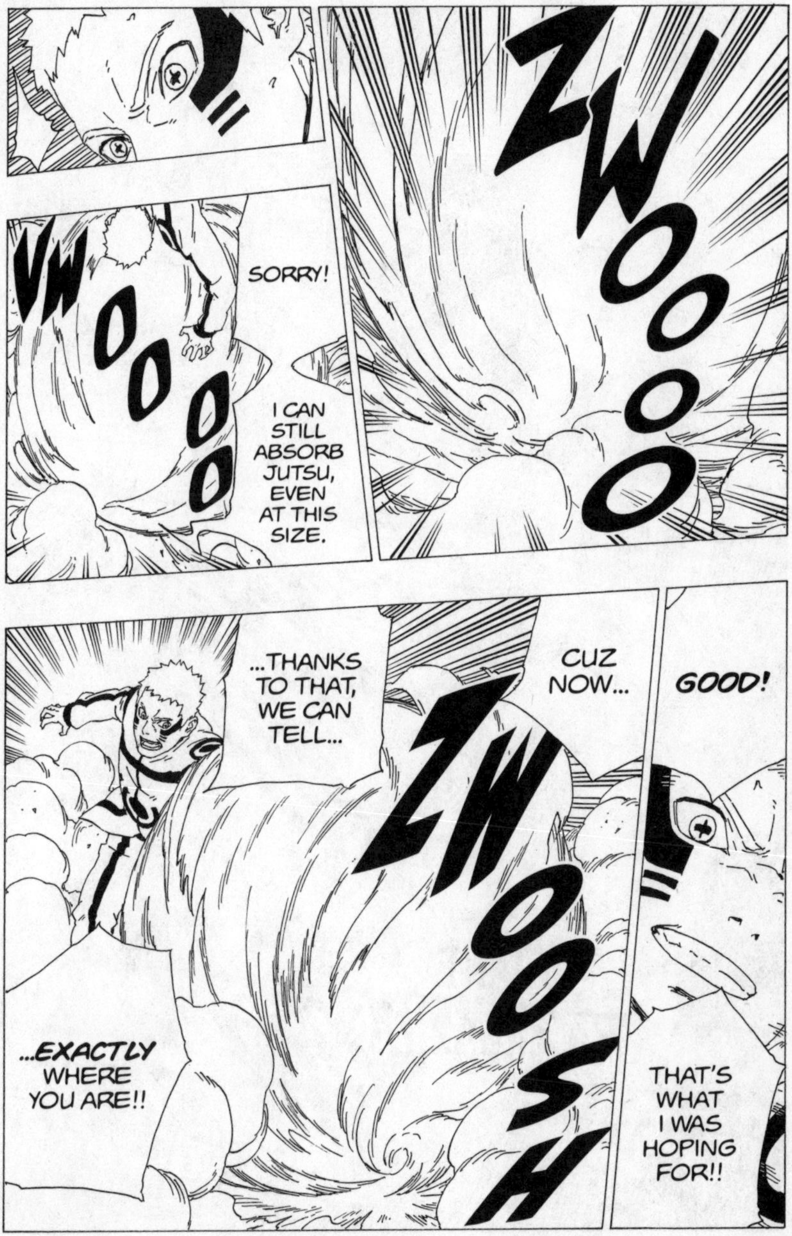
ZWOOOOO
SORRY!
VWOOOOO
I CAN STILL ABSORB JUTSU, EVEN AT THIS SIZE.
GOOD!
THAT'S WHAT I WAS HOPING FOR!!
CUZ NOW...
...THANKS TO THAT, WE CAN TELL...
ZWOOOSH
...EXACTLY WHERE YOU ARE!!

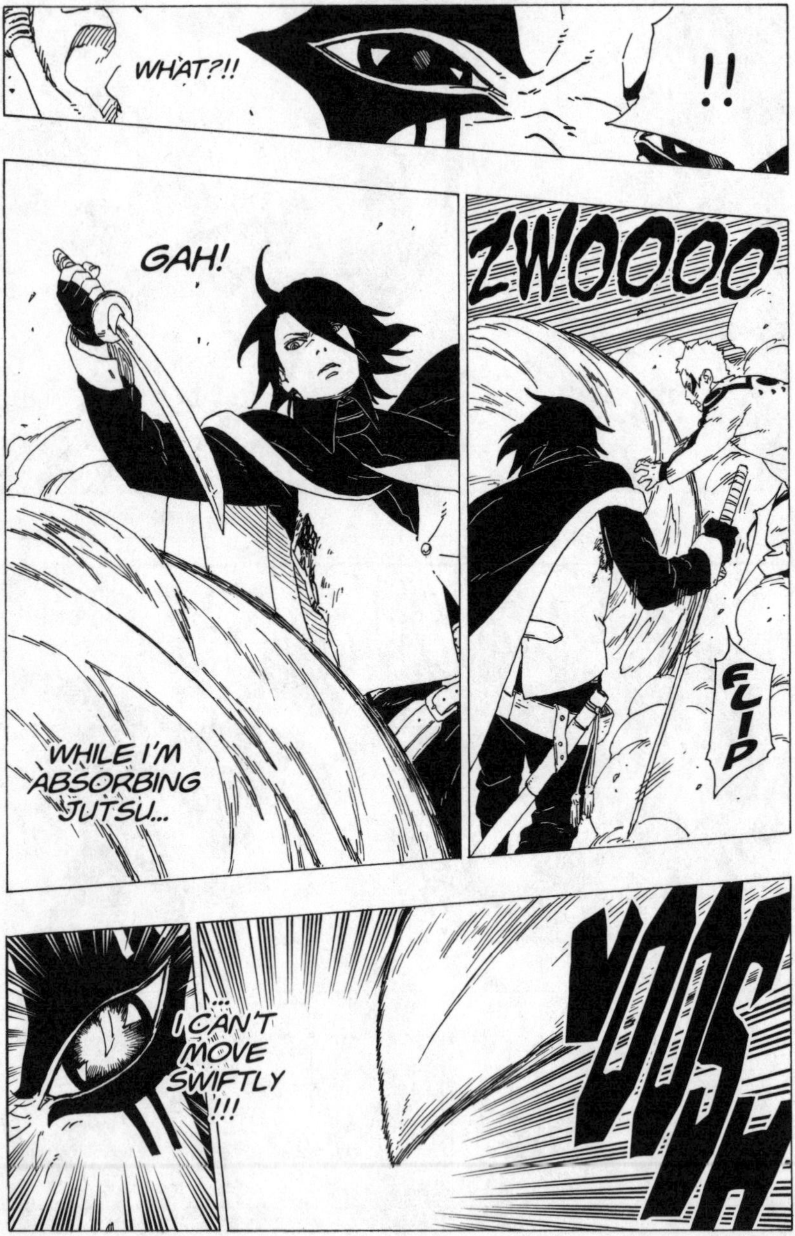
!!
WHAT?!!
ZWOOOO
FLIP
GAH!
WHILE I'M ABSORBING JUTSU...
VOOSH
... I CAN'T MOVE SWIFTLY !!!

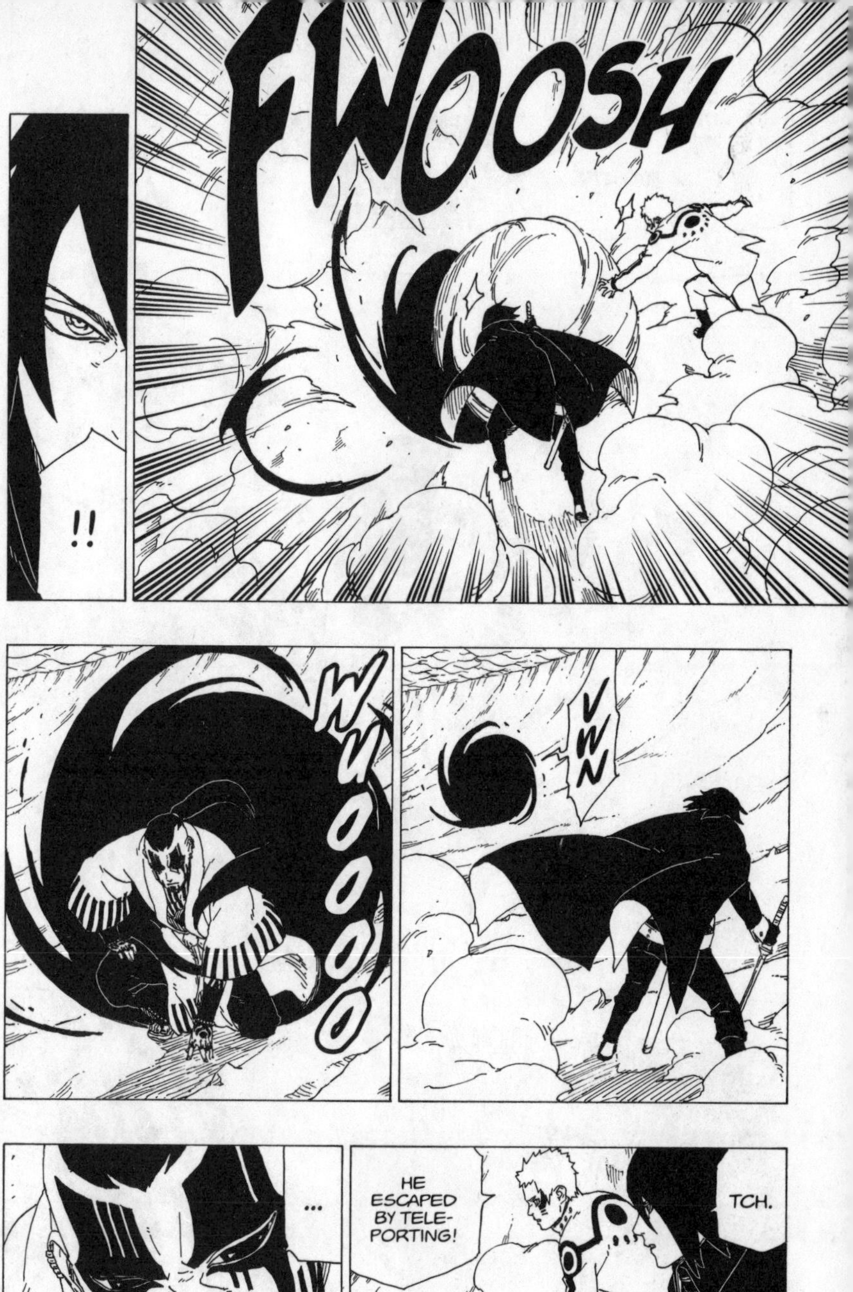
FWOOSH
!!
VWN
WUOOOO
TCH.
HE ESCAPED BY TELE-PORTING!
...

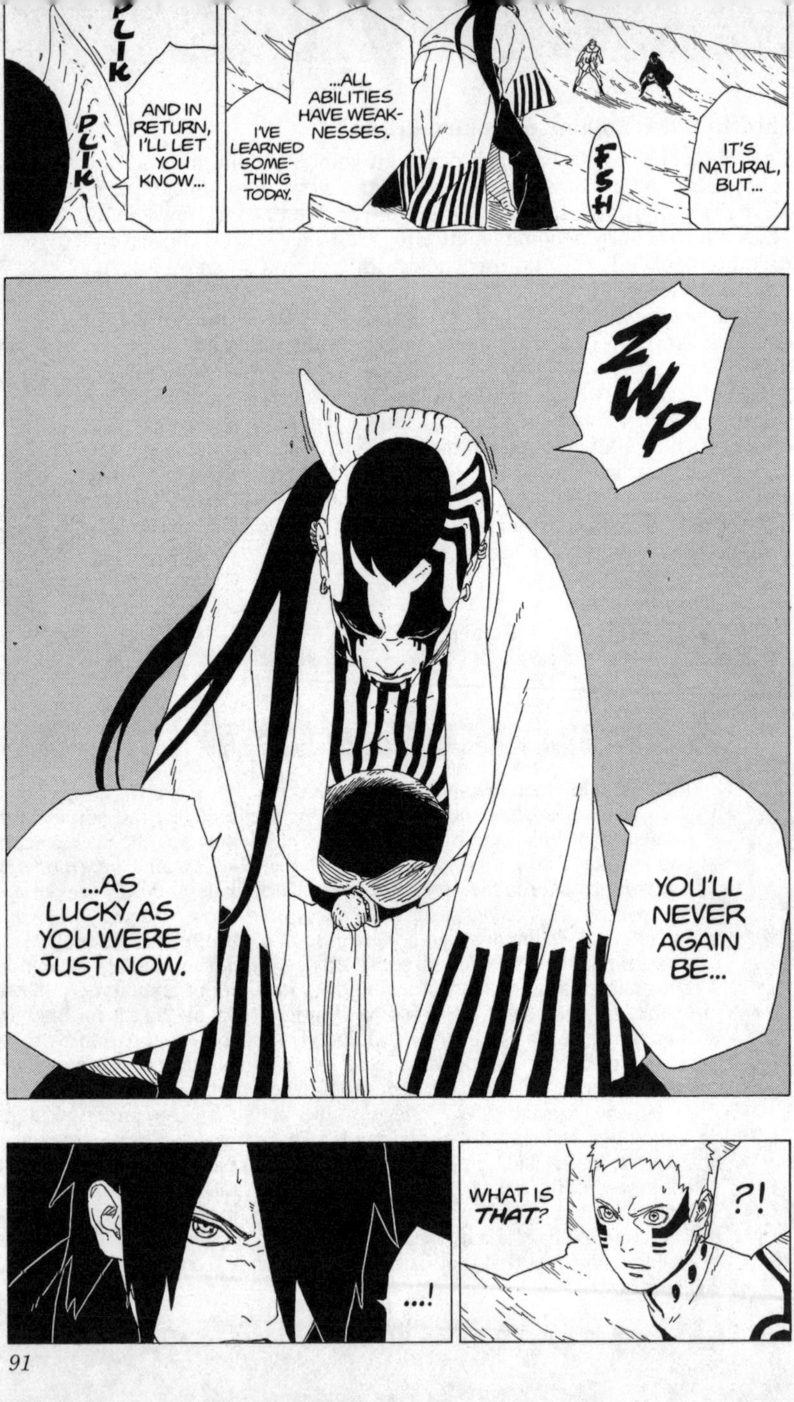
IT'S NATURAL, BUT...
FSH
...ALL ABILITIES HAVE WEAKNESSES.
I'VE LEARNED SOMETHING TODAY.
PLIK
PLIK
AND IN RETURN, I'LL LET YOU KNOW...
ZWP
YOU'LL NEVER AGAIN BE...
...AS LUCKY AS YOU WERE JUST NOW.
?!
WHAT IS *THAT*?
...!

Shinobi Hiden Column 6: Shinobi Crime

Only shinobi are able to crack down on shinobi crime. It's the only process that is practical, because no matter how many Village police officers are deployed, they would likely be unable to capture a shinobi. Thus, it has recently become practice for each Village to establish a unit called the Police Force and task them with cracking down on internal crime. Previously in Konoha Village, the Uchiha clan, which was on the losing side of political strife, was essentially forcibly assigned this task, but it is currently undertaken by the distantly related Fuuma clan (whose members do not possess sharingan). The Police Force's authority falls short of that wielded by the undercover Black Ops unit, and thus there exists tension between the two squads. Those who commit major crimes such as killing daimyo and overthrowing governments get put on wanted lists distributed across nations by the network of daimyo and are treated as international criminals. While they retain the right to a court trial, in many instances the shinobi's discretion to pronounce summary judgment on the scene is recognized.

Having said that, in instances of even greater crimes (such as coups d'état), there are cases where peremptory orders are issued by the perpetrators' homeland or Village to have them brought back by any means necessary and subjected to interrogation under the label of a trial. Hefty monetary rewards are offered for such international criminals, and they are pursued irrespective of Village. Most are shinobi, and those chasing after these underworld villains who grace Bingo Book pages are also shinobi. At the same time, the underworld constantly requires the abilities of shinobi. Drug cartels and human trafficking rings that cannot commission Villages utilize international criminals via under-the-table commissions and monetary awards. For example, **Akatsuki** had strong connections with the underworld. No matter the type of shinobi, they cannot operate independently of society. In order to differentiate them from rogue ninja, ninja who forsake their Village to be active in the underworld are sometimes referred to as "brigands." For example, **Mujina**, who were involved in the kidnapping of Tento, are representative of brigands. In addition, Uchiha Sasuke, who is a rogue ninja rather than a genin of his Village, could be considered a "brigand" as well, in terms of the big picture. The superiority of such freelance shinobi is acknowledged due to their freedom. The fact that they can survive as such is proof of their remarkable abilities.

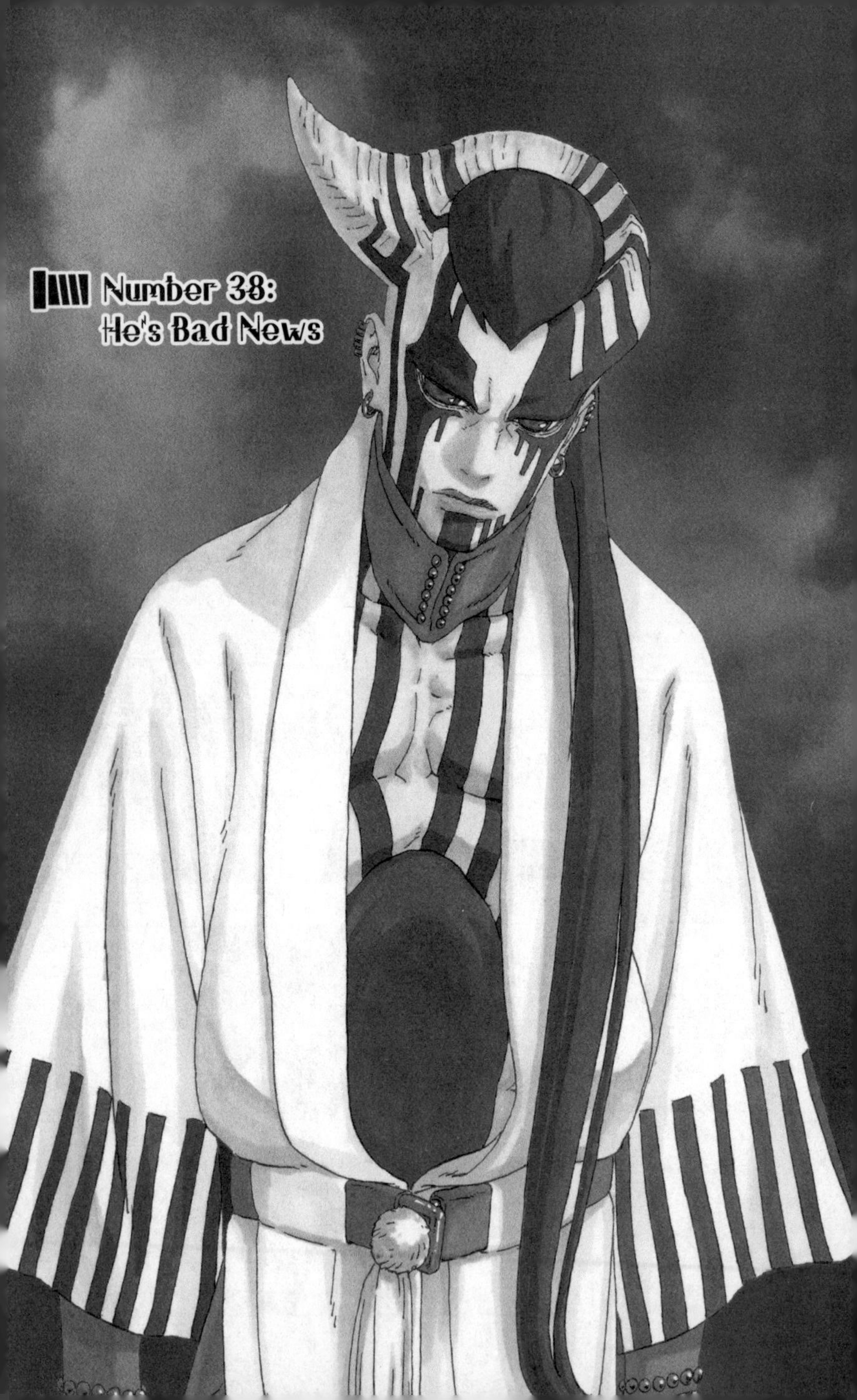
Number 38:
He's Bad News

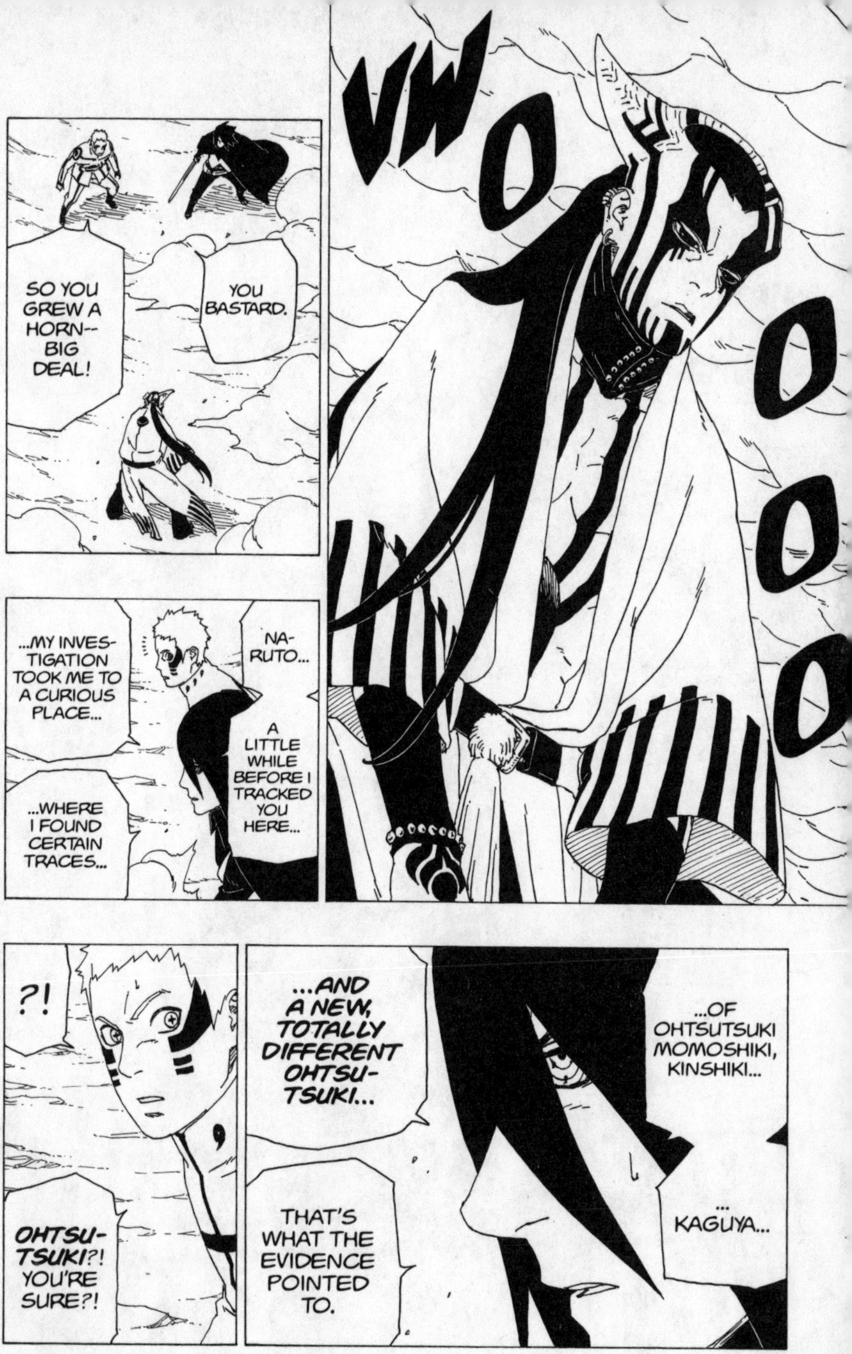
VWOOOOO
YOU BASTARD.
SO YOU GREW A HORN-- BIG DEAL!
NA-RUTO...
...MY INVES-TIGATION TOOK ME TO A CURIOUS PLACE...
A LITTLE WHILE BEFORE I TRACKED YOU HERE...
...WHERE I FOUND CERTAIN TRACES...
...OF OHTSUTSUKI MOMOSHIKI, KINSHIKI...
... KAGUYA...
...AND A NEW, TOTALLY DIFFERENT OHTSU-TSUKI...
THAT'S WHAT THE EVIDENCE POINTED TO.
?!
OHTSU-TSUKI?! YOU'RE SURE?!

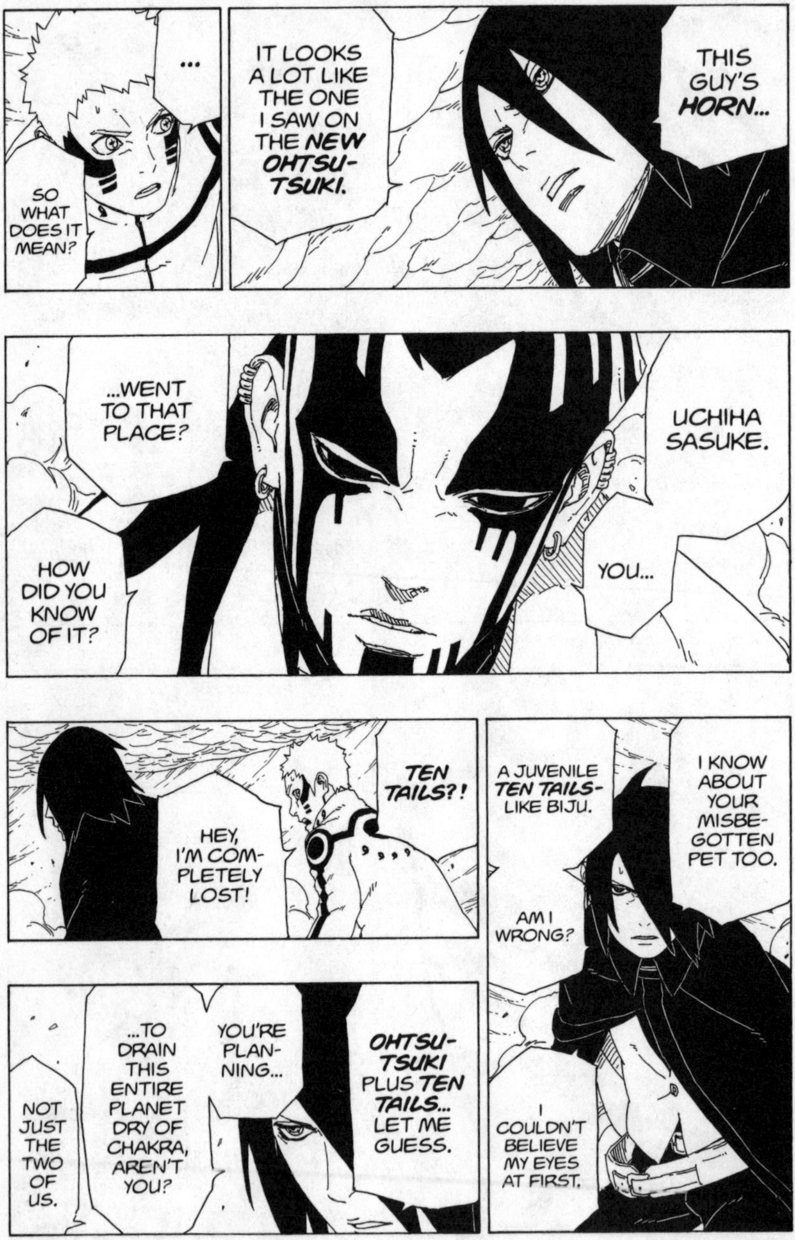
THIS GUY'S **HORN**...
IT LOOKS A LOT LIKE THE ONE I SAW ON THE ***NEW OHTSUTSUKI***.
...
SO WHAT DOES IT MEAN?
UCHIHA SASUKE.
YOU...
...WENT TO THAT PLACE?
HOW DID YOU KNOW OF IT?
I KNOW ABOUT YOUR MISBEGOTTEN PET TOO.
A JUVENILE ***TEN TAILS***-LIKE BIJU.
AM I WRONG?
I COULDN'T BELIEVE MY EYES AT FIRST.
TEN TAILS?!
HEY, I'M COMPLETELY LOST!
OHTSUTSUKI PLUS ***TEN TAILS***... LET ME GUESS.
YOU'RE PLANNING...
...TO DRAIN THIS ENTIRE PLANET DRY OF CHAKRA, AREN'T YOU?
NOT JUST THE TWO OF US.

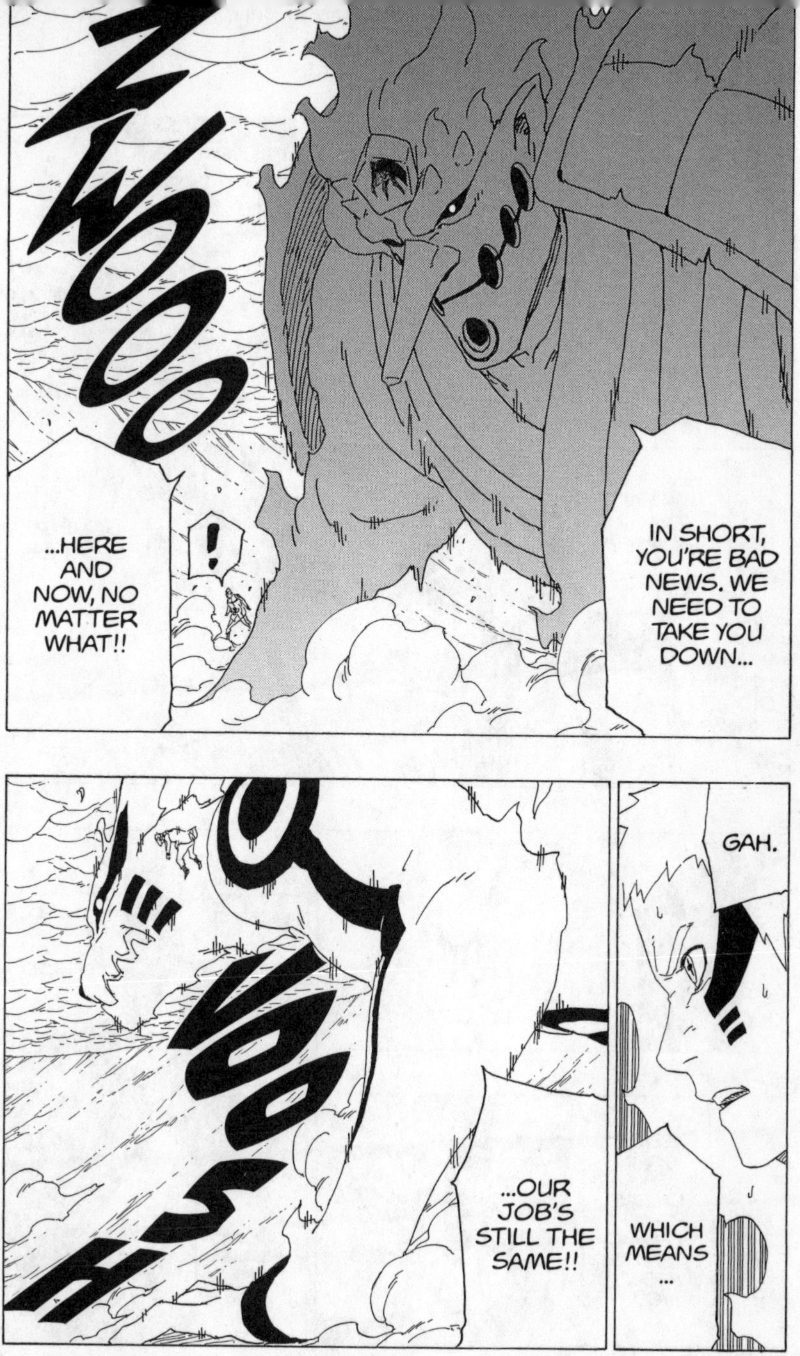

IN SHORT, YOU'RE BAD NEWS. WE NEED TO TAKE YOU DOWN...
...HERE AND NOW, NO MATTER WHAT!!
!
GAH.
WHICH MEANS ...
...OUR JOB'S STILL THE SAME!!

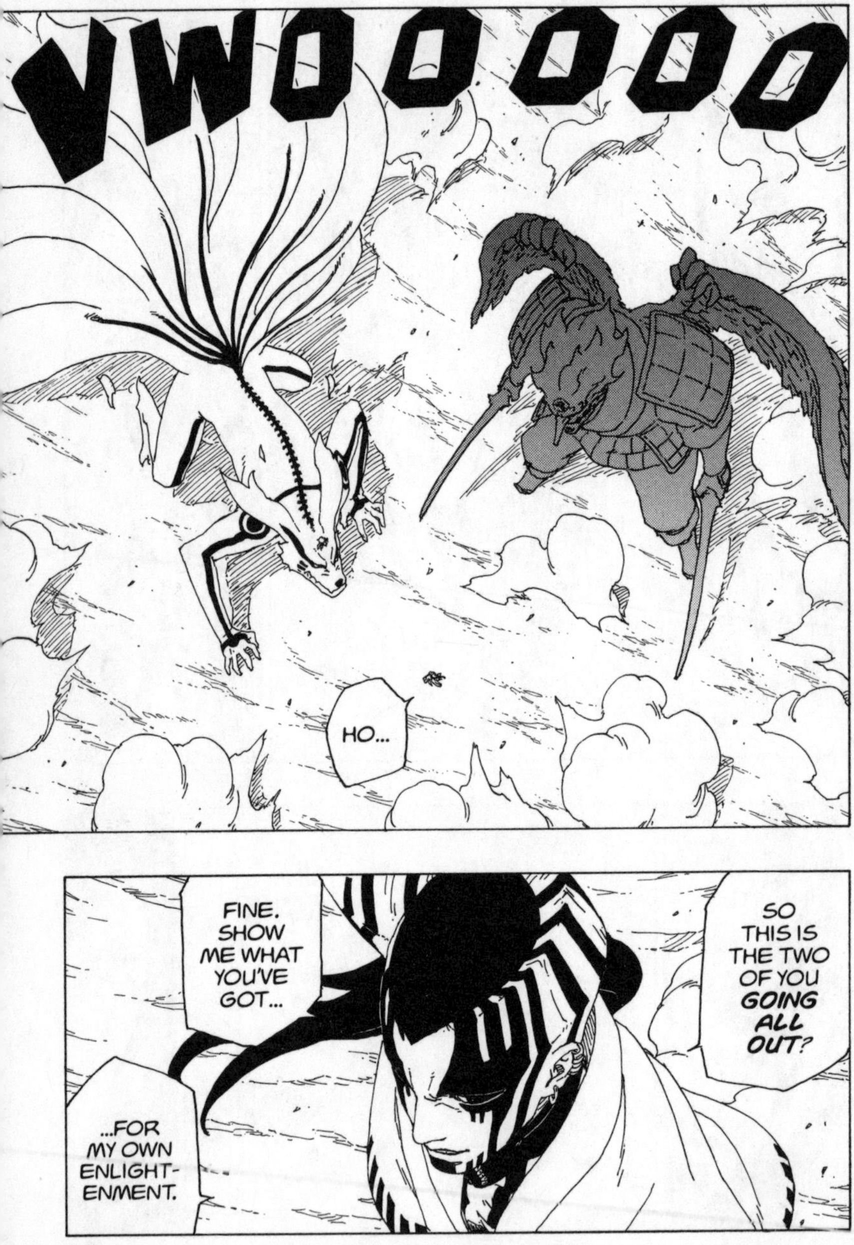
VWOOOOO
HO...
SO THIS IS THE TWO OF YOU GOING ALL OUT?
FINE. SHOW ME WHAT YOU'VE GOT...
...FOR MY OWN ENLIGHT- ENMENT.

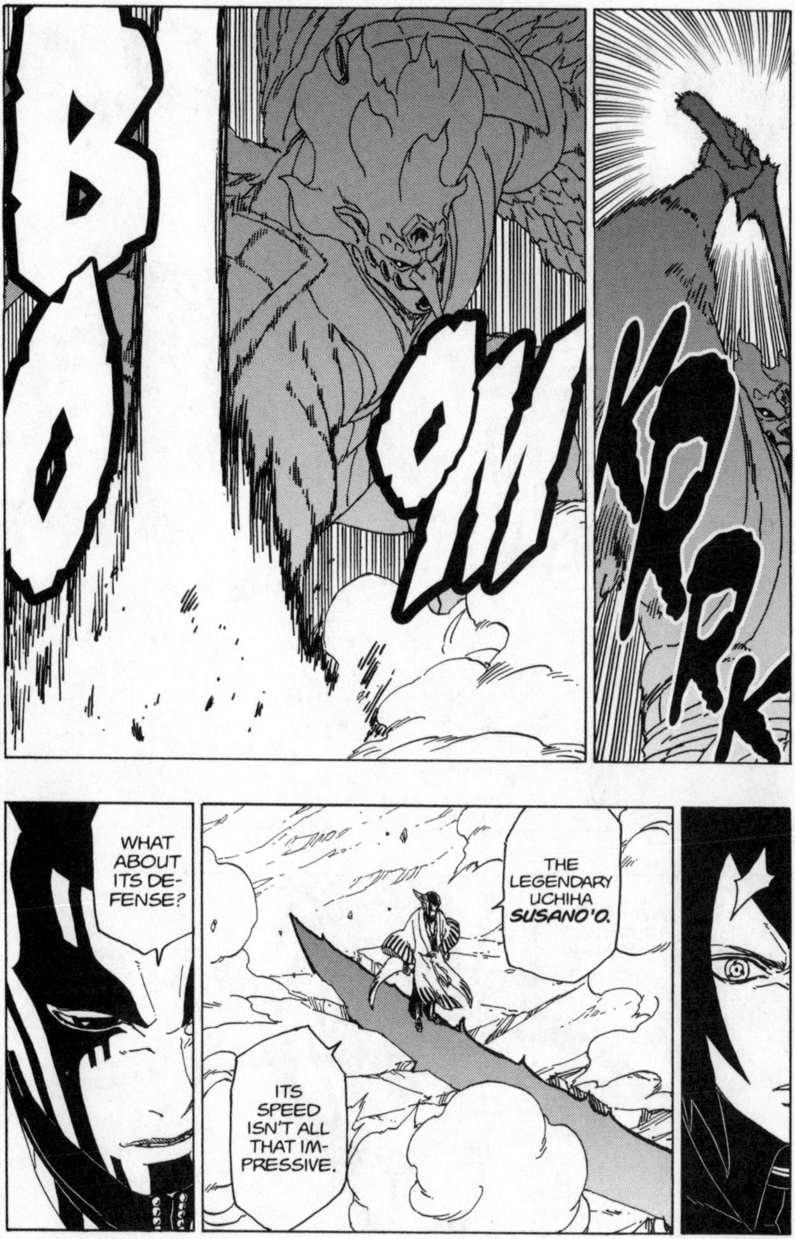
KRRK
BOOM
THE LEGENDARY UCHIHA *SUSANO'O.*
ITS SPEED ISN'T ALL THAT IMPRESSIVE.
WHAT ABOUT ITS DEFENSE?

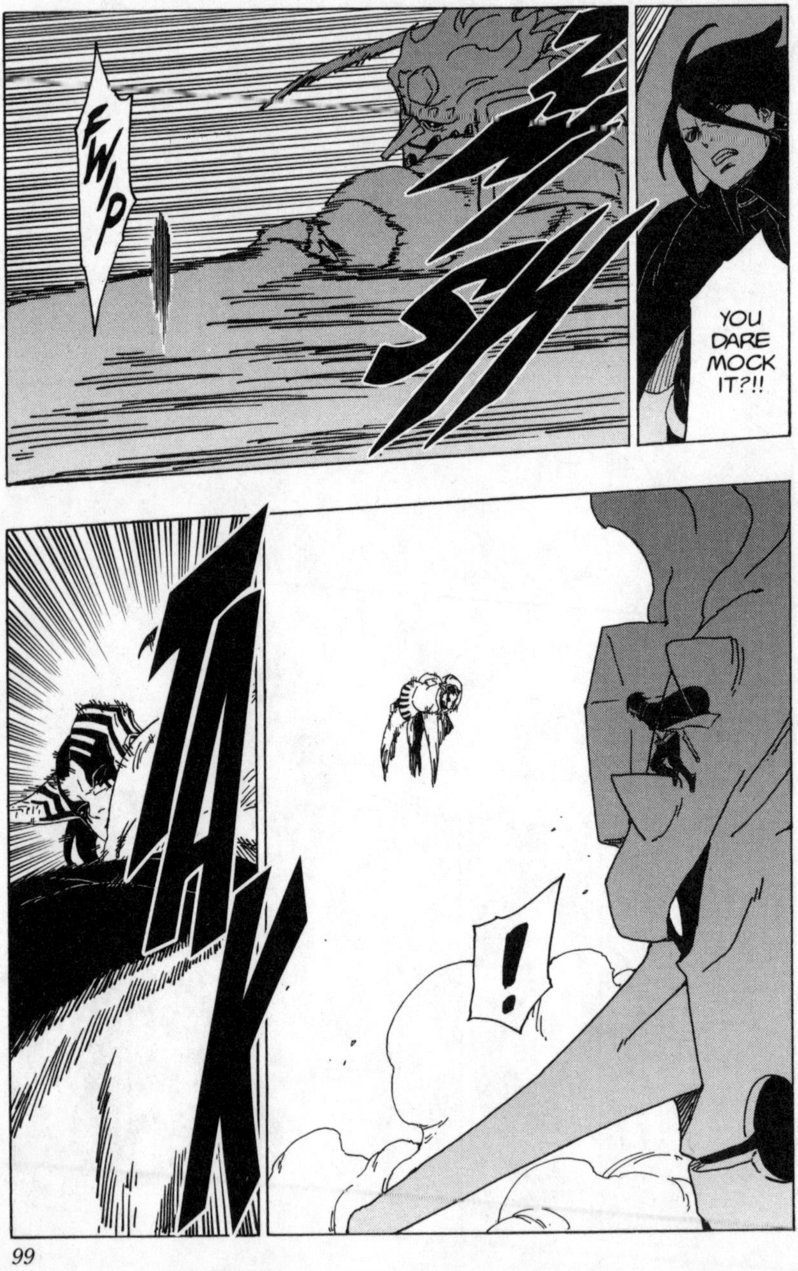
YOU DARE MOCK IT?!!
ZWISH
FWIP
!
TAK

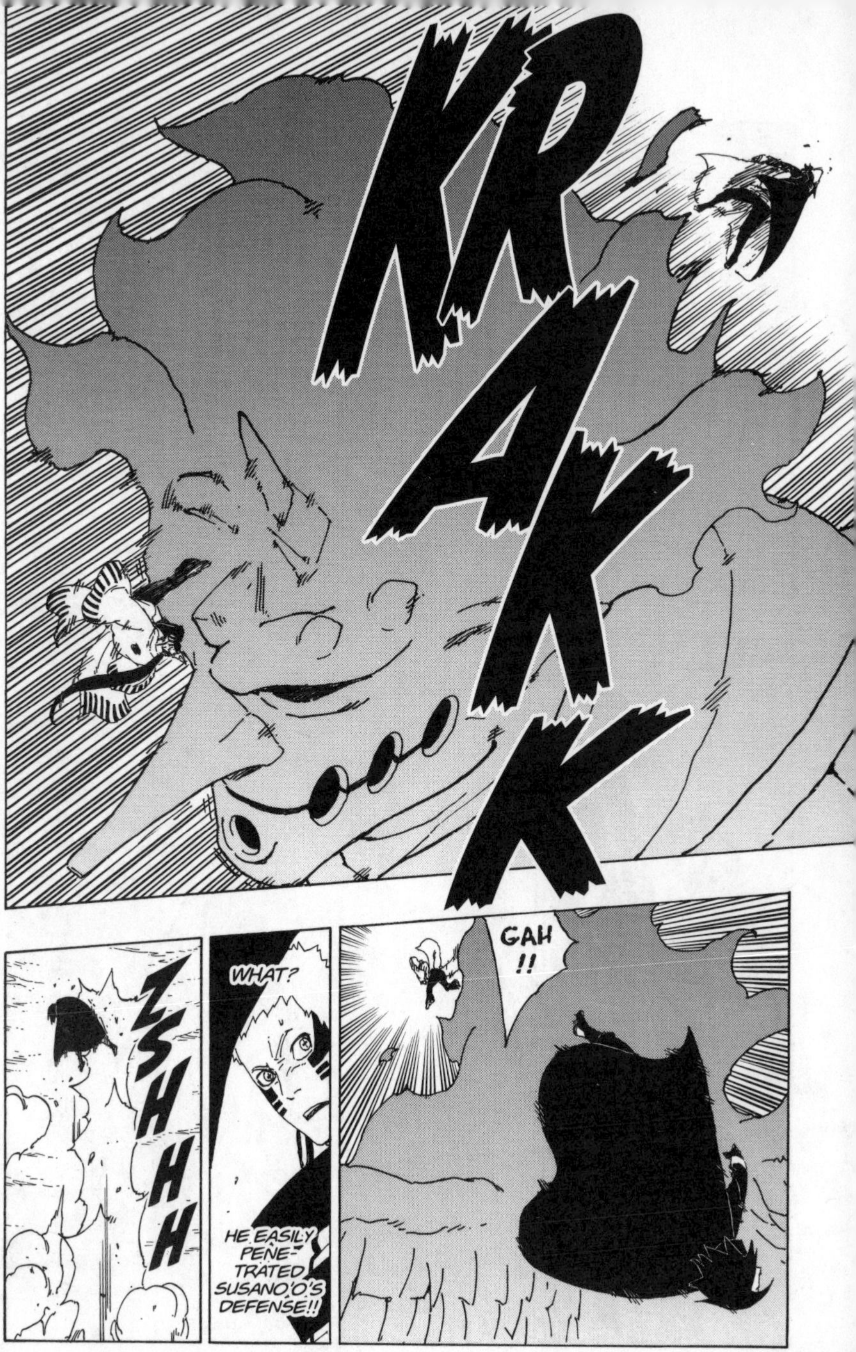
KRAAKK
GAH!!
WHAT?
HE EASILY PENE-TRATED SUSANO'O'S DEFENSE!!
ZSHHHH

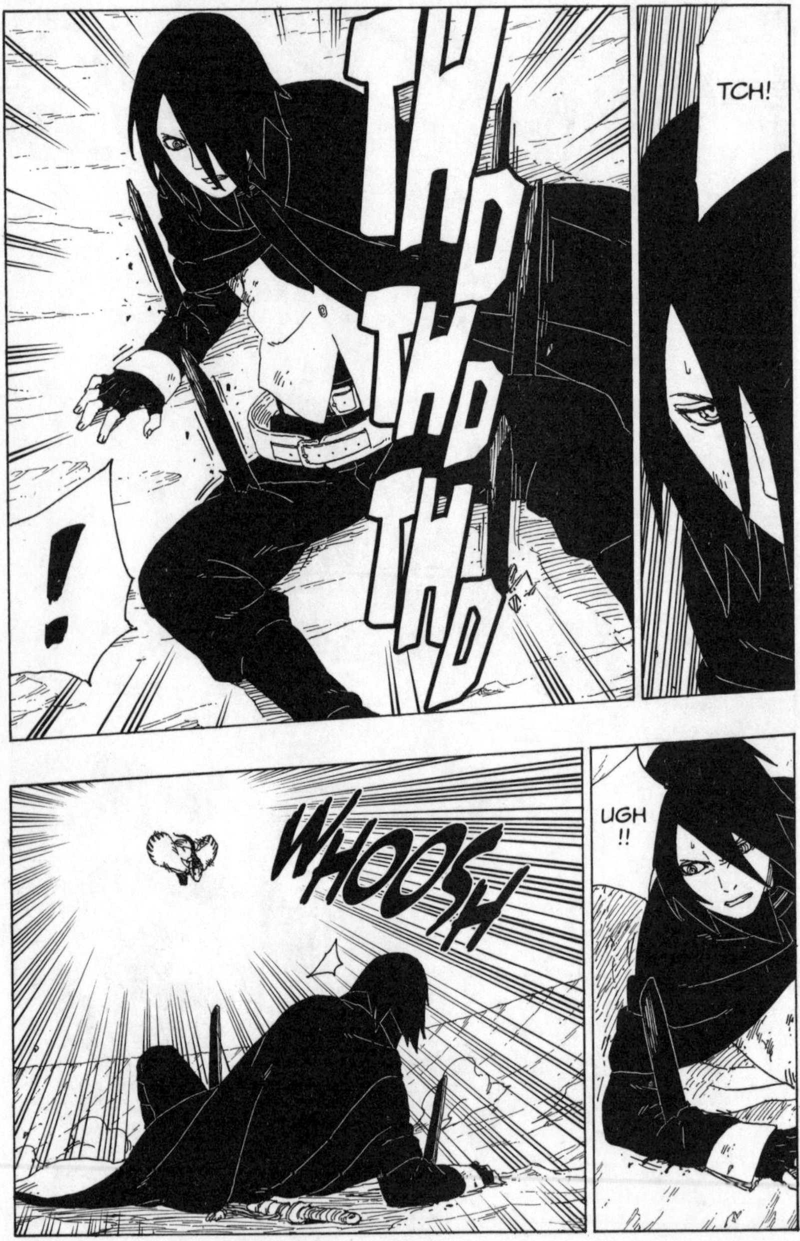
TCH!
THD THD THD THD
!
UGH !!
WHOOSH

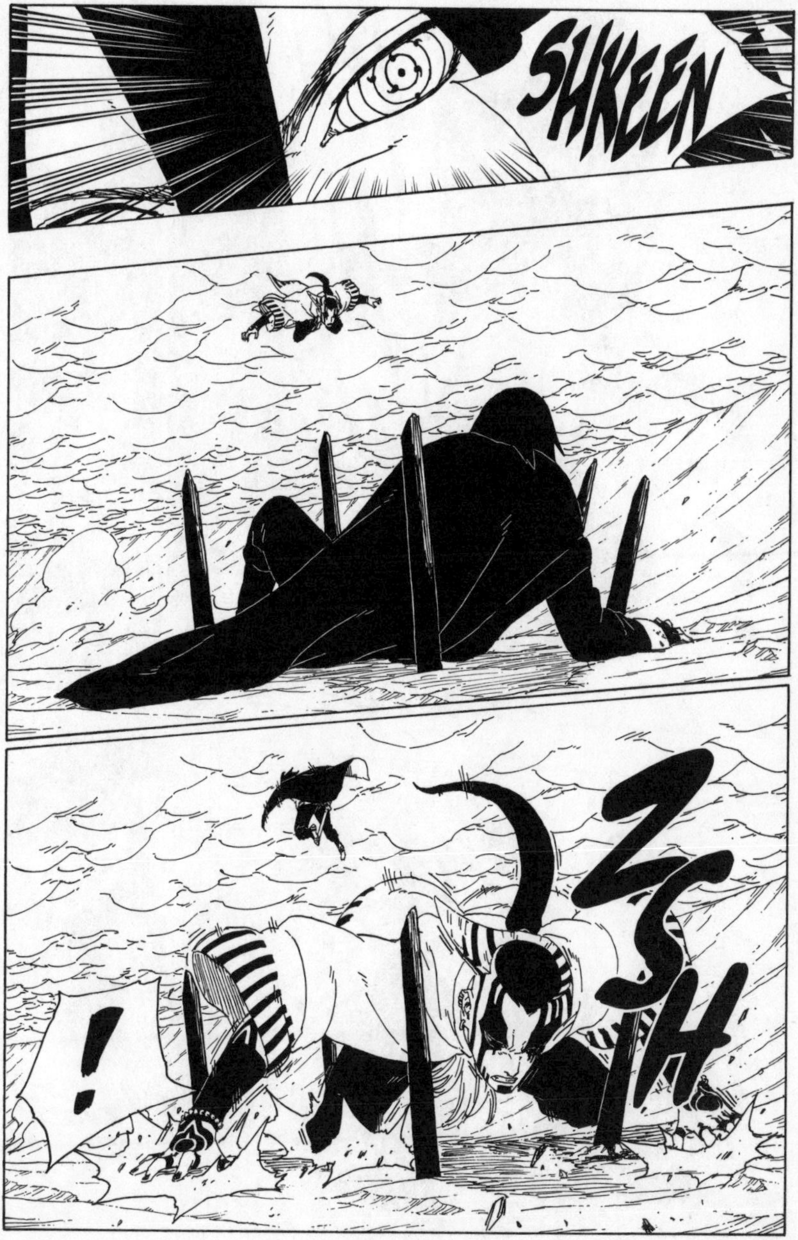

SHKEEN
ZSH
!

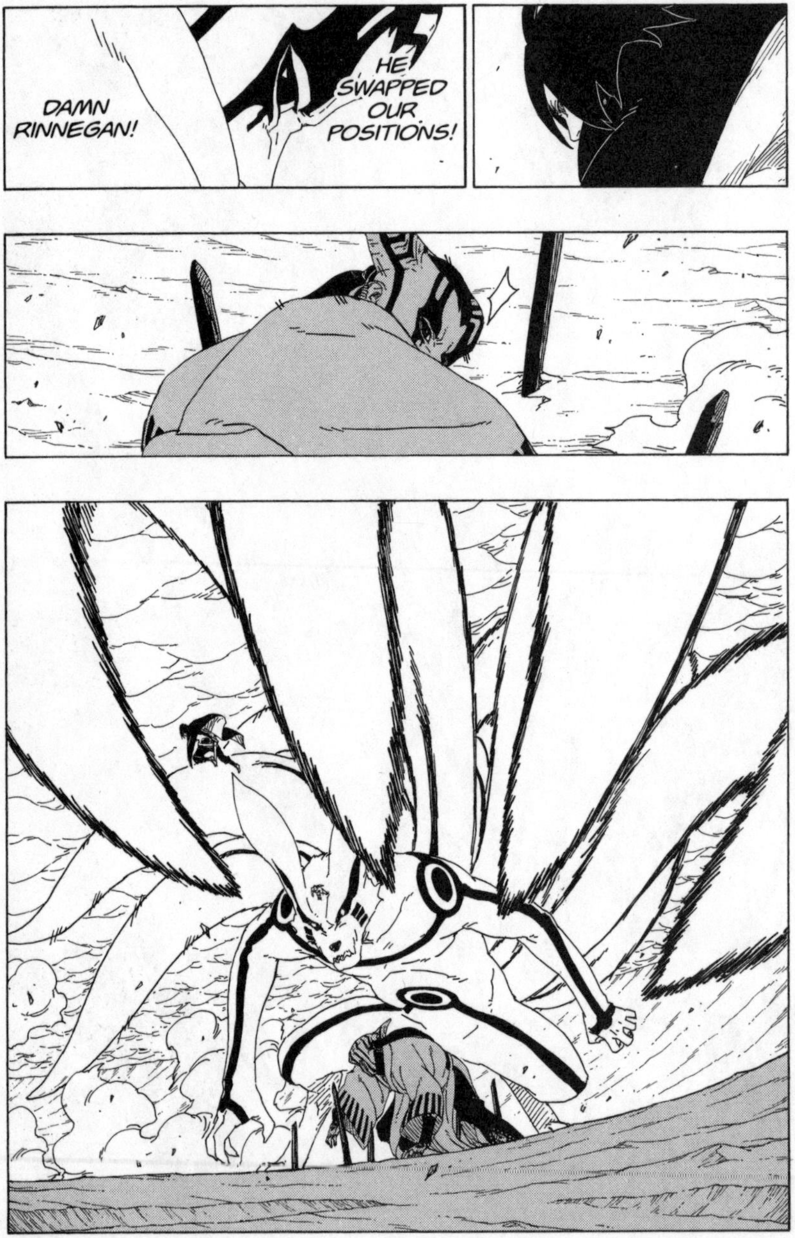
HE SWAPPED OUR POSITIONS!
DAMN RINNEGAN!

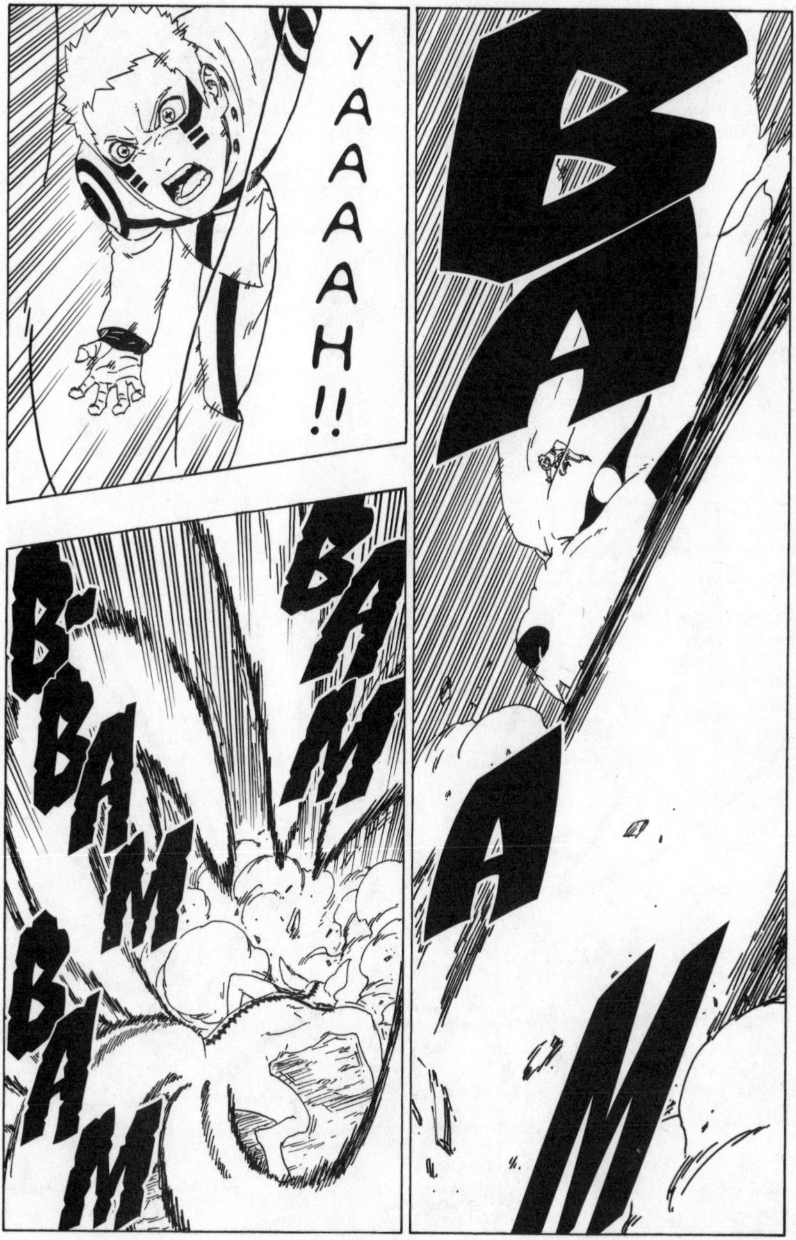
BAAAM
YAAAAH!!
BAM
B-BAM BAM

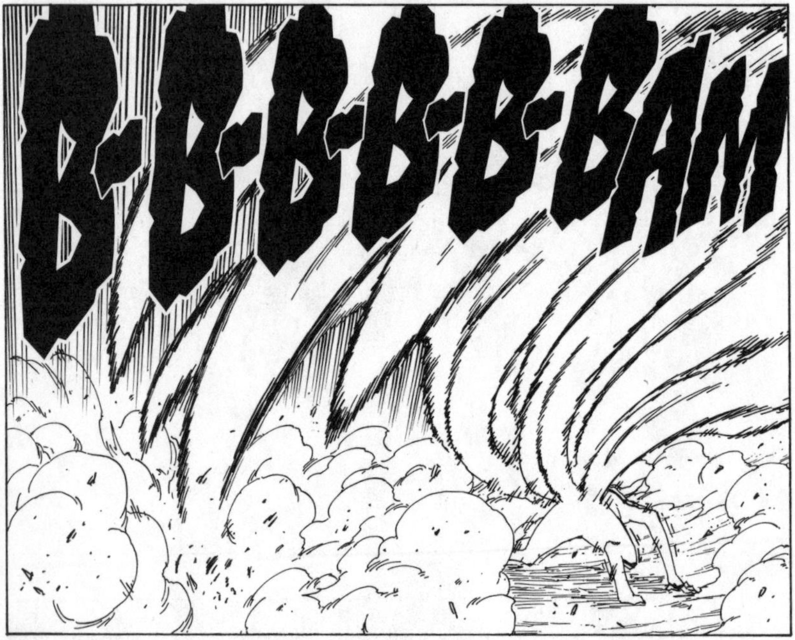
B-B-B-B-B-BAM

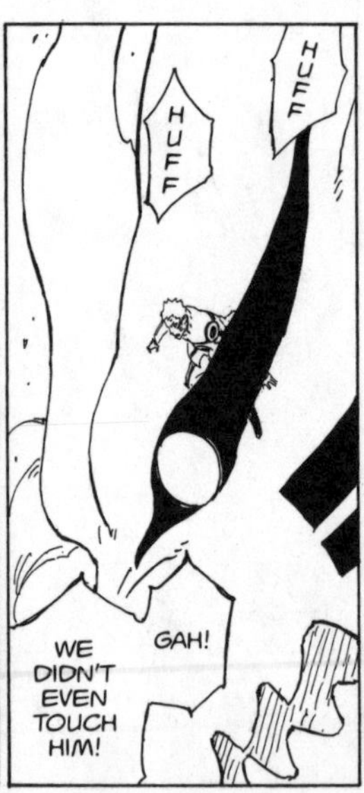
HUFF
HUFF
GAH!
WE DIDN'T EVEN TOUCH HIM!

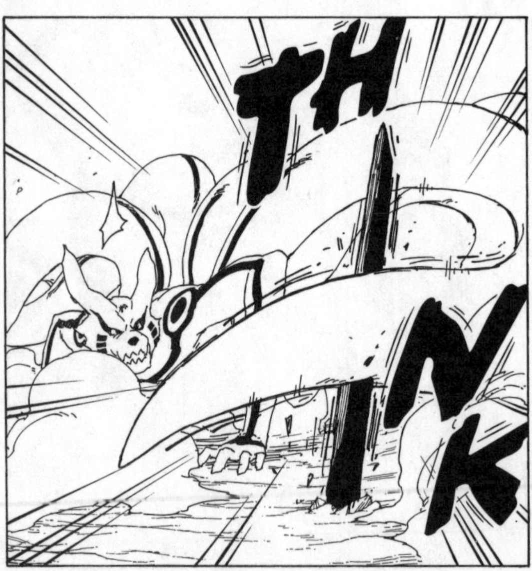
THINK

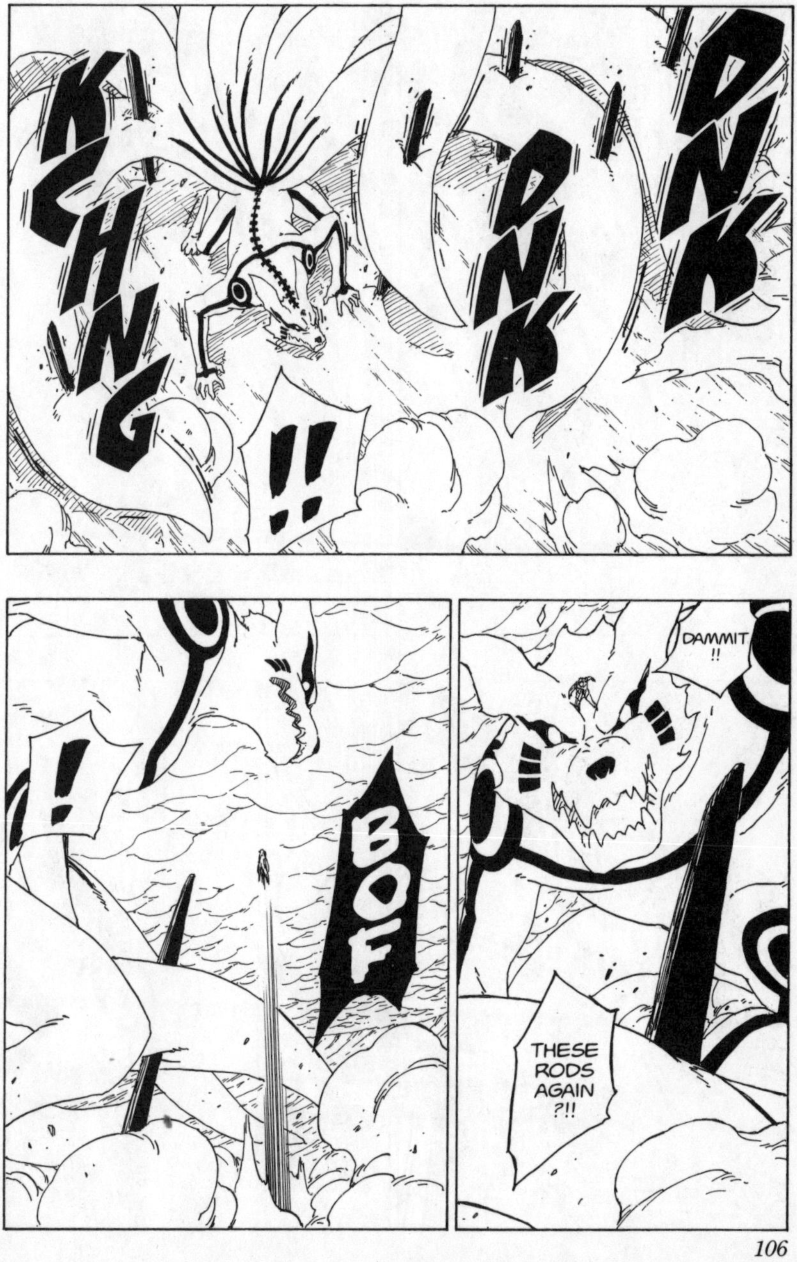
DNK
DNK
!!
KCHNG
DAMMIT!!
THESE RODS AGAIN?!!
BOF
!

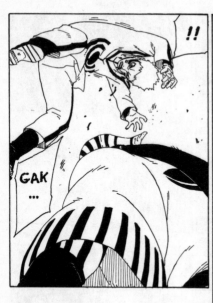

GAK
...

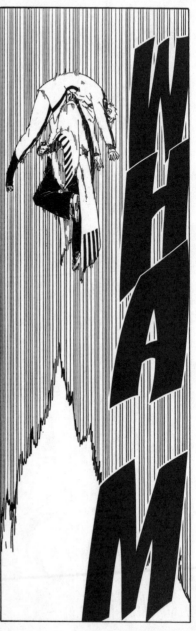

WHAM

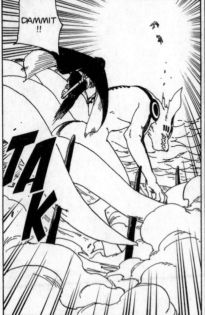

DAMMIT
!!

TA
KI

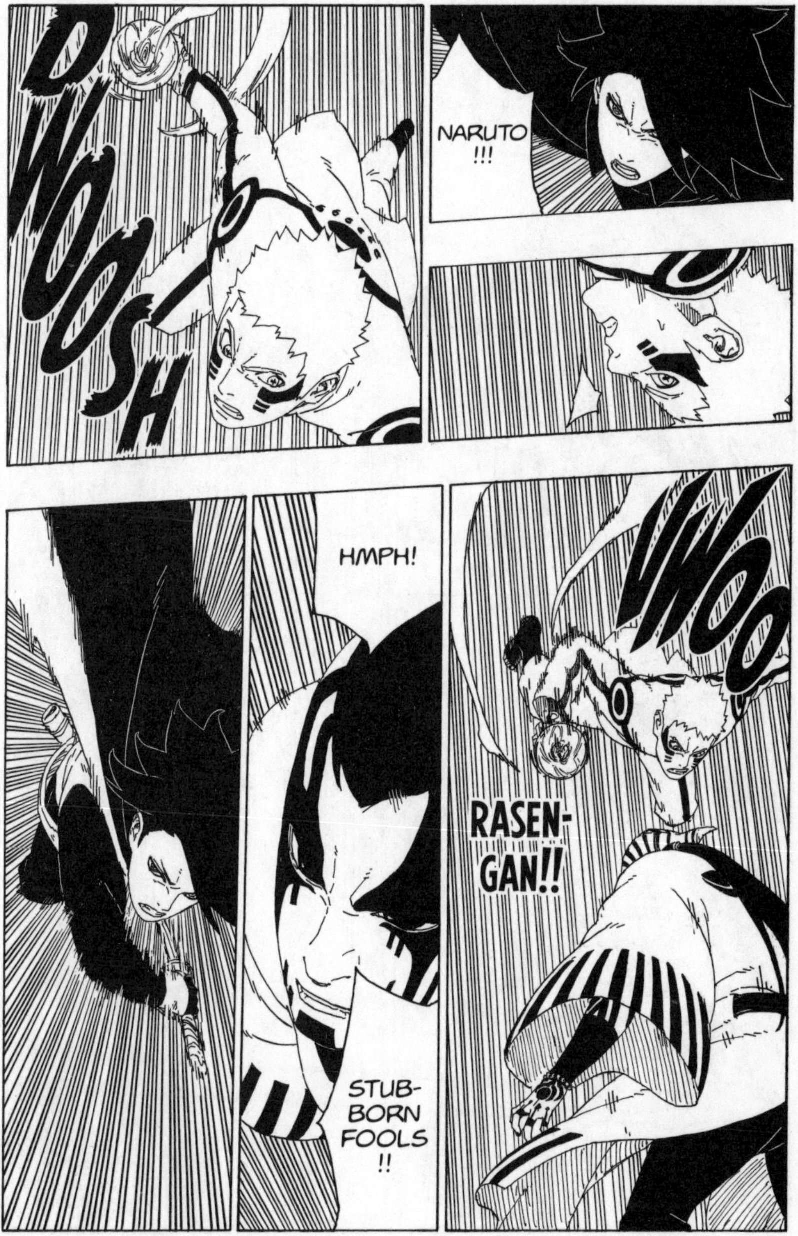
NARUTO !!!
DWOOSH
WOO
RASEN-GAN!!
HMPH!
STUB-BORN FOOLS !!

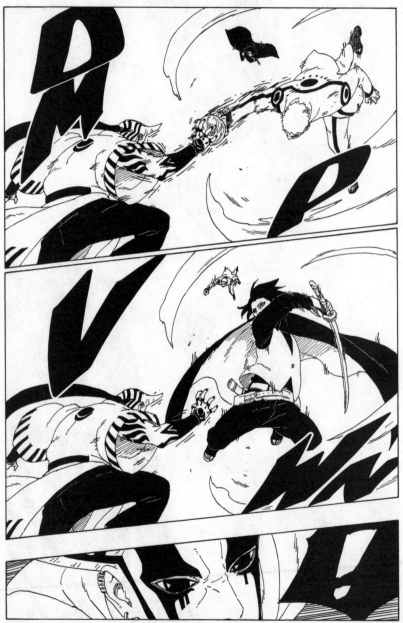

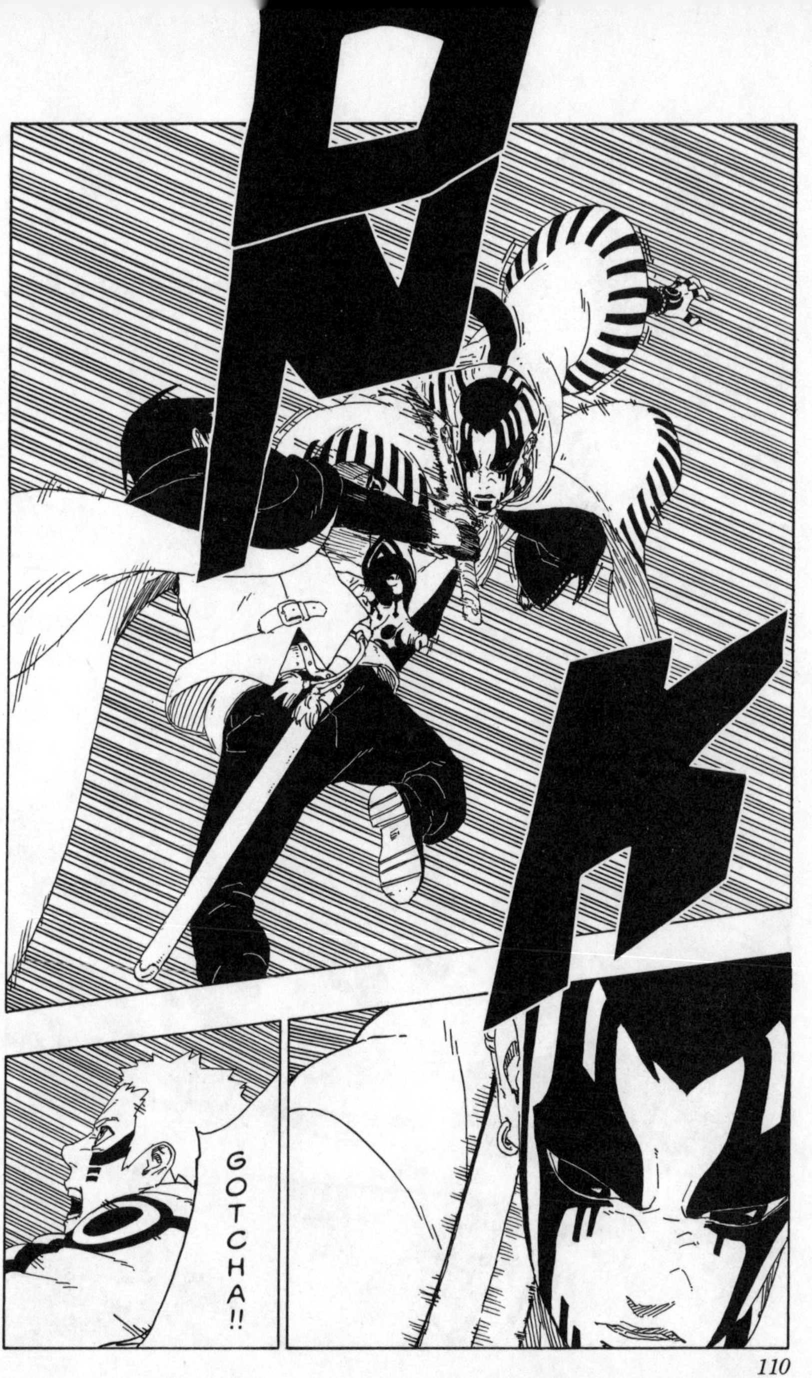
GOTCHA!!

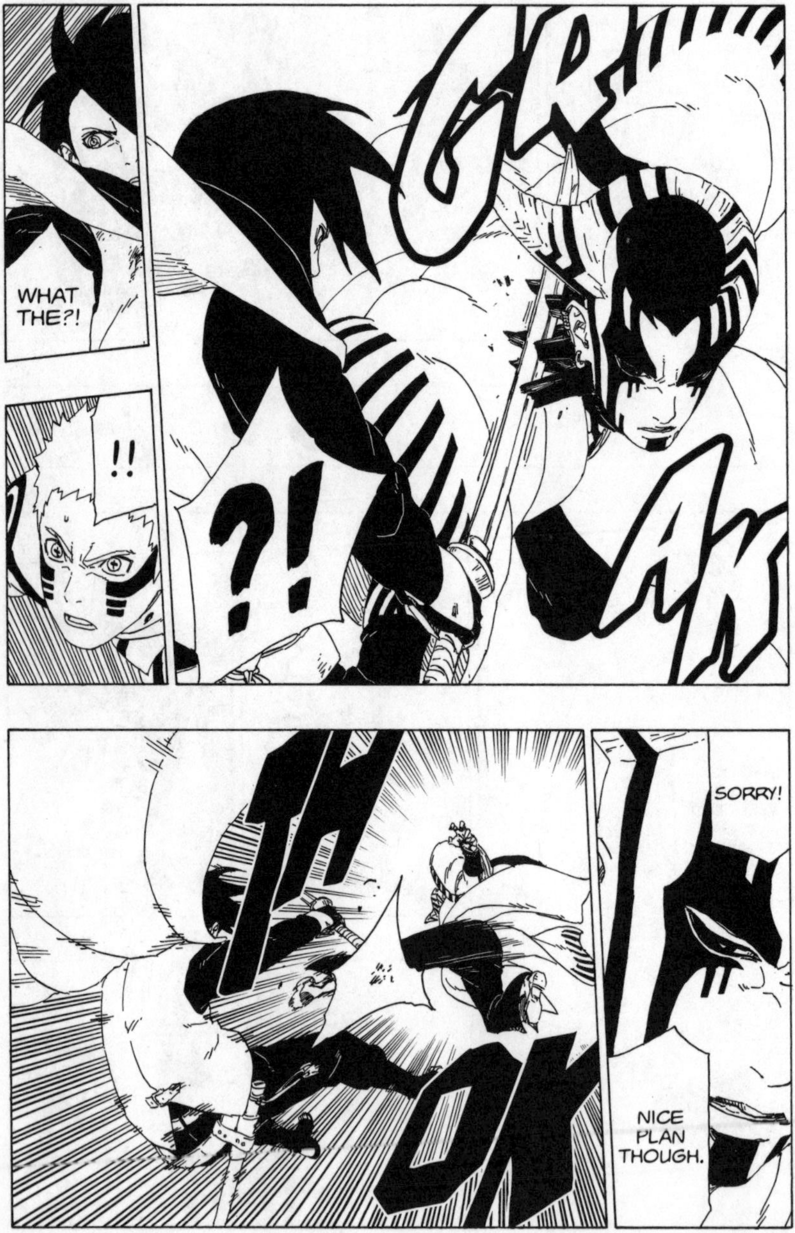
?!
WHAT THE?!
!!
SORRY!
NICE PLAN THOUGH.

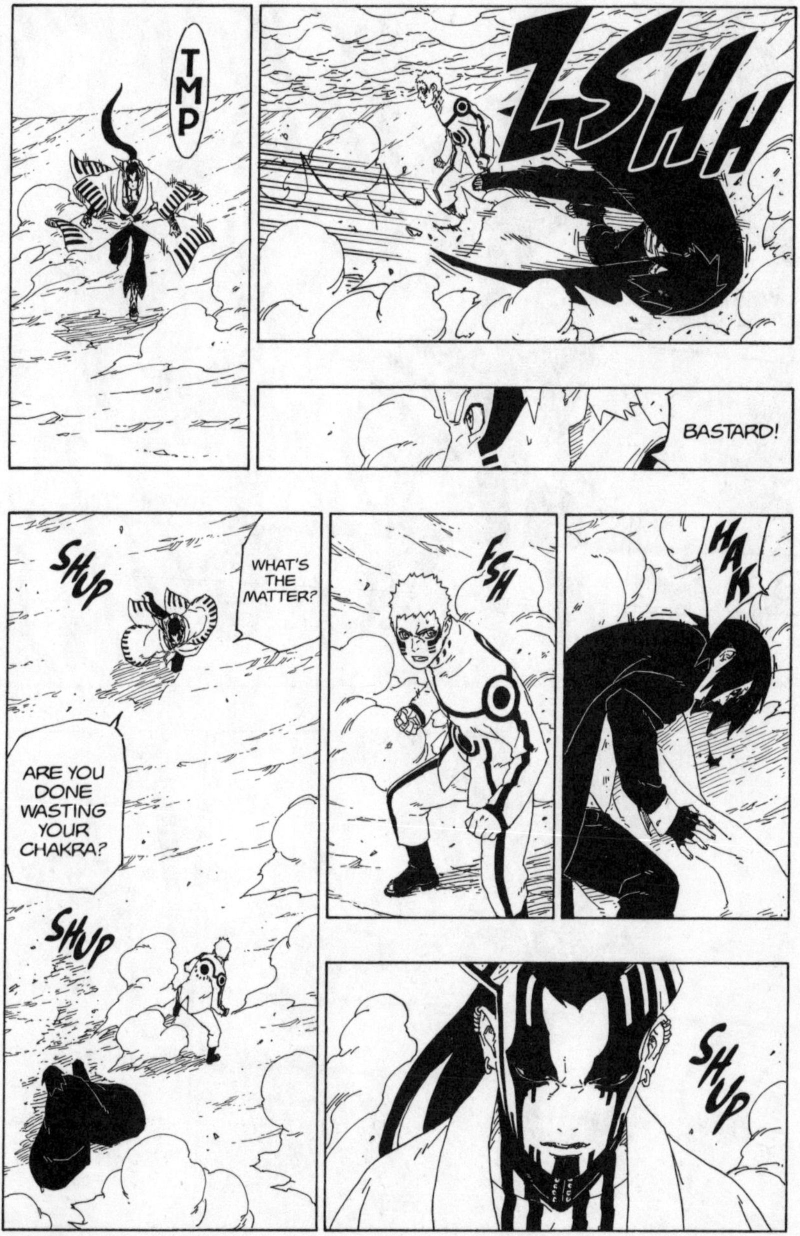
ZSHH
BASTARD!
TMP
HAK
FSH
SHUP
WHAT'S THE MATTER?
SHUP
ARE YOU DONE WASTING YOUR CHAKRA?
SHUP

TAK
GRP
WHAM
GOFF!!

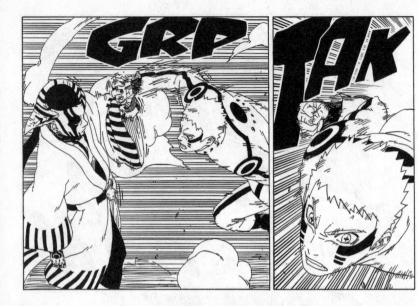

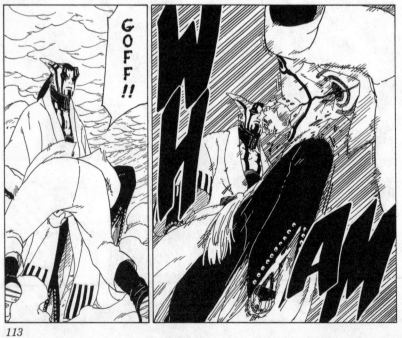

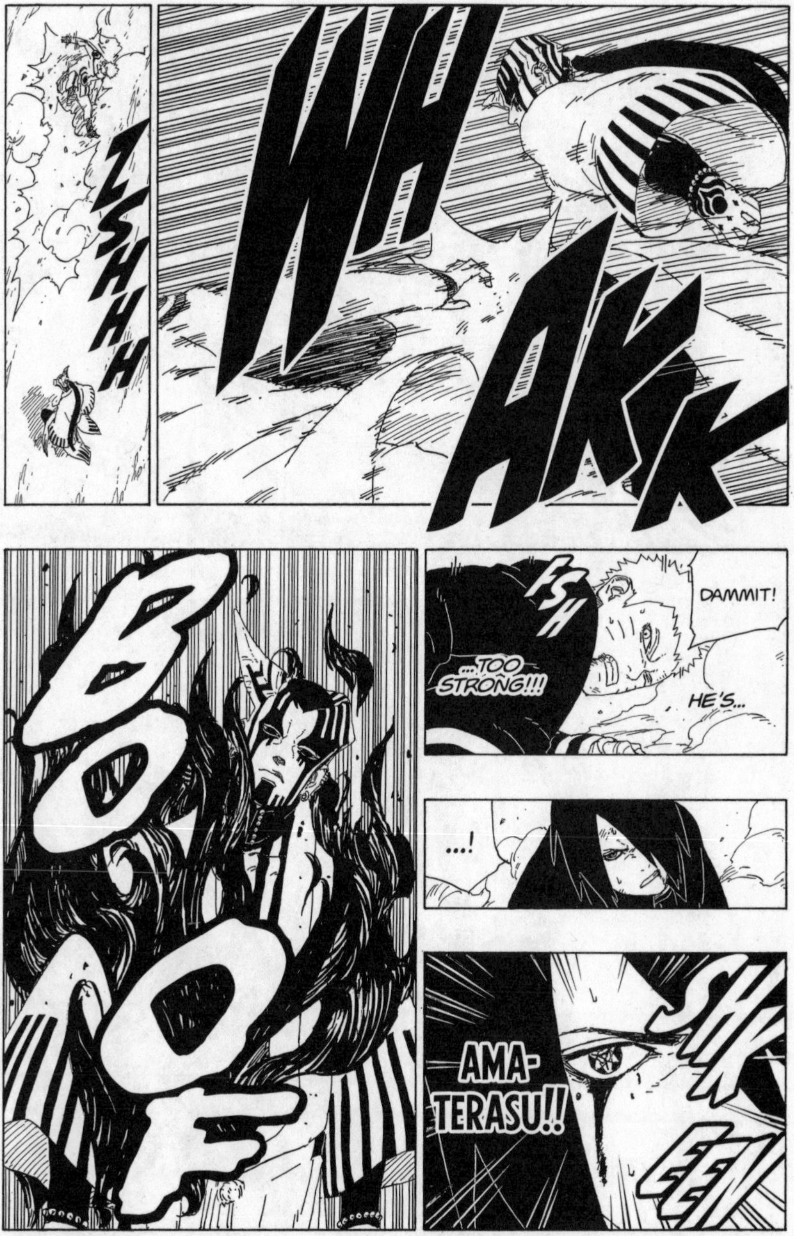
WHAKK
ZSHHHH
DAMMIT!
HE'S...
FSH
...TOO STRONG!!!
...!
SHK
EEN
AMA-TERASU!!
BOOF

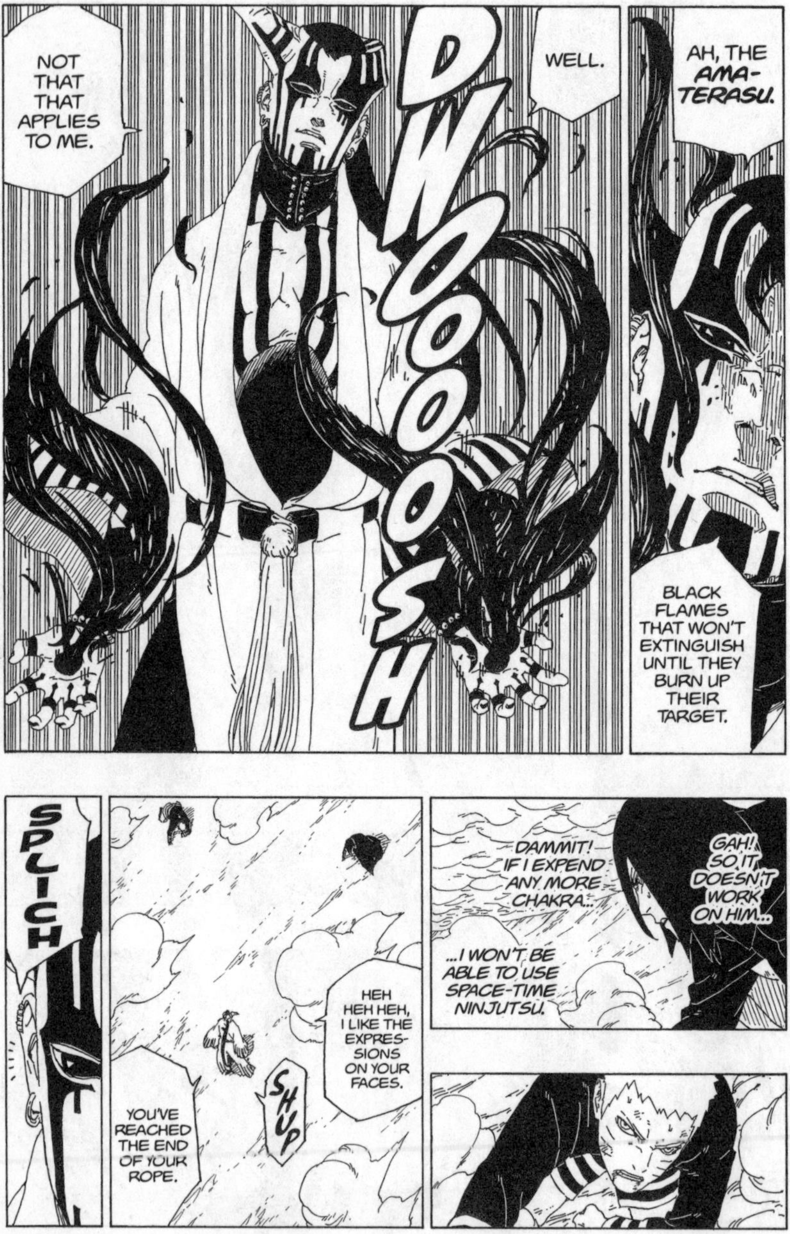
AH, THE AMATERASU.
BLACK FLAMES THAT WON'T EXTINGUISH UNTIL THEY BURN UP THEIR TARGET.
WELL.
DWOOOOOSH
NOT THAT THAT APPLIES TO ME.
GAH! SO IT DOESN'T WORK ON HIM...
DAMMIT! IF I EXPEND ANY MORE CHAKRA...
...I WON'T BE ABLE TO USE SPACE-TIME NINJUTSU.
HEH HEH HEH, I LIKE THE EXPRESSIONS ON YOUR FACES.
SHUP
YOU'VE REACHED THE END OF YOUR ROPE.
SPLICH

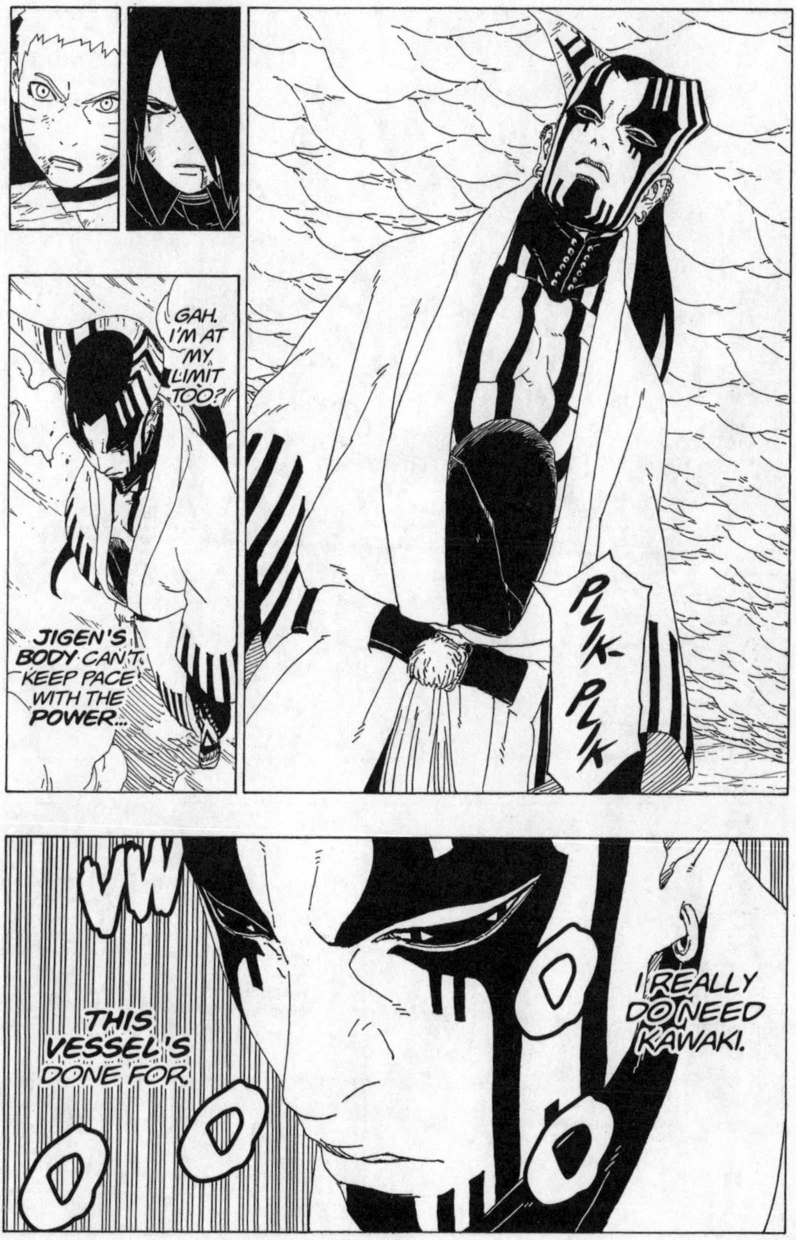
PLIK PLIK
GAH. I'M AT MY LIMIT TOO?
JIGEN'S BODY CAN'T KEEP PACE WITH THE POWER...
I REALLY DO NEED KAWAKI.
THIS VESSEL'S DONE FOR.

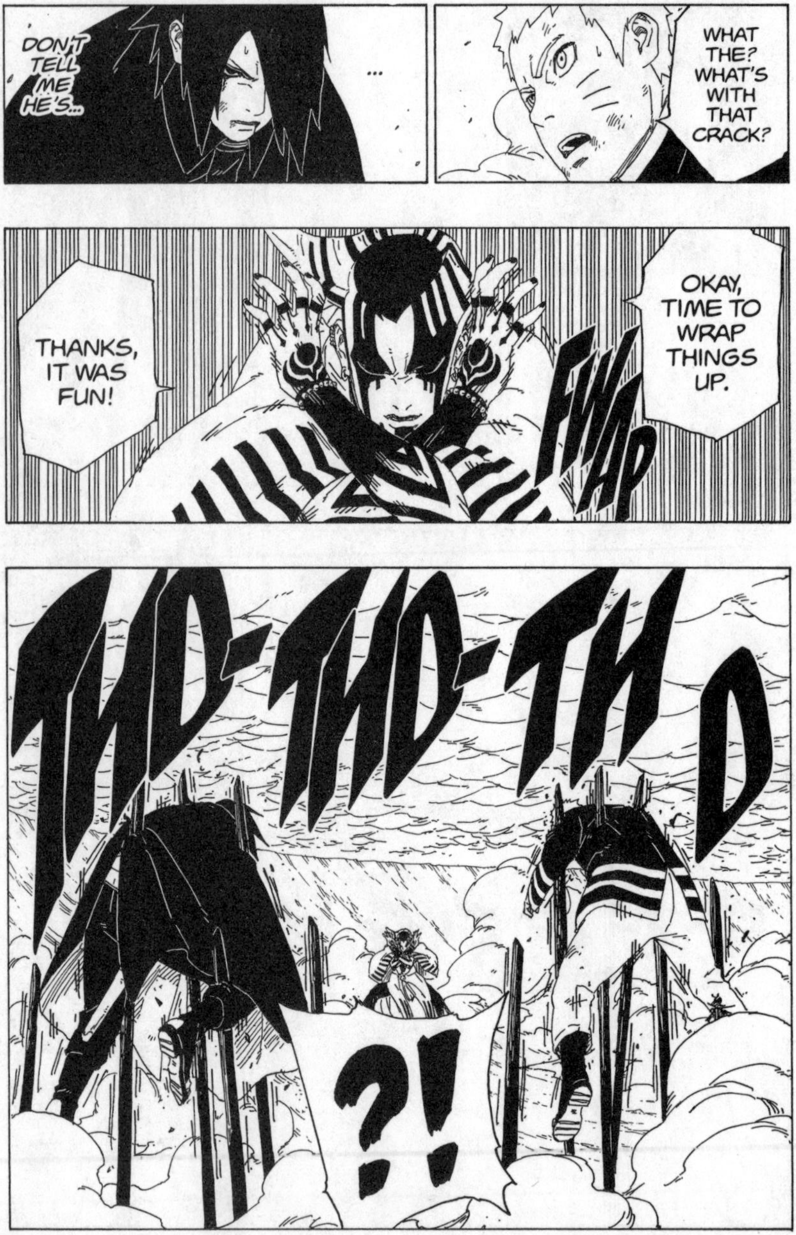
WHAT THE? WHAT'S WITH THAT CRACK?
...
DON'T TELL ME HE'S...
OKAY, TIME TO WRAP THINGS UP.
FWAP
THANKS, IT WAS FUN!
THD-THD-THD
?!

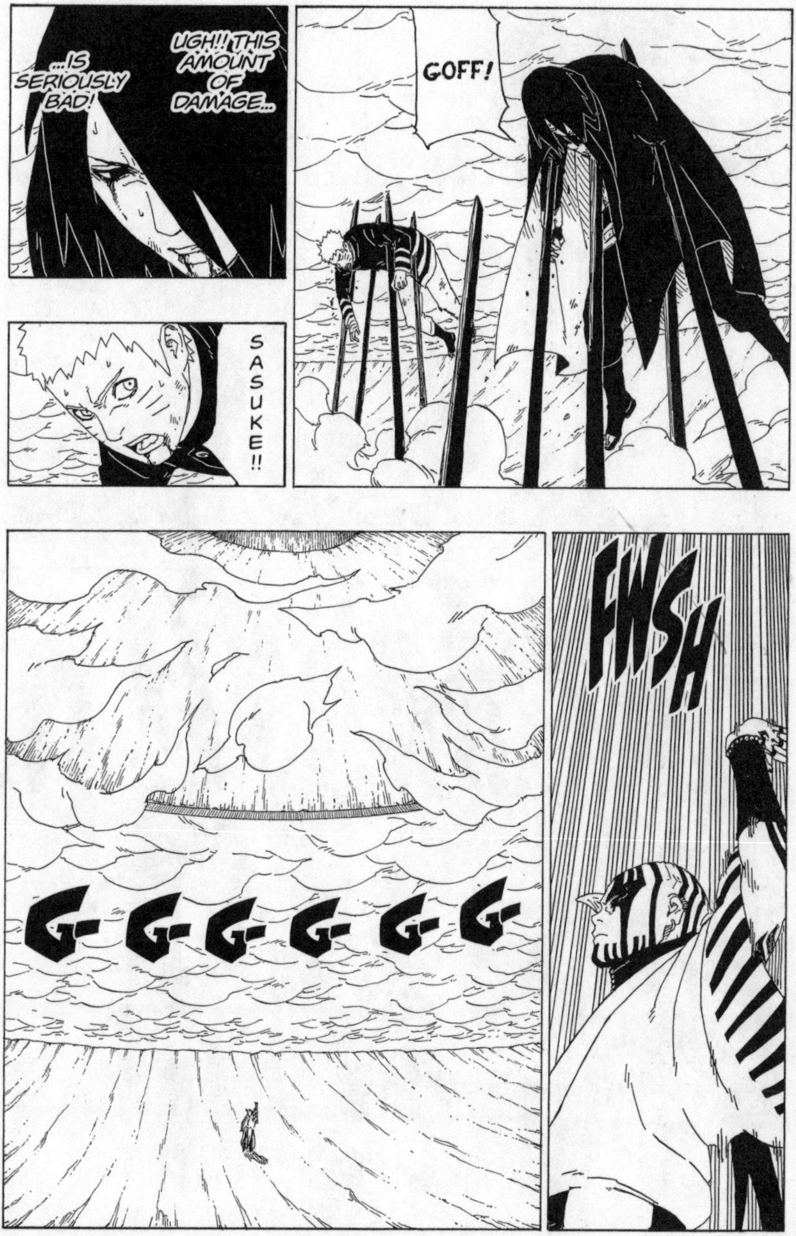
GOFF!
UGH!! THIS AMOUNT OF DAMAGE...
...IS SERIOUSLY BAD!
SASUKE!!
FWSH
G-G-G-G-G-G-

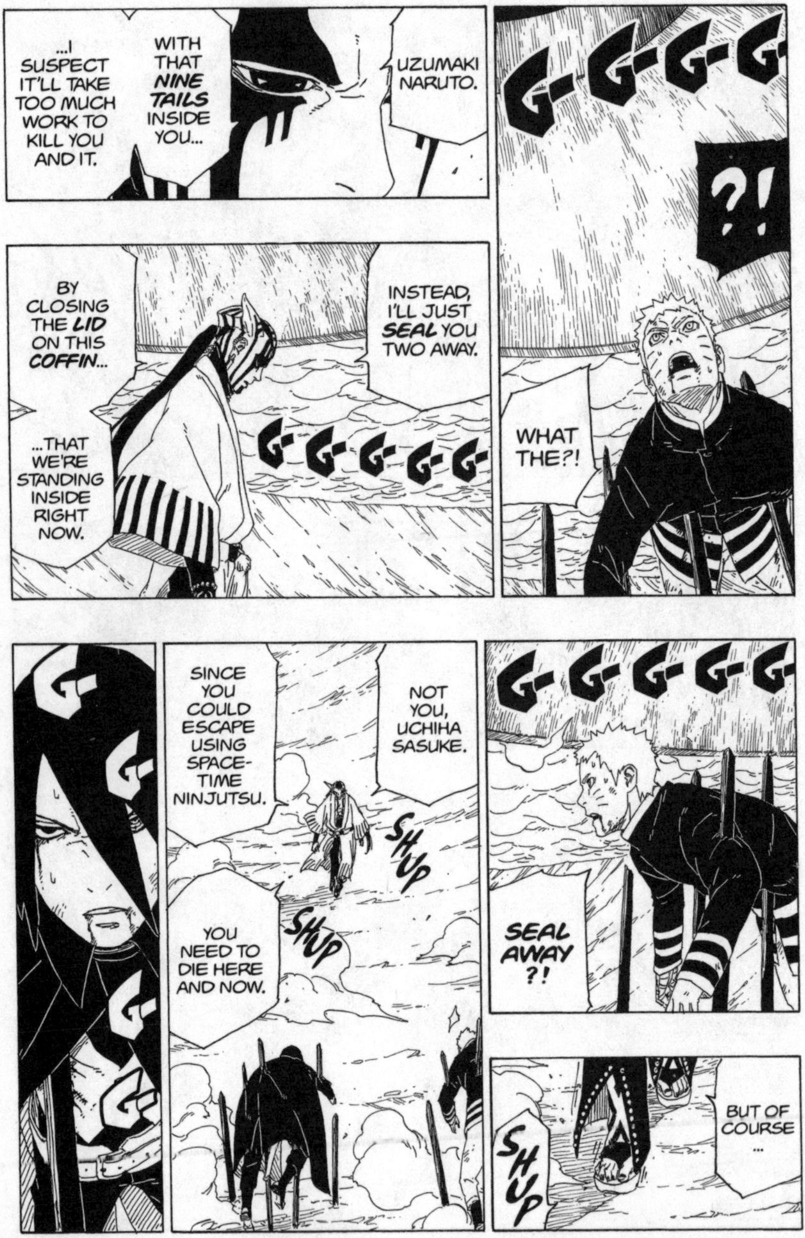
G-G-G-G-G-
?!
WHAT THE?!
UZUMAKI NARUTO.
WITH THAT NINE TAILS INSIDE YOU...
...I SUSPECT IT'LL TAKE TOO MUCH WORK TO KILL YOU AND IT.
INSTEAD, I'LL JUST SEAL YOU TWO AWAY.
G-G-G-G-G-
BY CLOSING THE LID ON THIS COFFIN...
...THAT WE'RE STANDING INSIDE RIGHT NOW.
G-G-G-G-G-
SEAL AWAY?!
BUT OF COURSE...
SHUP
NOT YOU, UCHIHA SASUKE.
SINCE YOU COULD ESCAPE USING SPACE-TIME NINJUTSU.
SHUP
YOU NEED TO DIE HERE AND NOW.
SHUP
G-
G-
G-
G-

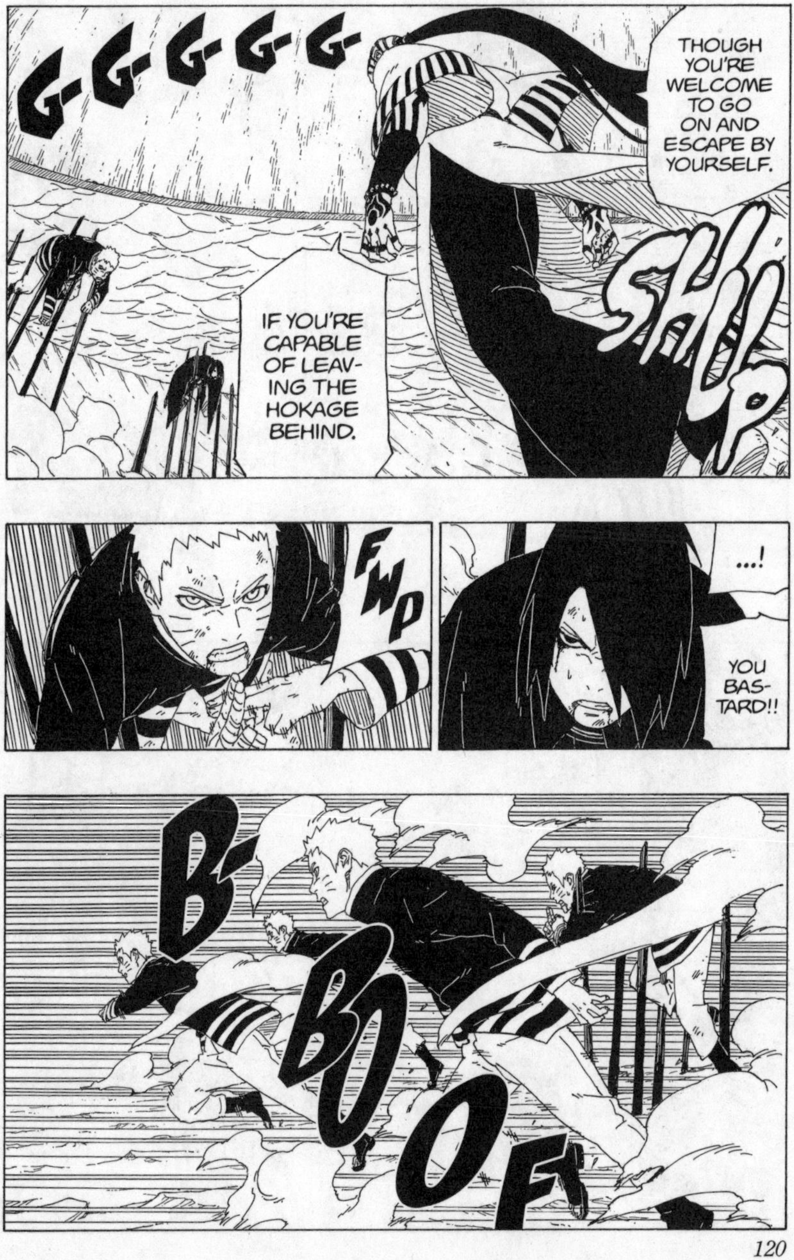
THOUGH YOU'RE WELCOME TO GO ON AND ESCAPE BY YOURSELF.
G-G-G-G-G-
SHUP
IF YOU'RE CAPABLE OF LEAV-ING THE HOKAGE BEHIND.
...!
YOU BAS-TARD!!
FWP
B-BOOOF

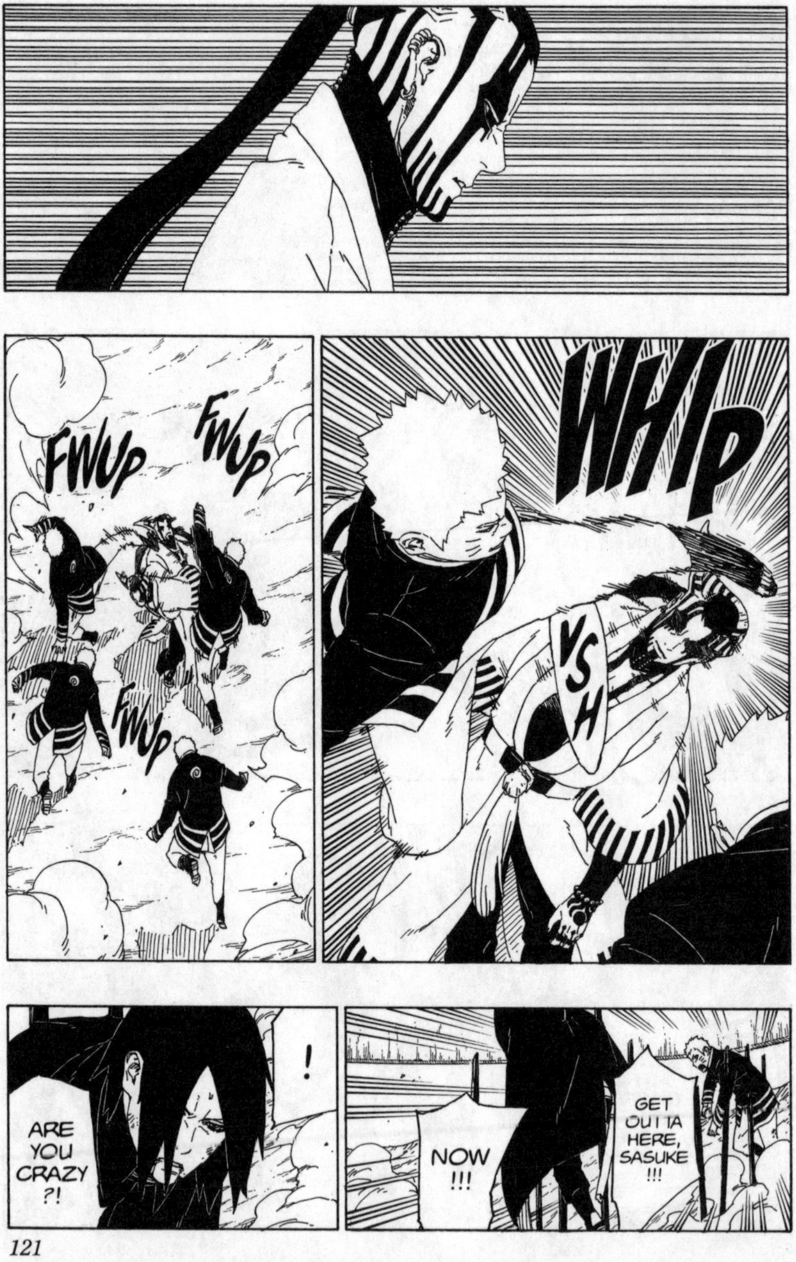
WHIP
VSH
FWUP
FWUP
FWUP
GET OUTTA HERE, SASUKE!!!
NOW!!!
!
ARE YOU CRAZY?!

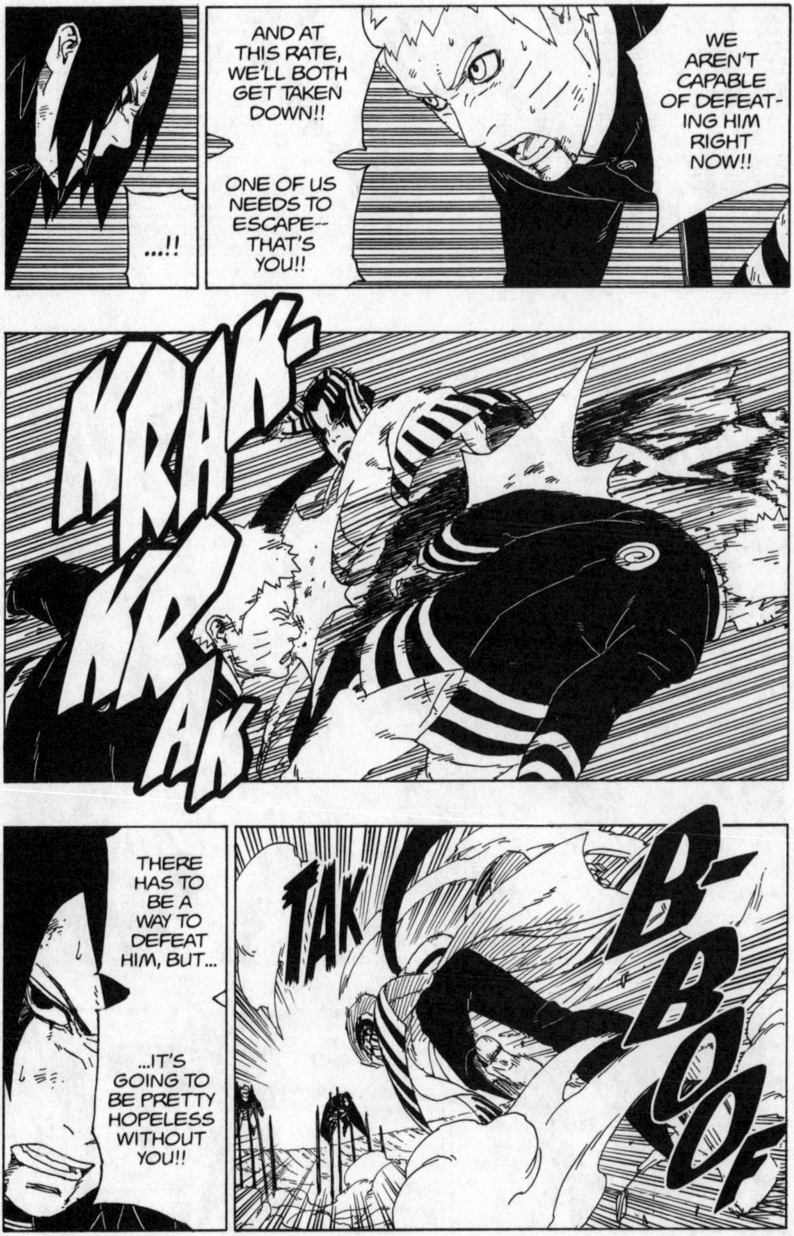
WE AREN'T CAPABLE OF DEFEATING HIM RIGHT NOW!!
AND AT THIS RATE, WE'LL BOTH GET TAKEN DOWN!!
ONE OF US NEEDS TO ESCAPE--THAT'S YOU!!
...!!
KRAK KRAK
B-BOOF
TAK
THERE HAS TO BE A WAY TO DEFEAT HIM, BUT...
...IT'S GOING TO BE PRETTY HOPELESS WITHOUT YOU!!

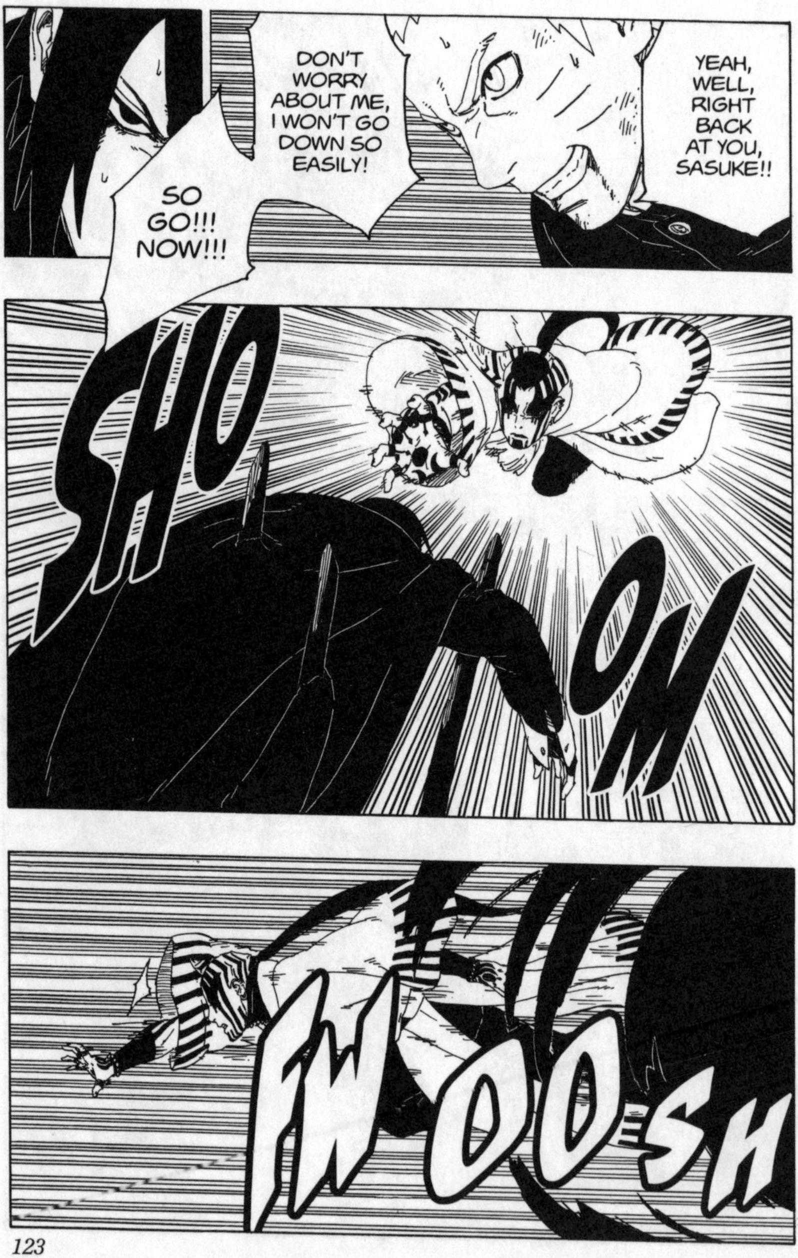
YEAH, WELL, RIGHT BACK AT YOU, SASUKE!!
DON'T WORRY ABOUT ME, I WON'T GO DOWN SO EASILY!
SO GO!!! NOW!!!
SHOOM
WHOOSH

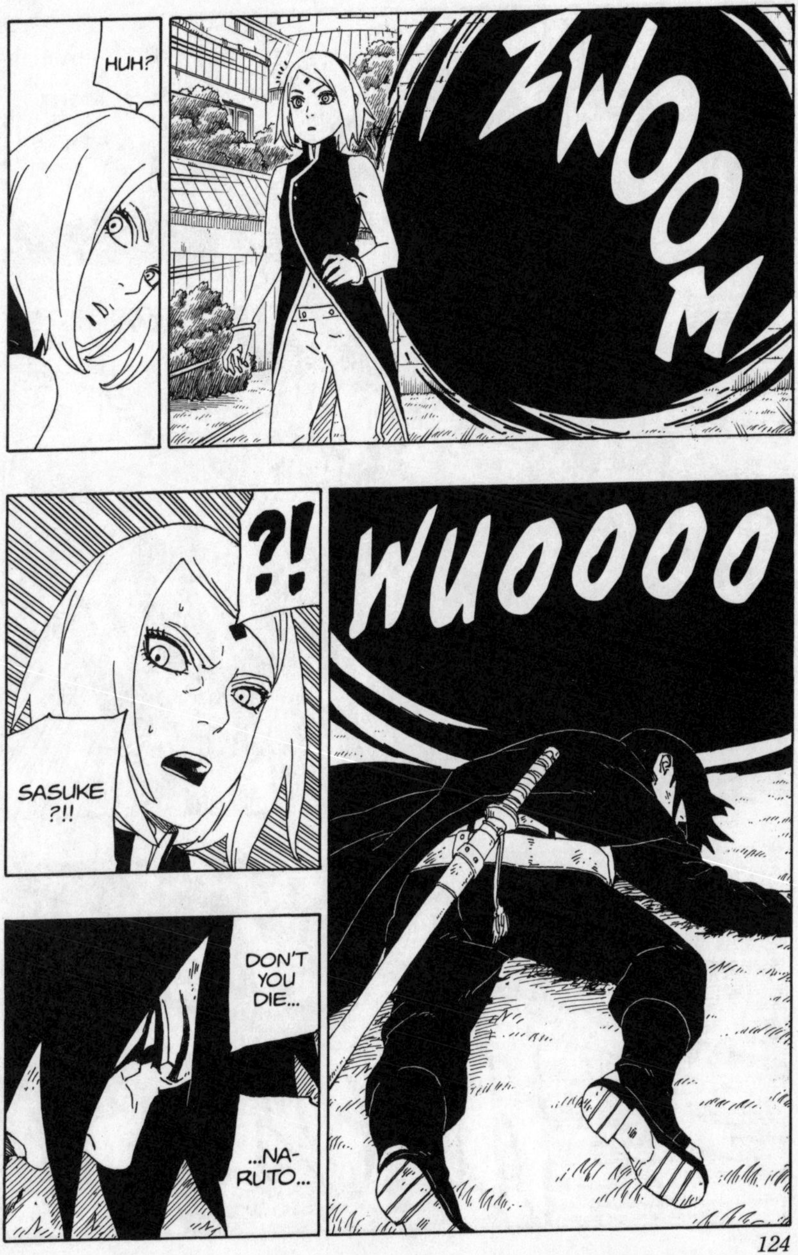
ZWOOM
HUH?
WUOOOO
?!
SASUKE ?!!
DON'T YOU DIE...
...NA-RUTO...

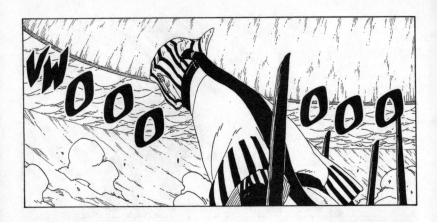

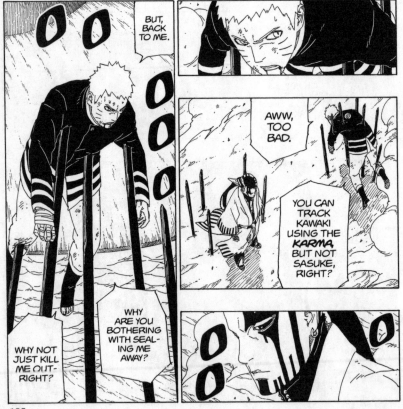

BUT, BACK TO ME.

AWW, TOO BAD.

YOU CAN TRACK KAWAKI USING THE *KARMA*, BUT NOT SASUKE, RIGHT?

WHY ARE YOU BOTHERING WITH SEALING ME AWAY?

WHY NOT JUST KILL ME OUTRIGHT?

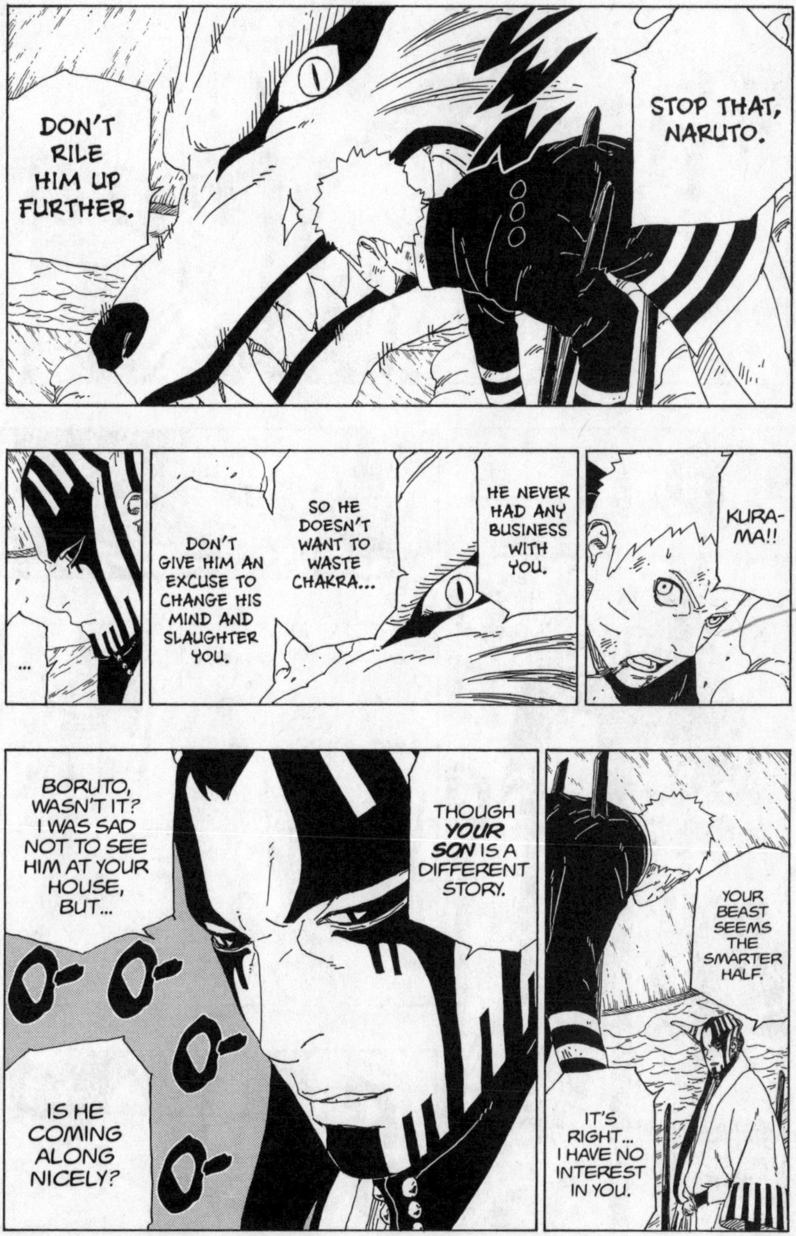
STOP THAT, NARUTO.
DON'T RILE HIM UP FURTHER.
KURA-MA!!
HE NEVER HAD ANY BUSINESS WITH YOU.
SO HE DOESN'T WANT TO WASTE CHAKRA...
DON'T GIVE HIM AN EXCUSE TO CHANGE HIS MIND AND SLAUGHTER YOU.
...
YOUR BEAST SEEMS THE SMARTER HALF.
IT'S RIGHT... I HAVE NO INTEREST IN YOU.
THOUGH *YOUR SON* IS A DIFFERENT STORY.
BORUTO, WASN'T IT? I WAS SAD NOT TO SEE HIM AT YOUR HOUSE, BUT...
IS HE COMING ALONG NICELY?

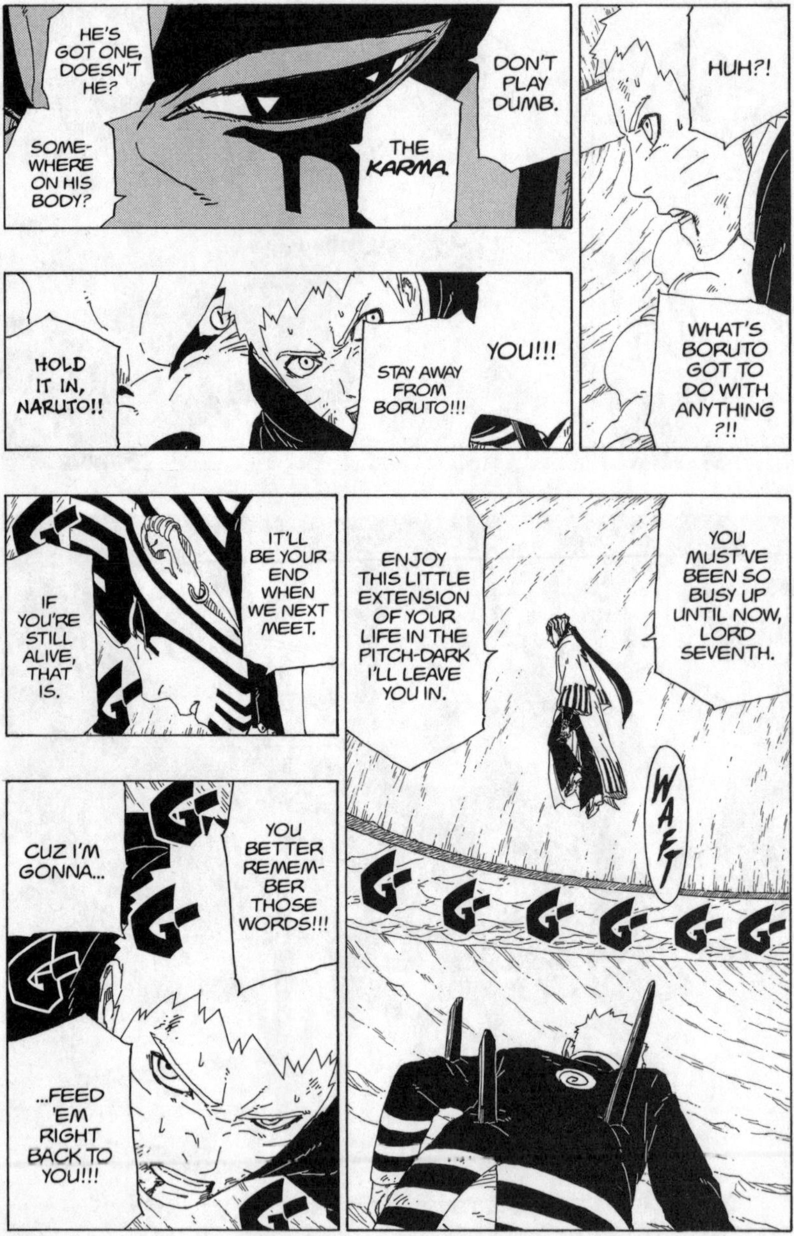
HUH?!
WHAT'S BORUTO GOT TO DO WITH ANYTHING?!!
DON'T PLAY DUMB.
THE *KARMA.*
HE'S GOT ONE, DOESN'T HE?
SOME-WHERE ON HIS BODY?
YOU!!!
STAY AWAY FROM BORUTO!!!
HOLD IT IN, NARUTO!!
YOU MUST'VE BEEN SO BUSY UP UNTIL NOW, LORD SEVENTH.
ENJOY THIS LITTLE EXTENSION OF YOUR LIFE IN THE PITCH-DARK I'LL LEAVE YOU IN.
WAFT
G- G- G- G- G- G-
IT'LL BE YOUR END WHEN WE NEXT MEET.
IF YOU'RE STILL ALIVE, THAT IS.
G- G-
YOU BETTER REMEMBER THOSE WORDS!!!
CUZ I'M GONNA...
G- G- G-
...FEED 'EM RIGHT BACK TO YOU!!!
G-

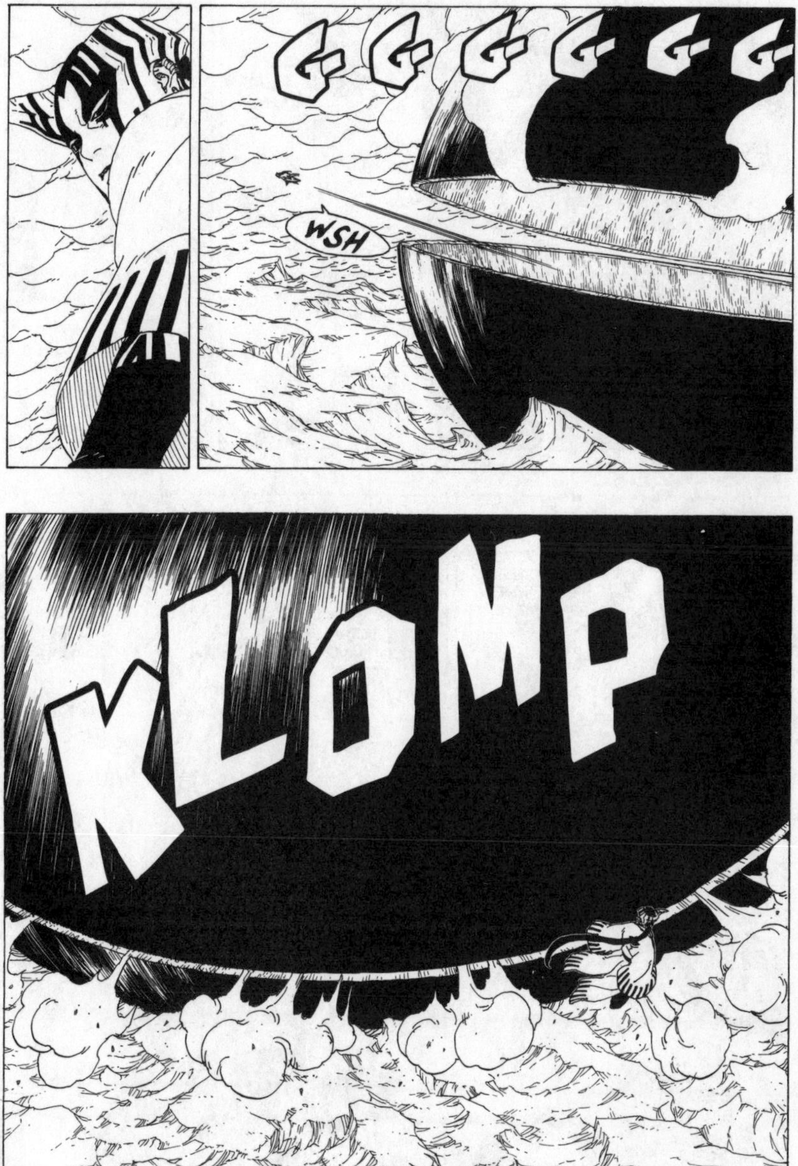
G-G-G-G-G-G
WSH
KLOMP

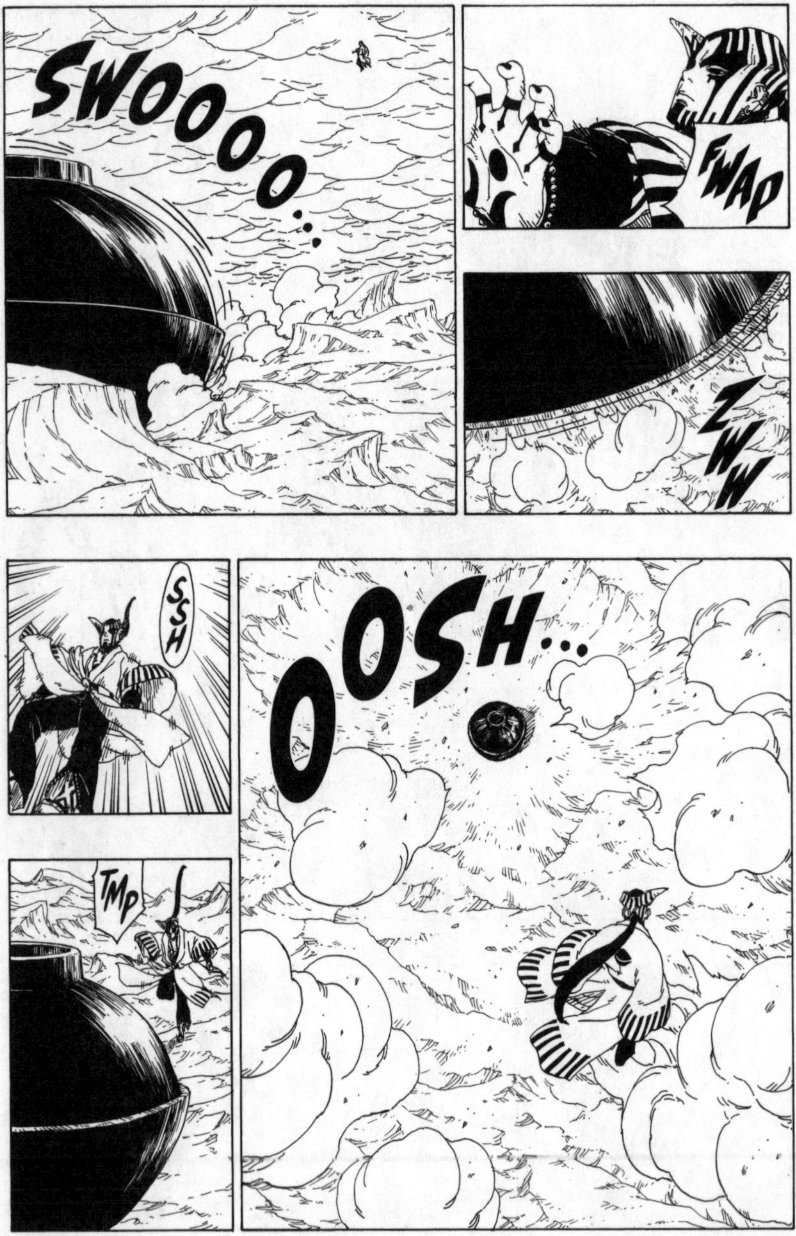
FWAP
ZWW
SWOOOO...
OOSH...
SSH
TMP

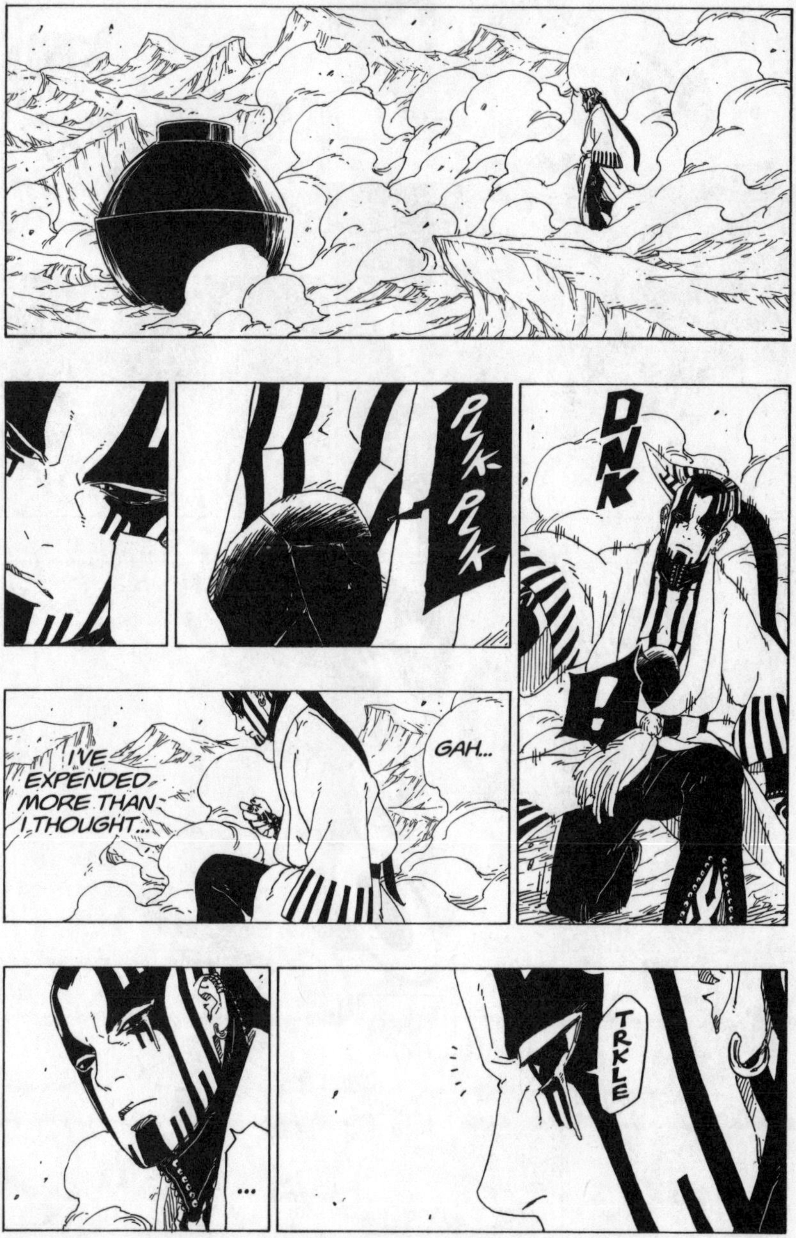
DNK
!
PLIK PLIK
GAH...
I'VE EXPENDED MORE THAN I THOUGHT...
TRKLE
...

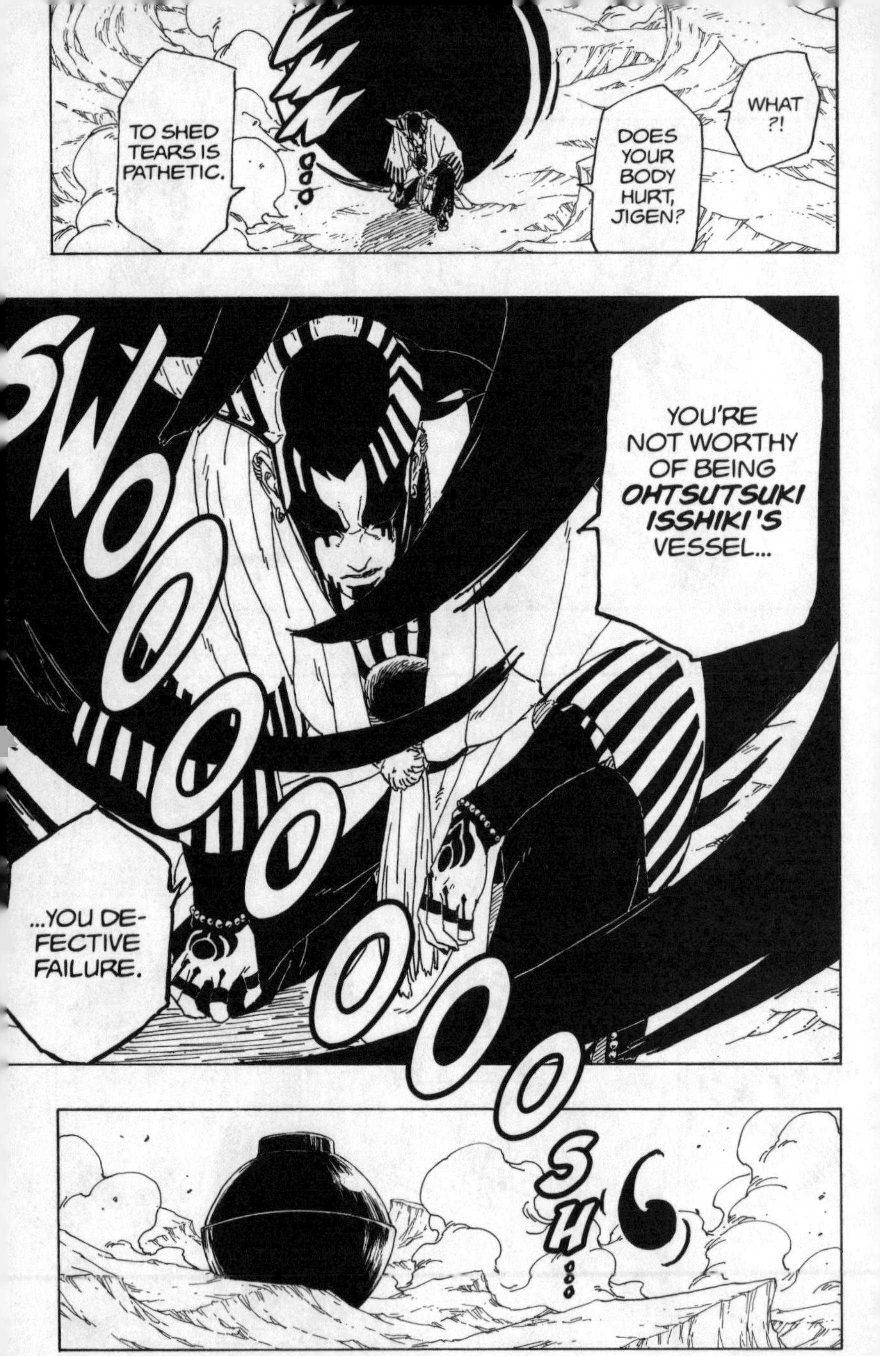
WHAT?!
DOES YOUR BODY HURT, JIGEN?
TO SHED TEARS IS PATHETIC.
YOU'RE NOT WORTHY OF BEING ***OHTSUTSUKI ISSHIKI'S*** VESSEL...
...YOU DEFECTIVE FAILURE.
SWOOOOOOOOOSH...

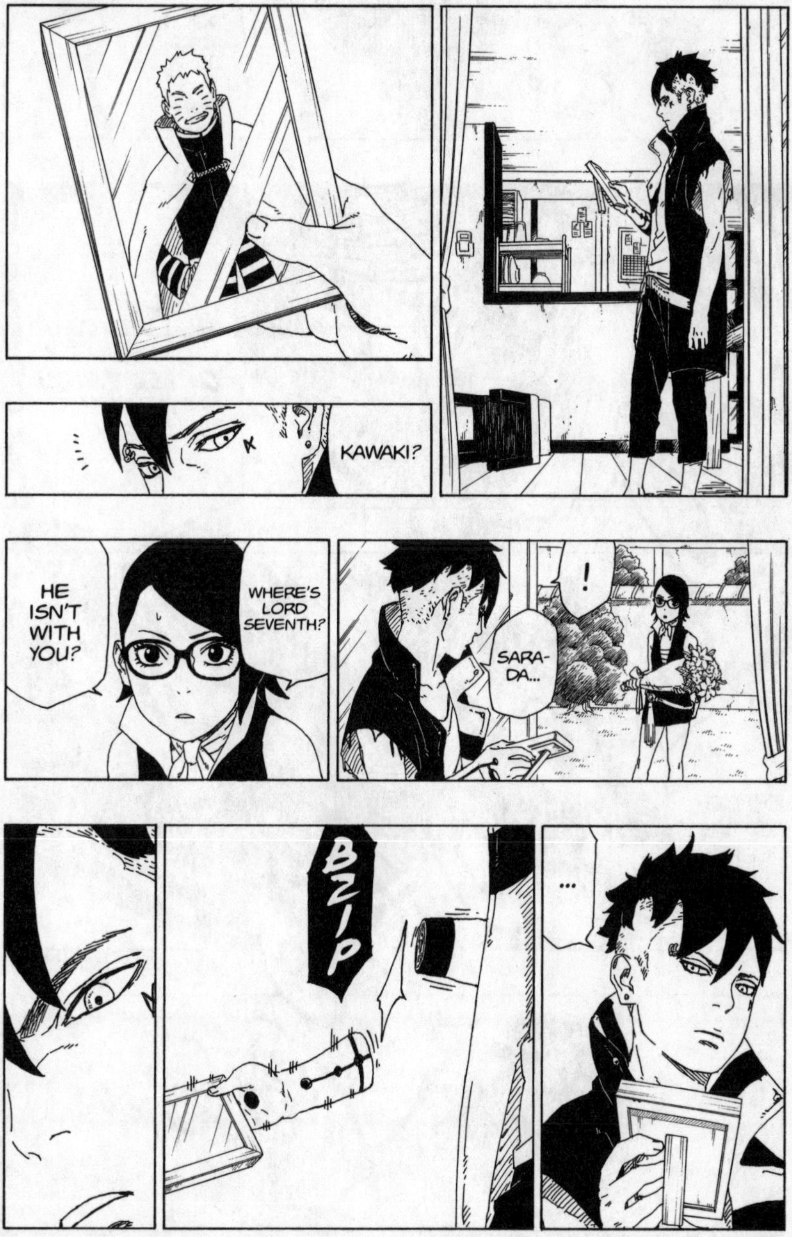

KAWAKI?
!
SARADA...
WHERE'S LORD SEVENTH?
HE ISN'T WITH YOU?
...
BZIP

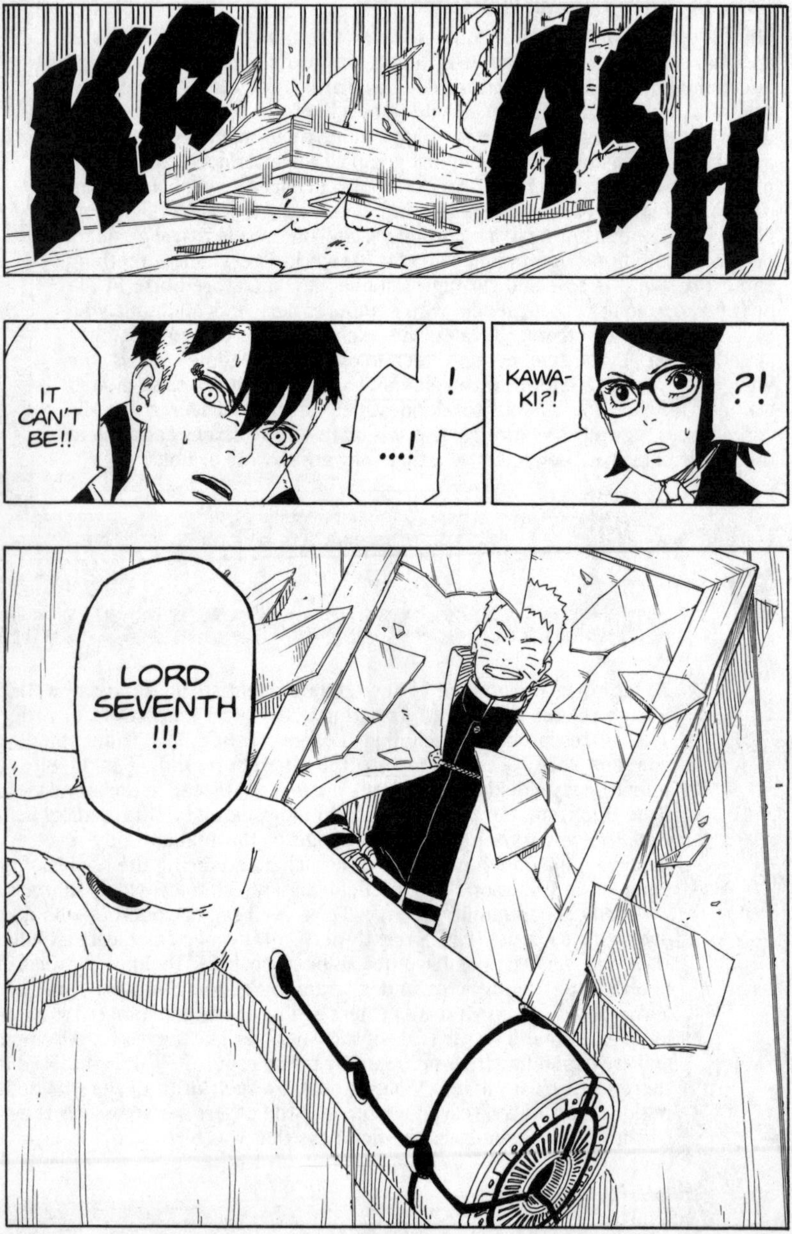
KRASH
?!
KAWAKI?!
!
...!
IT CAN'T BE!!
LORD SEVENTH!!!

Shinobi Hiden Column 7: Science

Shinobi can be outstanding scientists as well. Orochimaru, Yakushi Kabuto and Katasuke are representative examples, but even otherwise, all front-line shinobi (excluding exceptions such as Naruto) possess well-rounded scientific knowledge. This can be said to be a byproduct of them trying to understand all things in nature in order to hone their jutsu. Because being a ninja involves using jutsu, they must grasp all the interlaced factors that make up the world, plus many are genuinely curious as well. One cannot use jutsu that one does not understand. One can use Raikiri (Lightning Blade) because one knows what lightning is, and one is able to use genjutsu because one fathoms how people perceive the world. Every time something about the world is revealed through science, new jutsu are born. In the near future, ninjutsu that meddle with computer networks and ninja who can manipulate electronic devices will likely emerge. Or perhaps they already exist. Such science and technology is spreading across the Villagers' world in addition to the shinobi world. In past wartime eras, it was not unusual for shinobi to clandestinely attend Villager academic conferences, as well as vice versa. Every Hidden Village listens carefully to the words of brilliant scientists, whether they are shinobi or not.

To rephrase, the number of outstanding scientists possessed by a Hidden Village relates directly to its rating. Extraction maneuvers in order to secure researchers (including coarse tactics like kidnapping) are commonplace occurrences in the shinobi world. For if one can scientifically elucidate an enemy's jutsu, it could lead to unilateral victory. In addition, shinobi science and technology extend to the medical field as well. These past ten years, knowledge of the human body revealed by medical ninja (much of it gained by slicing and dicing the bodies of both enemies and allies on the battlefield) has started to be widely shared with the medical community at large. Thus, even regular doctors who do not use medical ninjutsu can currently perform advanced medical procedures. However, such strides have not all been positive. Technology regarding potent drugs being kept under wraps by Hidden Villages came to be leaked, leading to evil drug dealers selling those substances. Such drug lords have wealth on the scale of small nations, like the old Gato Company, and are expanding their influence by hiring rogue ninja. It is rumored that there even exist Hidden Villages built by such drug dealers in remote regions. Part of the reason Naruto and the others are so busy is they are battling such scoundrels, the darkness that was birthed by peace, every day.

Number 39: Proof

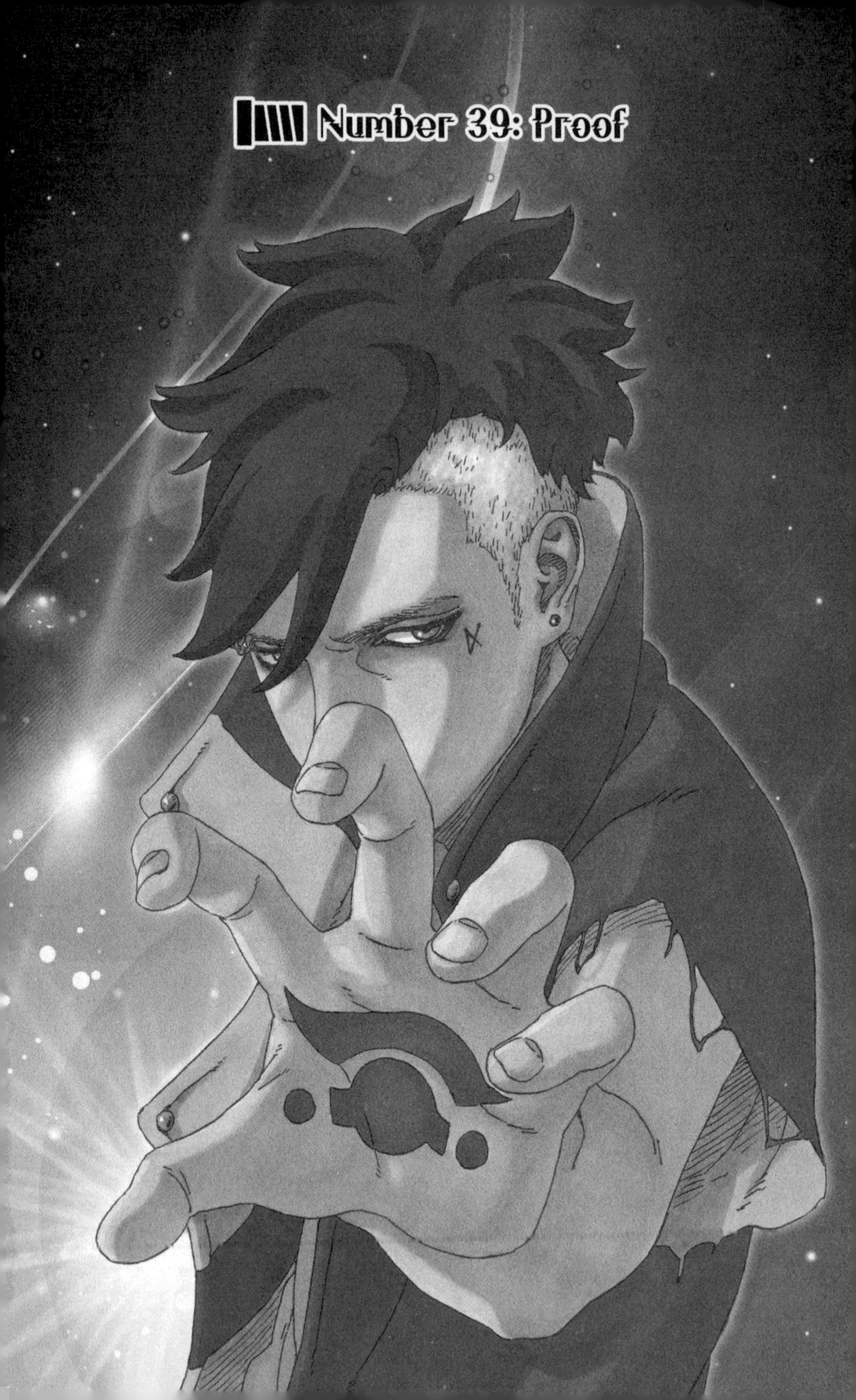

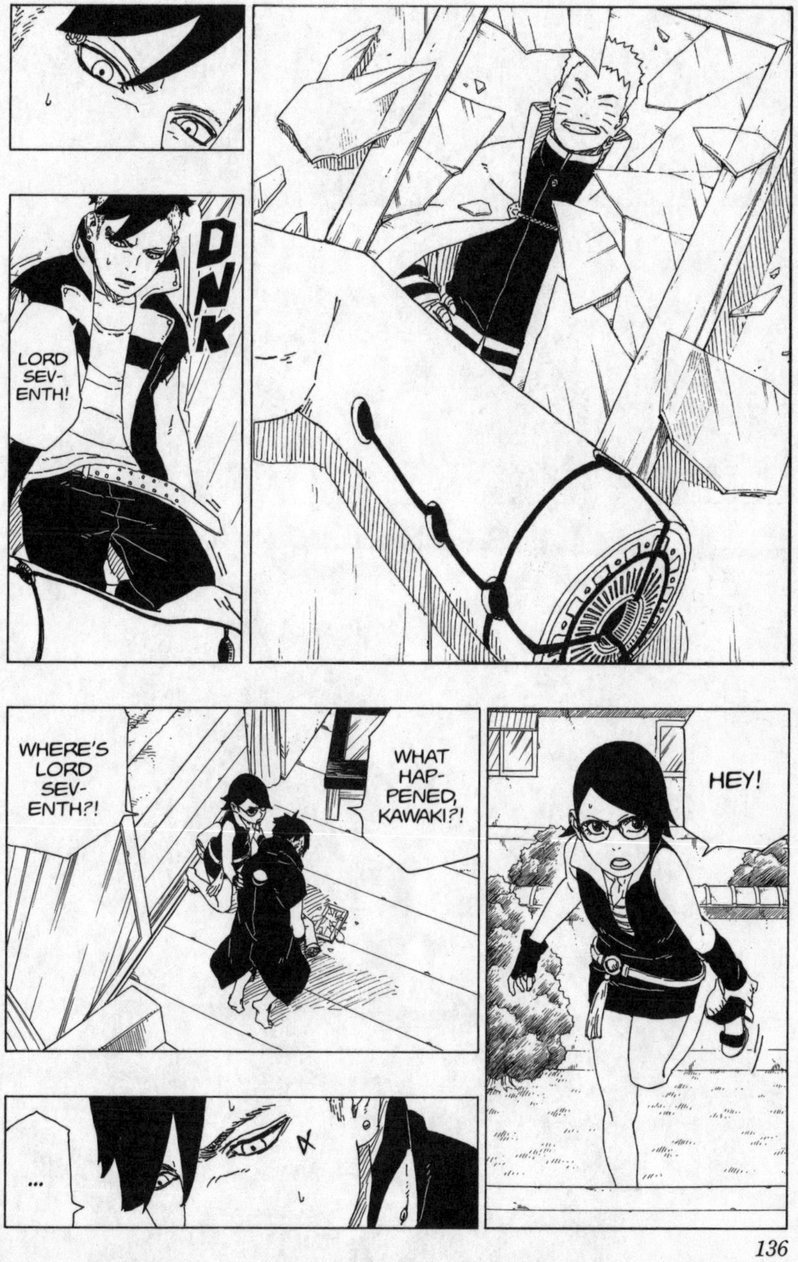
DNK
LORD SEVENTH!
HEY!
WHAT HAPPENED, KAWAKI?!
WHERE'S LORD SEVENTH?!
...

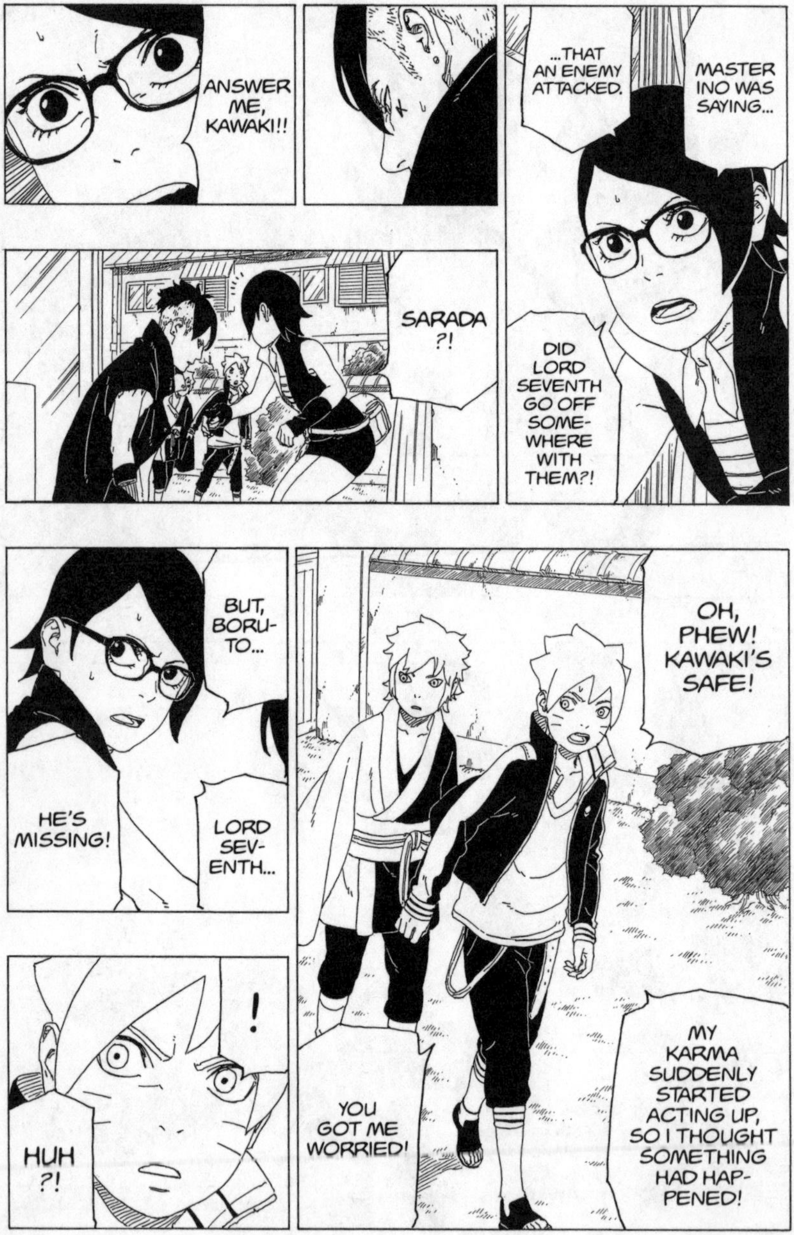
MASTER INO WAS SAYING...
...THAT AN ENEMY ATTACKED.
DID LORD SEVENTH GO OFF SOME-WHERE WITH THEM?!
ANSWER ME, KAWAKI!!
SARADA ?!
OH, PHEW! KAWAKI'S SAFE!
MY KARMA SUDDENLY STARTED ACTING UP, SO I THOUGHT SOMETHING HAD HAP-PENED!
YOU GOT ME WORRIED!
BUT, BORU-TO...
LORD SEV-ENTH...
HE'S MISSING!
!
HUH ?!

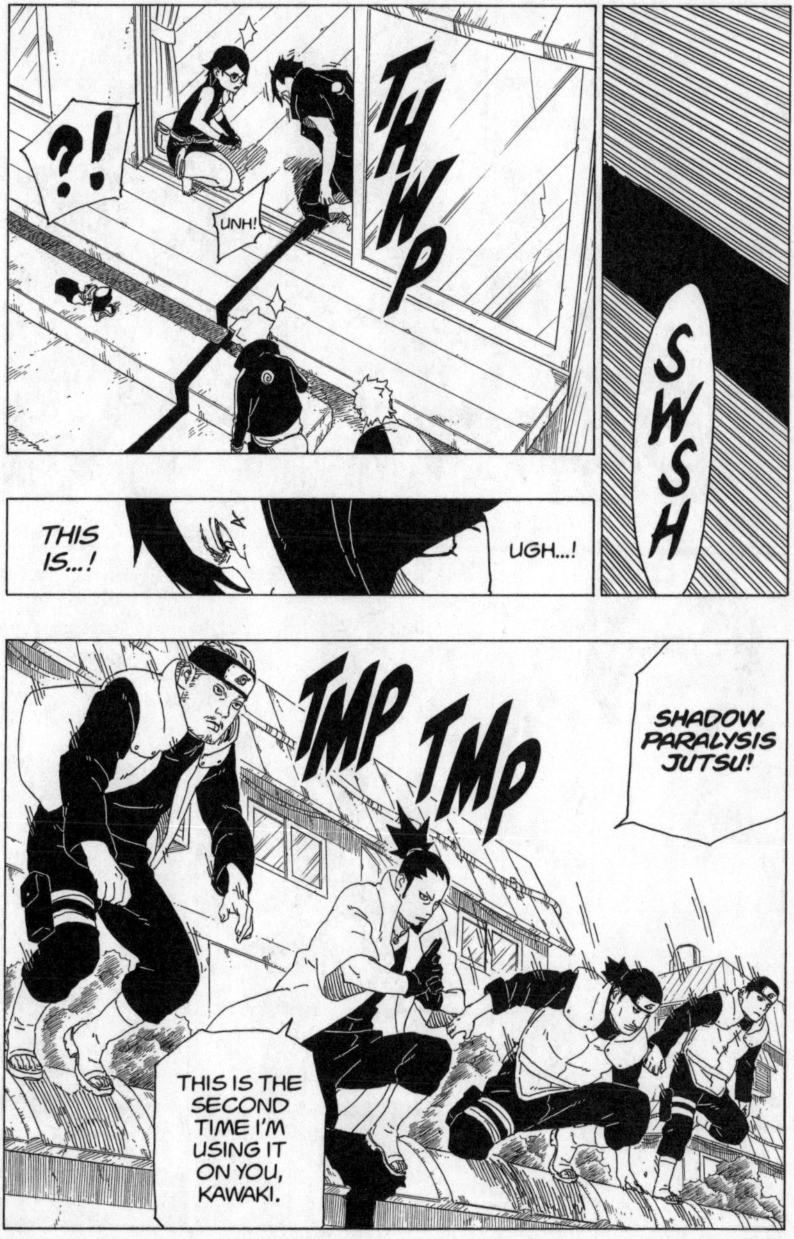
SWSH
THWP
?!
UNH!
UGH...!
THIS IS...!
SHADOW PARALYSIS JUTSU!
TMP TMP
THIS IS THE SECOND TIME I'M USING IT ON YOU, KAWAKI.

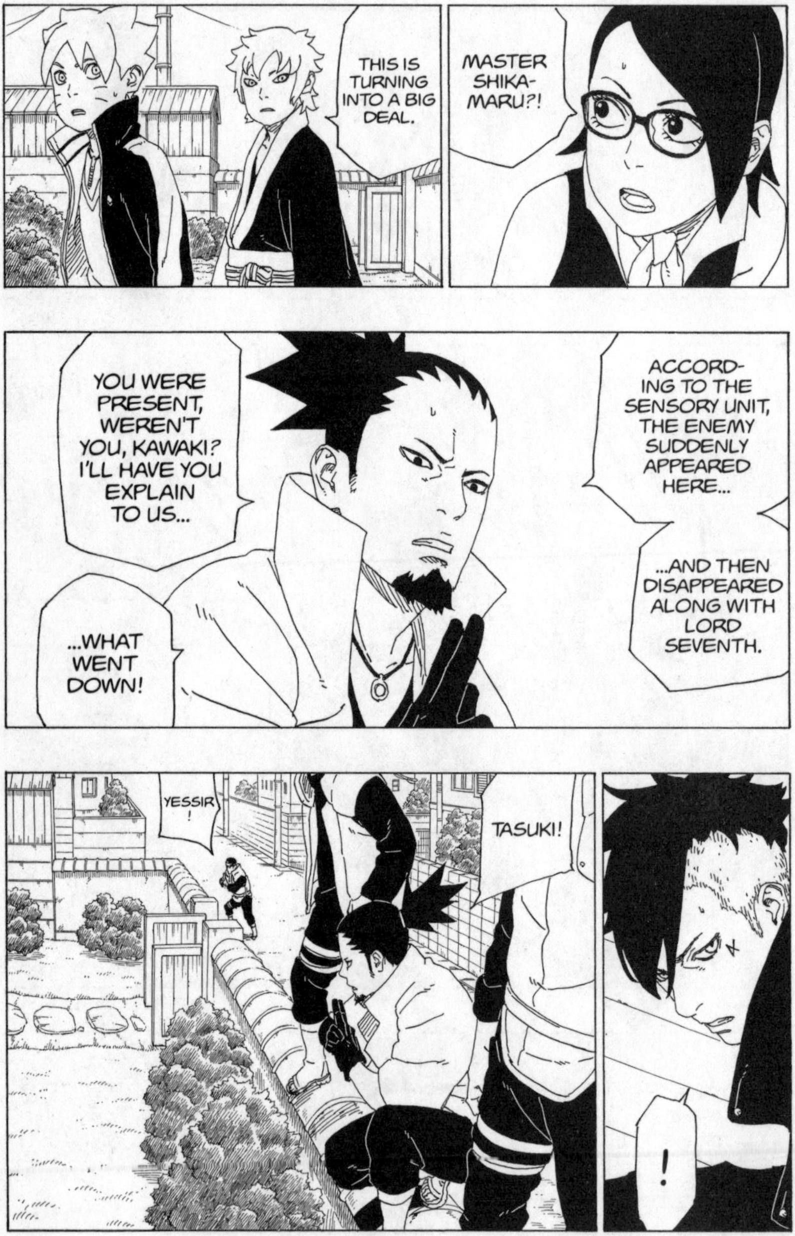
MASTER SHIKA-MARU?!
THIS IS TURNING INTO A BIG DEAL.
ACCORD-ING TO THE SENSORY UNIT, THE ENEMY SUDDENLY APPEARED HERE...
...AND THEN DISAPPEARED ALONG WITH LORD SEVENTH.
YOU WERE PRESENT, WEREN'T YOU, KAWAKI? I'LL HAVE YOU EXPLAIN TO US...
...WHAT WENT DOWN!
!
TASUKI!
YESSIR!

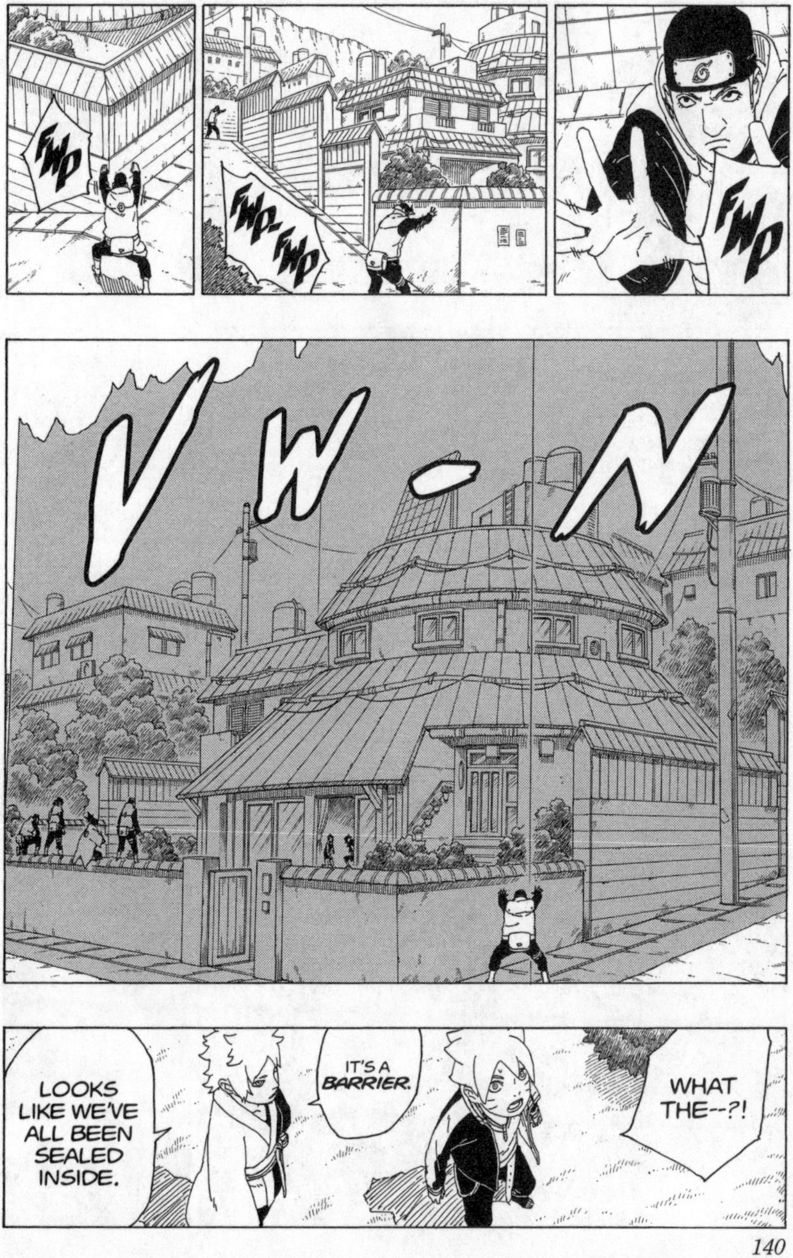
FWP
FWP-FWP
FWP
VW-N
WHAT THE--?!
IT'S A BARRIER.
LOOKS LIKE WE'VE ALL BEEN SEALED INSIDE.

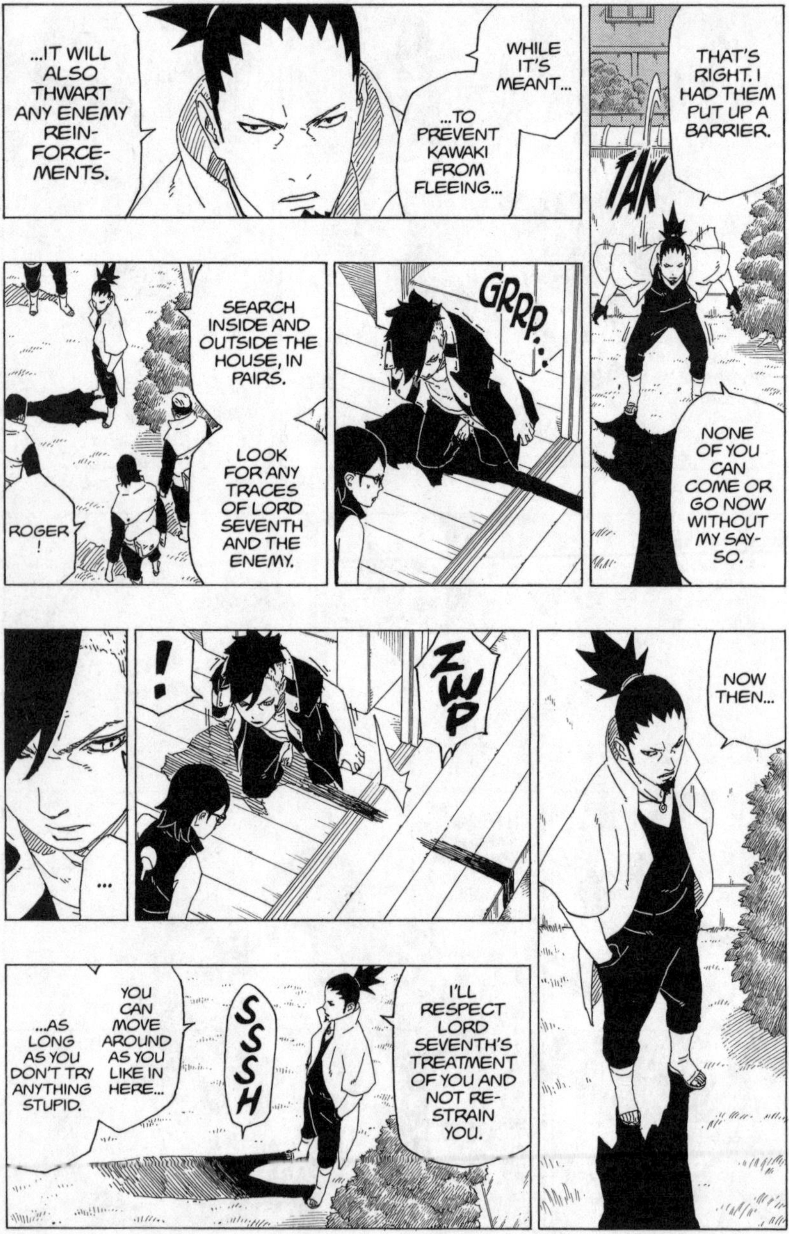
TAK
THAT'S RIGHT. I HAD THEM PUT UP A BARRIER.
NONE OF YOU CAN COME OR GO NOW WITHOUT MY SAY-SO.
WHILE IT'S MEANT...
...TO PREVENT KAWAKI FROM FLEEING...
...IT WILL ALSO THWART ANY ENEMY REIN-FORCE-MENTS.
GRRP...
SEARCH INSIDE AND OUTSIDE THE HOUSE, IN PAIRS.
LOOK FOR ANY TRACES OF LORD SEVENTH AND THE ENEMY.
ROGER!
NOW THEN...
ZWP
!
...
I'LL RESPECT LORD SEVENTH'S TREATMENT OF YOU AND NOT RE-STRAIN YOU.
SSSH
YOU CAN MOVE AROUND AS YOU LIKE IN HERE...
...AS LONG AS YOU DON'T TRY ANYTHING STUPID.

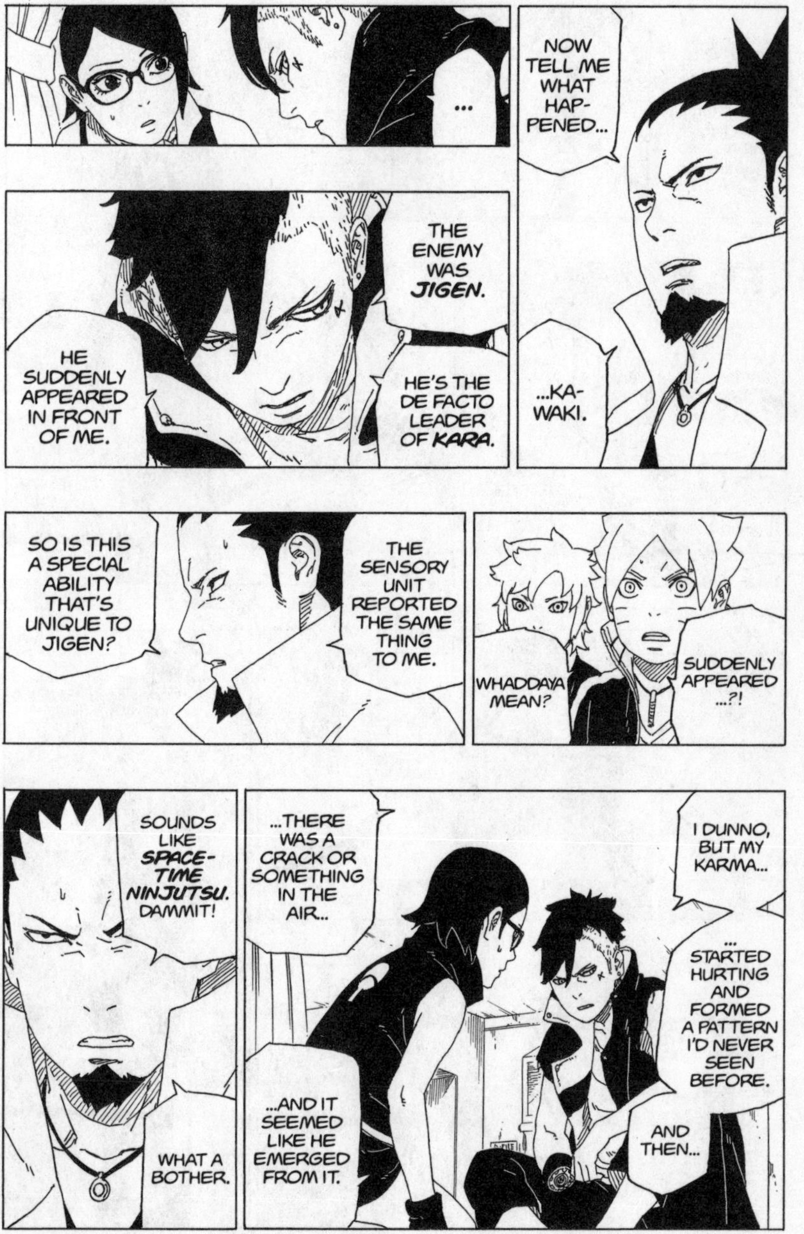
NOW TELL ME WHAT HAPPENED...
...
...KAWAKI.
THE ENEMY WAS JIGEN.
HE'S THE DE FACTO LEADER OF KARA.
HE SUDDENLY APPEARED IN FRONT OF ME.
SUDDENLY APPEARED...?!
WHADDAYA MEAN?
THE SENSORY UNIT REPORTED THE SAME THING TO ME.
SO IS THIS A SPECIAL ABILITY THAT'S UNIQUE TO JIGEN?
I DUNNO, BUT MY KARMA...
...STARTED HURTING AND FORMED A PATTERN I'D NEVER SEEN BEFORE.
AND THEN...
...THERE WAS A CRACK OR SOMETHING IN THE AIR...
...AND IT SEEMED LIKE HE EMERGED FROM IT.
SOUNDS LIKE SPACE-TIME NINJUTSU. DAMMIT!
WHAT A BOTHER.

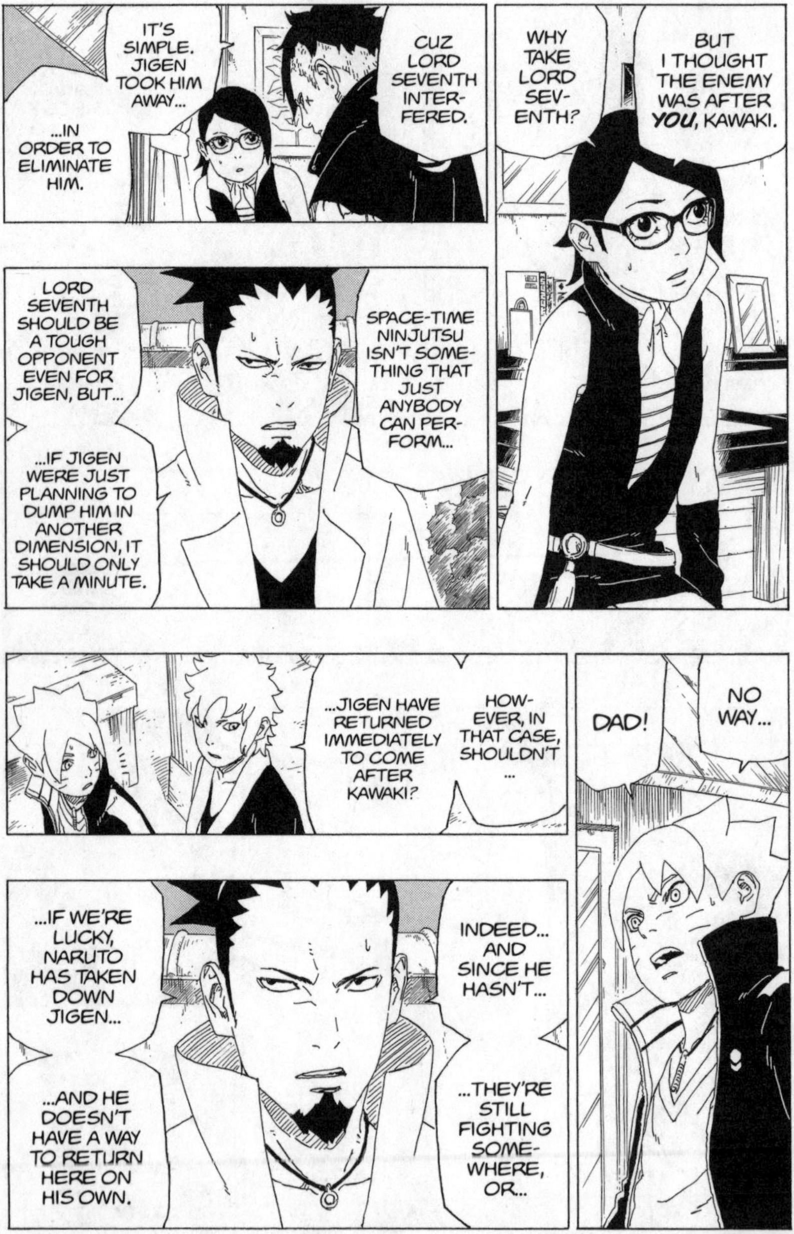
BUT I THOUGHT THE ENEMY WAS AFTER *YOU*, KAWAKI.
WHY TAKE LORD SEVENTH?
CUZ LORD SEVENTH INTERFERED.
IT'S SIMPLE. JIGEN TOOK HIM AWAY...
...IN ORDER TO ELIMINATE HIM.
SPACE-TIME NINJUTSU ISN'T SOMETHING THAT JUST ANYBODY CAN PERFORM...
LORD SEVENTH SHOULD BE A TOUGH OPPONENT EVEN FOR JIGEN, BUT...
...IF JIGEN WERE JUST PLANNING TO DUMP HIM IN ANOTHER DIMENSION, IT SHOULD ONLY TAKE A MINUTE.
NO WAY...
DAD!
HOWEVER, IN THAT CASE, SHOULDN'T ...
...JIGEN HAVE RETURNED IMMEDIATELY TO COME AFTER KAWAKI?
INDEED... AND SINCE HE HASN'T...
...IF WE'RE LUCKY, NARUTO HAS TAKEN DOWN JIGEN...
...AND HE DOESN'T HAVE A WAY TO RETURN HERE ON HIS OWN.
...THEY'RE STILL FIGHTING SOMEWHERE, OR...

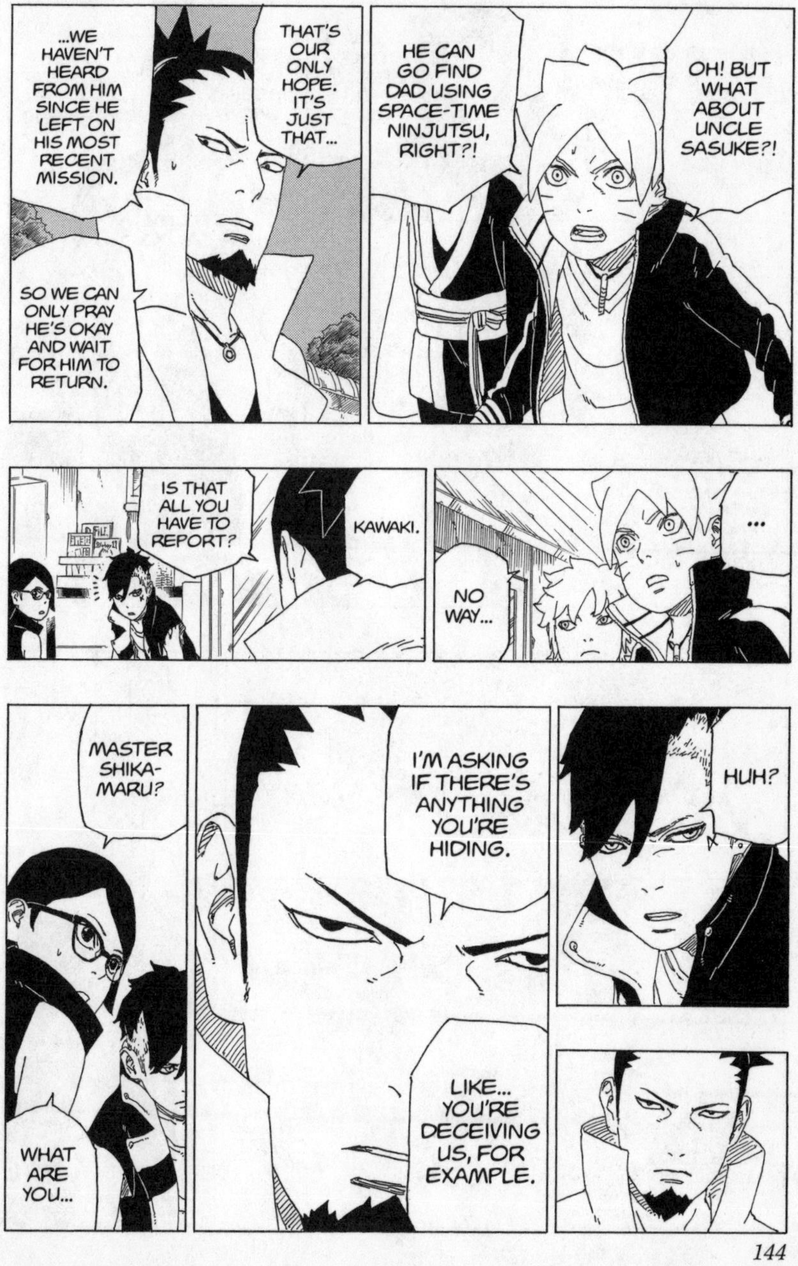
OH! BUT WHAT ABOUT UNCLE SASUKE?!
HE CAN GO FIND DAD USING SPACE-TIME NINJUTSU, RIGHT?!
THAT'S OUR ONLY HOPE. IT'S JUST THAT...
...WE HAVEN'T HEARD FROM HIM SINCE HE LEFT ON HIS MOST RECENT MISSION.
SO WE CAN ONLY PRAY HE'S OKAY AND WAIT FOR HIM TO RETURN.
...
NO WAY...
KAWAKI.
IS THAT ALL YOU HAVE TO REPORT?
HUH?
I'M ASKING IF THERE'S ANYTHING YOU'RE HIDING.
LIKE... YOU'RE DECEIVING US, FOR EXAMPLE.
MASTER SHIKAMARU?
WHAT ARE YOU...

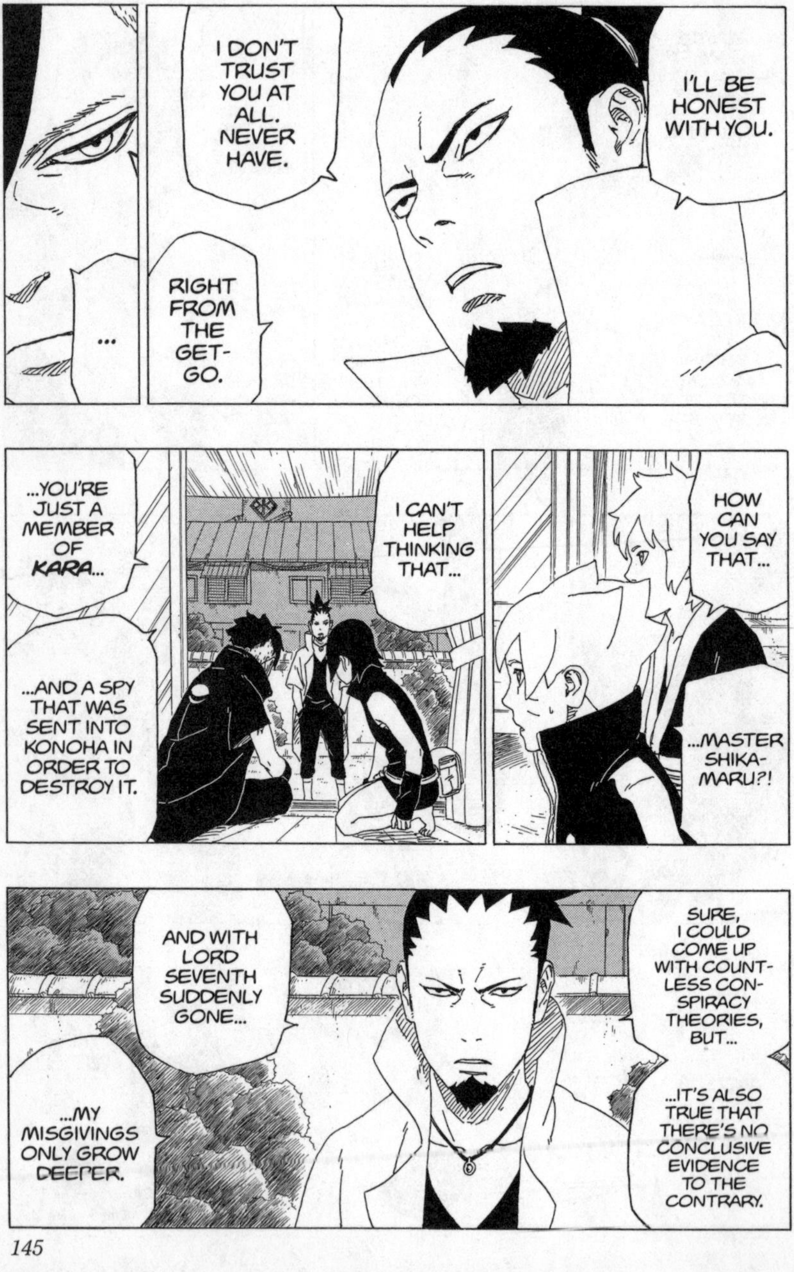
I'LL BE HONEST WITH YOU.
I DON'T TRUST YOU AT ALL. NEVER HAVE.
RIGHT FROM THE GET-GO.
...
HOW CAN YOU SAY THAT...
...MASTER SHIKAMARU?!
I CAN'T HELP THINKING THAT...
...YOU'RE JUST A MEMBER OF *KARA*...
...AND A SPY THAT WAS SENT INTO KONOHA IN ORDER TO DESTROY IT.
SURE, I COULD COME UP WITH COUNTLESS CONSPIRACY THEORIES, BUT...
...IT'S ALSO TRUE THAT THERE'S NO CONCLUSIVE EVIDENCE TO THE CONTRARY.
AND WITH LORD SEVENTH SUDDENLY GONE...
...MY MISGIVINGS ONLY GROW DEEPER.

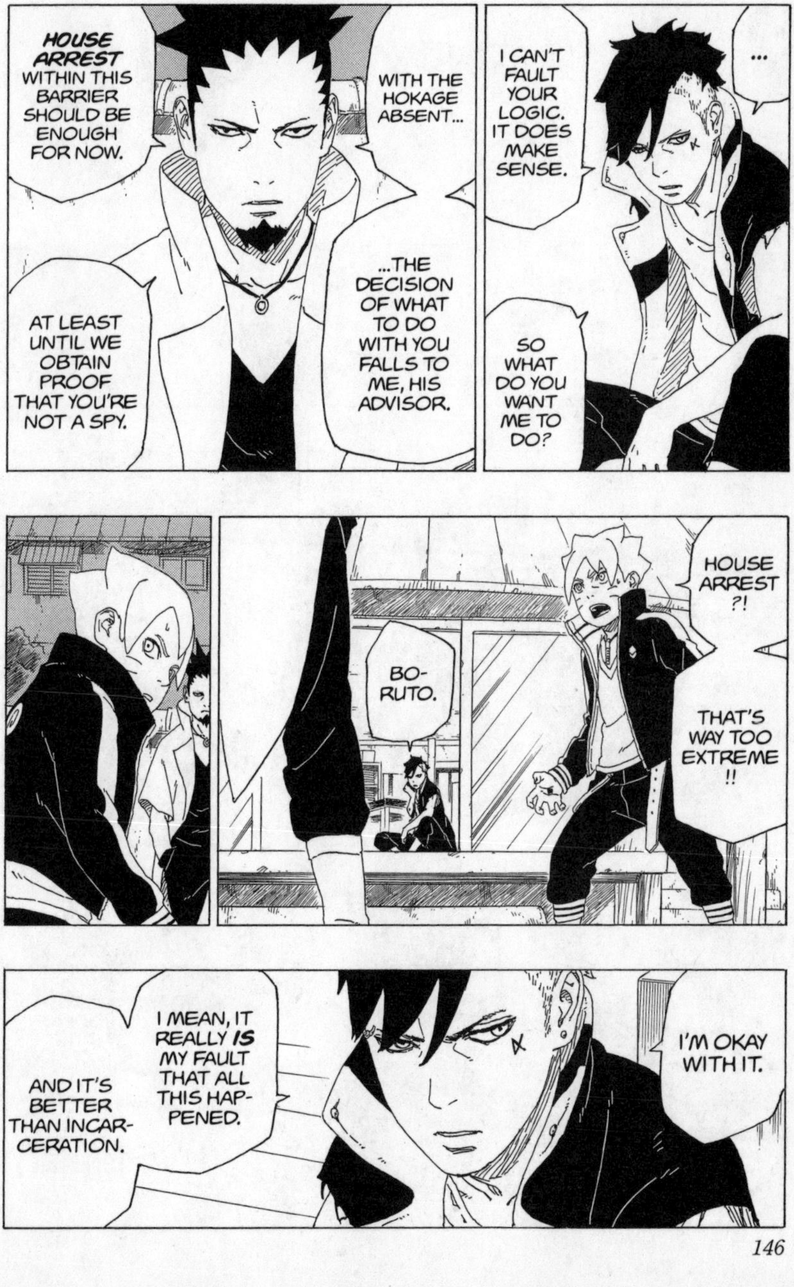
...
I CAN'T FAULT YOUR LOGIC. IT DOES MAKE SENSE.
SO WHAT DO YOU WANT ME TO DO?
WITH THE HOKAGE ABSENT...
...THE DECISION OF WHAT TO DO WITH YOU FALLS TO ME, HIS ADVISOR.
HOUSE ARREST WITHIN THIS BARRIER SHOULD BE ENOUGH FOR NOW.
AT LEAST UNTIL WE OBTAIN PROOF THAT YOU'RE NOT A SPY.
HOUSE ARREST ?!
THAT'S WAY TOO EXTREME !!
BO- RUTO.
I'M OKAY WITH IT.
I MEAN, IT REALLY *IS* MY FAULT THAT ALL THIS HAP- PENED.
AND IT'S BETTER THAN INCAR- CERATION.

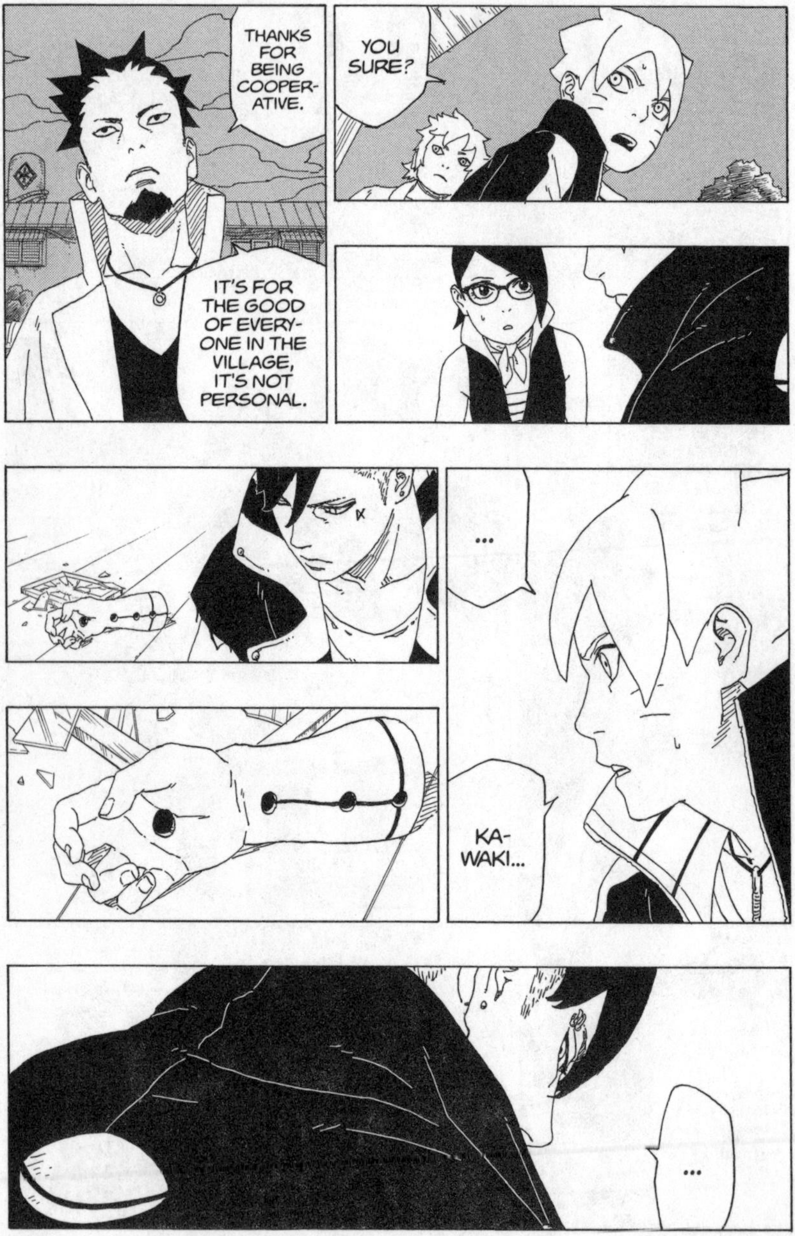
YOU SURE?
THANKS FOR BEING COOPER-ATIVE.
IT'S FOR THE GOOD OF EVERY-ONE IN THE VILLAGE, IT'S NOT PERSONAL.
...
KA-WAKI...
...

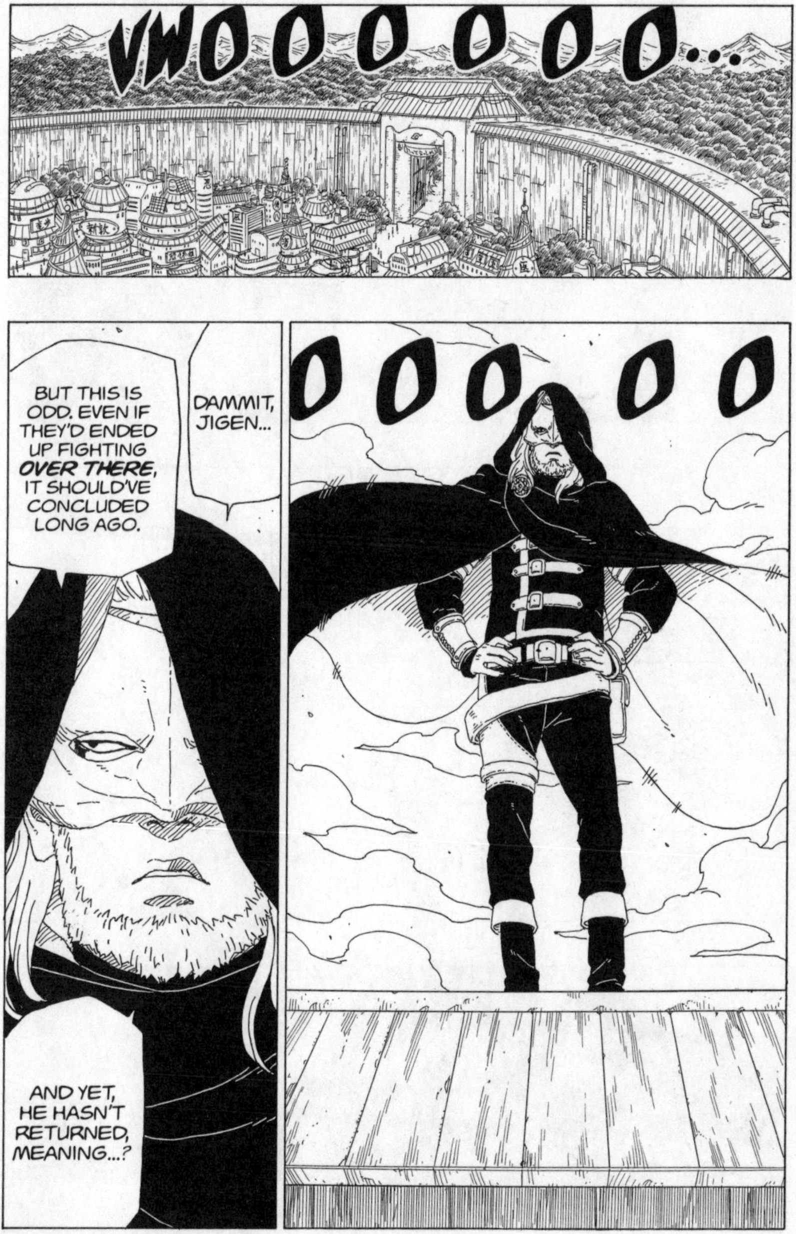
VWOOOO OOOO...
OOOOO
DAMMIT, JIGEN...
BUT THIS IS ODD. EVEN IF THEY'D ENDED UP FIGHTING **OVER THERE**, IT SHOULD'VE CONCLUDED LONG AGO.
AND YET, HE HASN'T RETURNED, MEANING...?

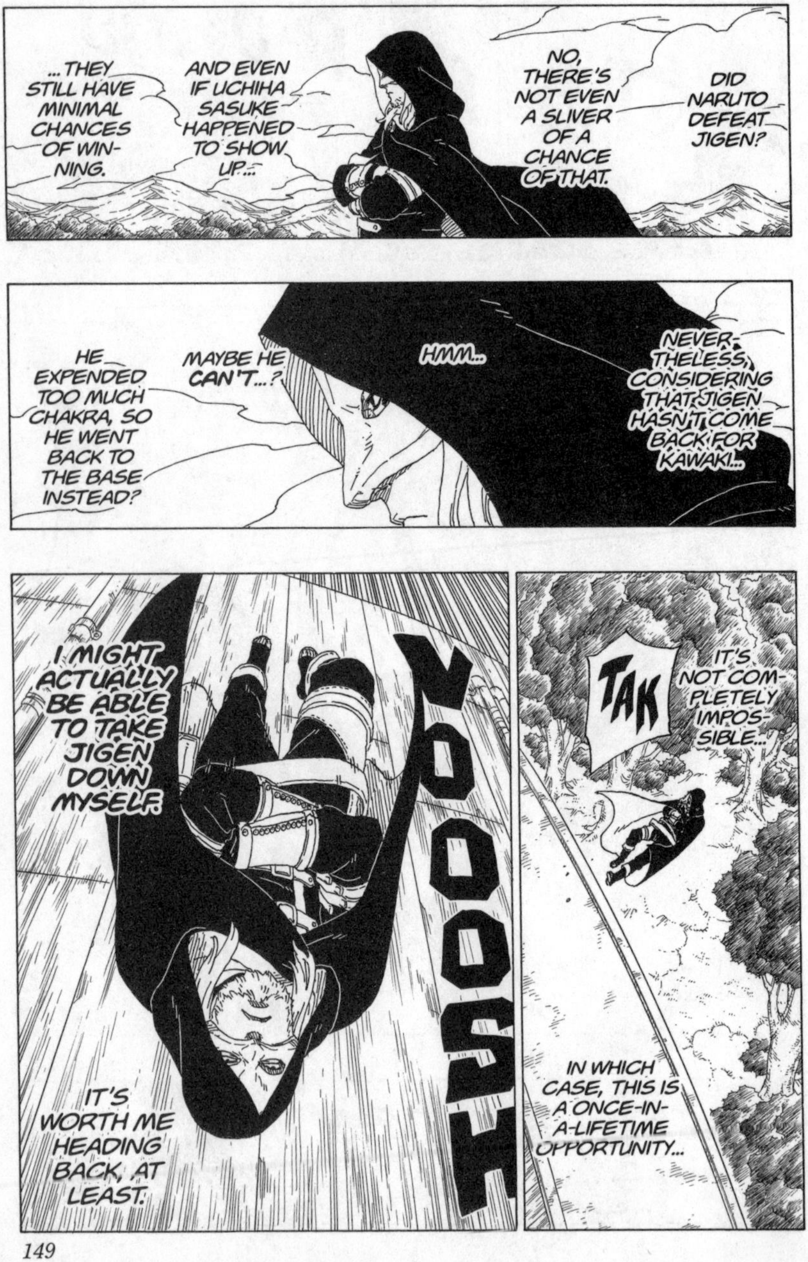
DID NARUTO DEFEAT JIGEN?
NO, THERE'S NOT EVEN A SLIVER OF A CHANCE OF THAT.
AND EVEN IF UCHIHA SASUKE HAPPENED TO SHOW UP...
...THEY STILL HAVE MINIMAL CHANCES OF WINNING.
NEVERTHELESS, CONSIDERING THAT JIGEN HASN'T COME BACK FOR KAWAKI...
HMM...
MAYBE HE CAN'T...?
HE EXPENDED TOO MUCH CHAKRA, SO HE WENT BACK TO THE BASE INSTEAD?
TAK
IT'S NOT COMPLETELY IMPOSSIBLE...
IN WHICH CASE, THIS IS A ONCE-IN-A-LIFETIME OPPORTUNITY...
I MIGHT ACTUALLY BE ABLE TO TAKE JIGEN DOWN MYSELF.
WOOSH
IT'S WORTH ME HEADING BACK, AT LEAST.

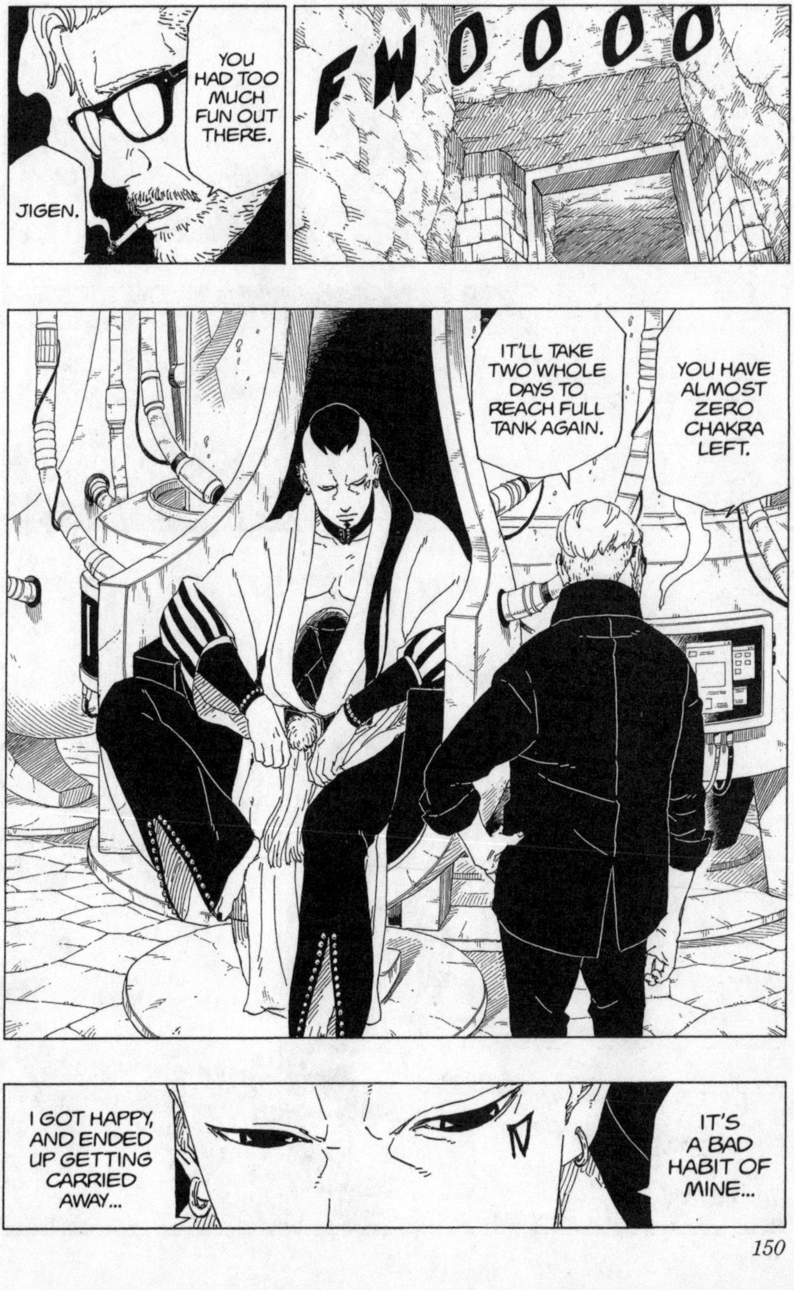
FWOOOO
YOU HAD TOO MUCH FUN OUT THERE.
JIGEN.
YOU HAVE ALMOST ZERO CHAKRA LEFT.
IT'LL TAKE TWO WHOLE DAYS TO REACH FULL TANK AGAIN.
IT'S A BAD HABIT OF MINE...
I GOT HAPPY, AND ENDED UP GETTING CARRIED AWAY...

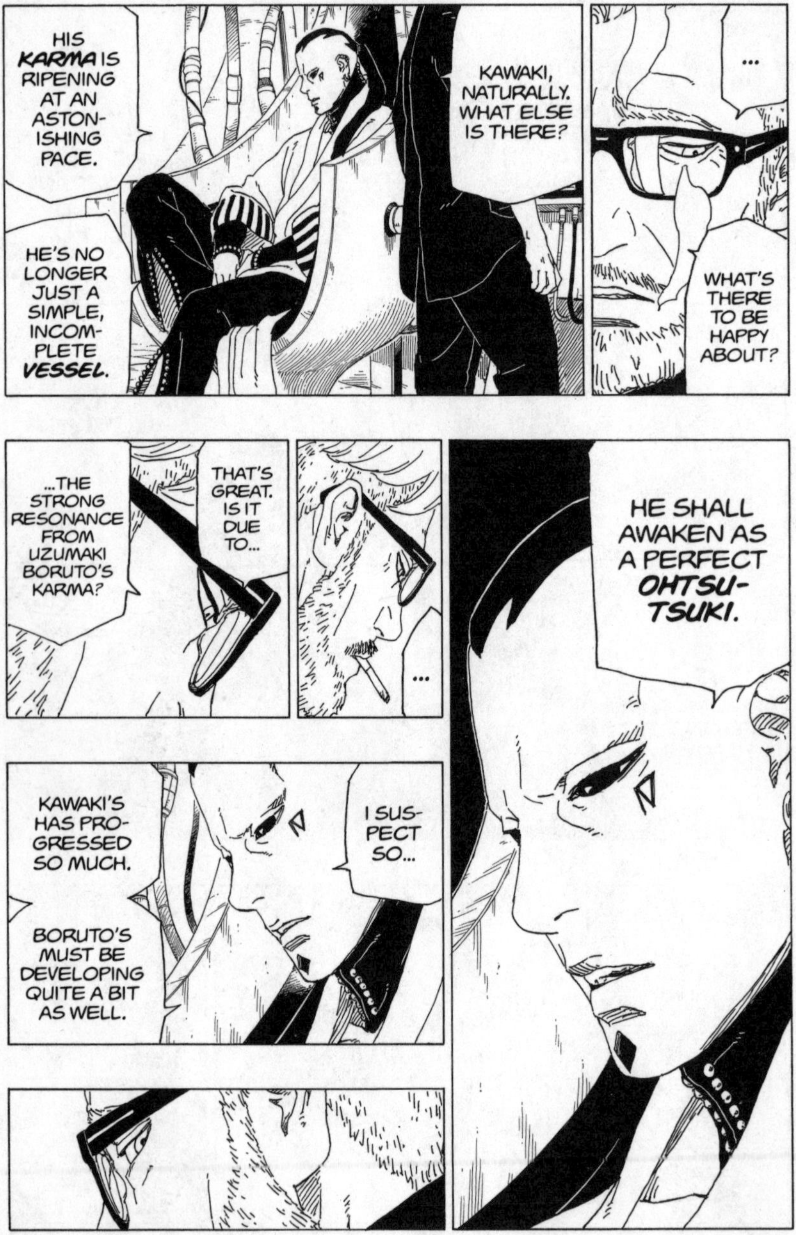

...
WHAT'S THERE TO BE HAPPY ABOUT?
KAWAKI, NATURALLY. WHAT ELSE IS THERE?
HIS KARMA IS RIPENING AT AN ASTONISHING PACE.
HE'S NO LONGER JUST A SIMPLE, INCOMPLETE VESSEL.
HE SHALL AWAKEN AS A PERFECT OHTSUTSUKI.
THAT'S GREAT. IS IT DUE TO...
...
...THE STRONG RESONANCE FROM UZUMAKI BORUTO'S KARMA?
I SUSPECT SO...
KAWAKI'S HAS PROGRESSED SO MUCH.
BORUTO'S MUST BE DEVELOPING QUITE A BIT AS WELL.

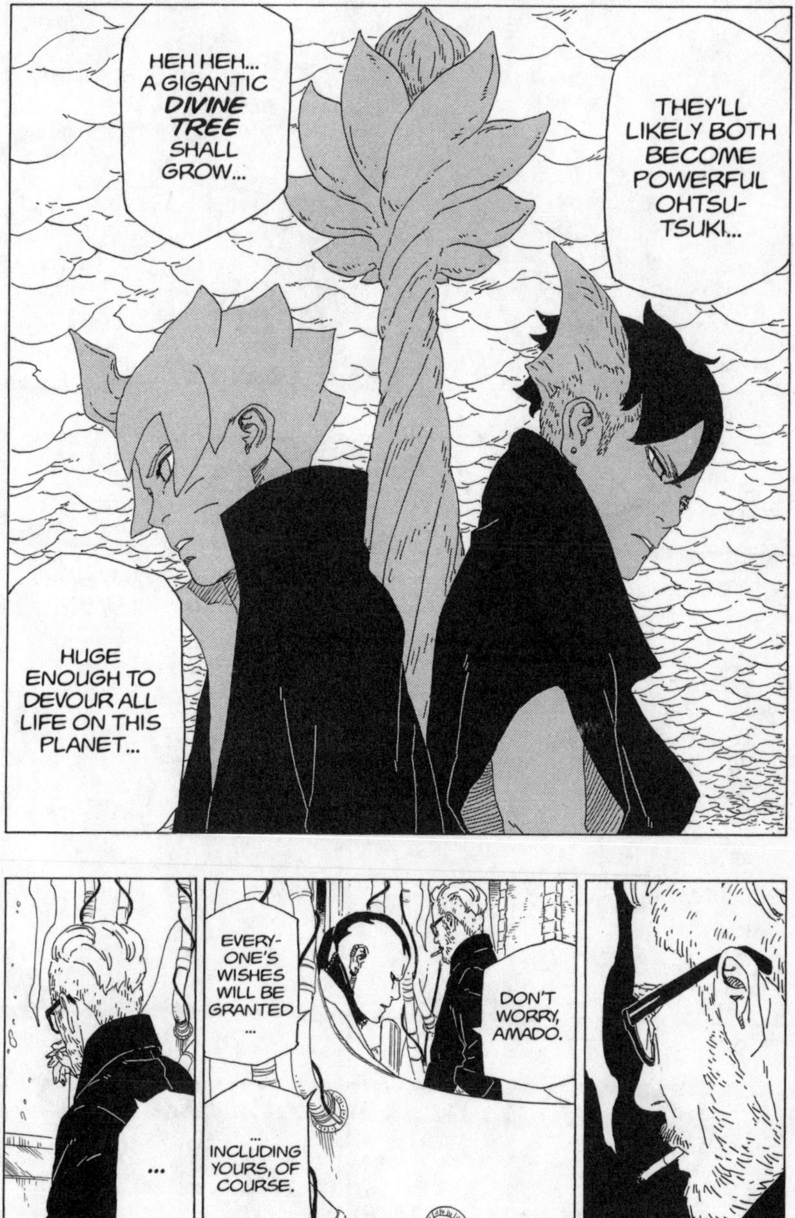
THEY'LL LIKELY BOTH BECOME POWERFUL OHTSU-TSUKI...
HEH HEH... A GIGANTIC DIVINE TREE SHALL GROW...
HUGE ENOUGH TO DEVOUR ALL LIFE ON THIS PLANET...
DON'T WORRY, AMADO.
EVERY-ONE'S WISHES WILL BE GRANTED ...
... INCLUDING YOURS, OF COURSE.
...

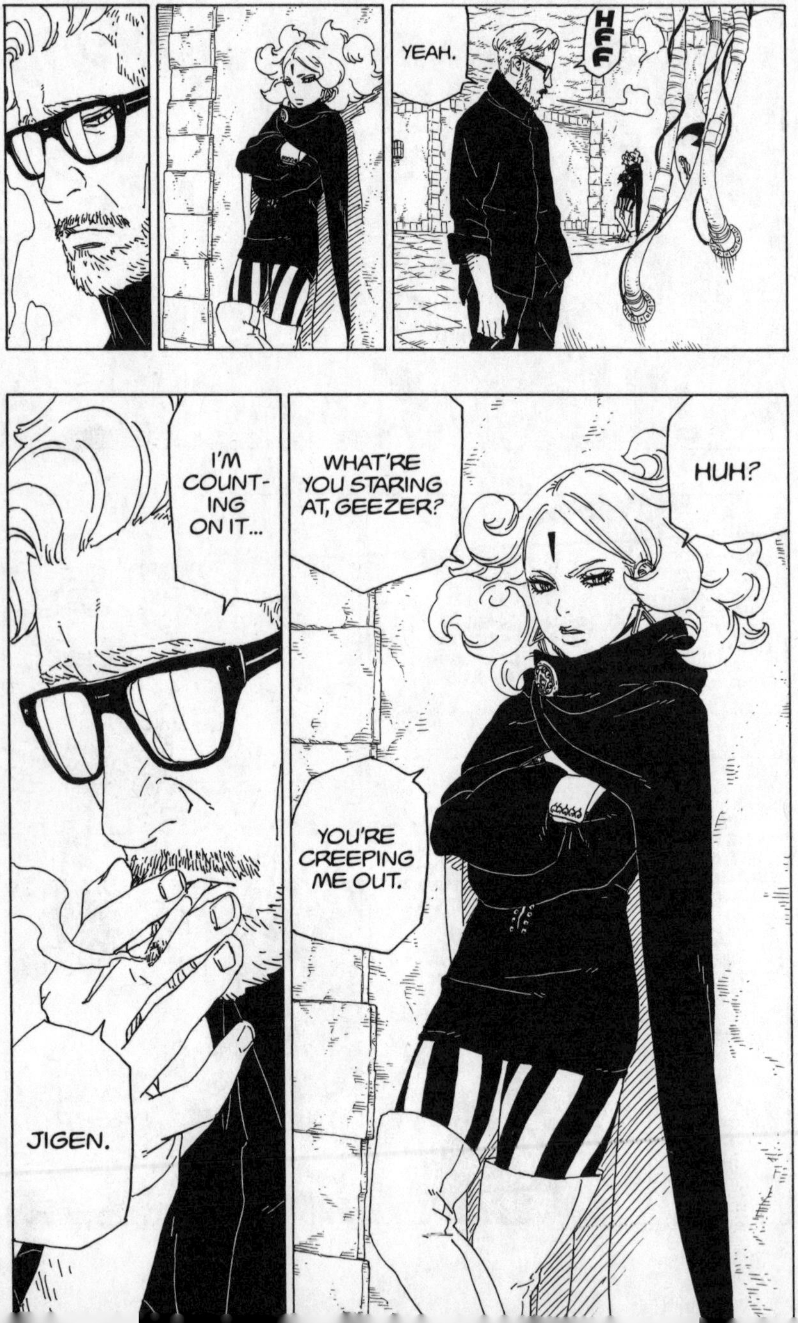
HFF
YEAH.
HUH?
WHAT'RE YOU STARING AT, GEEZER?
YOU'RE CREEPING ME OUT.
I'M COUNT-ING ON IT...
JIGEN.

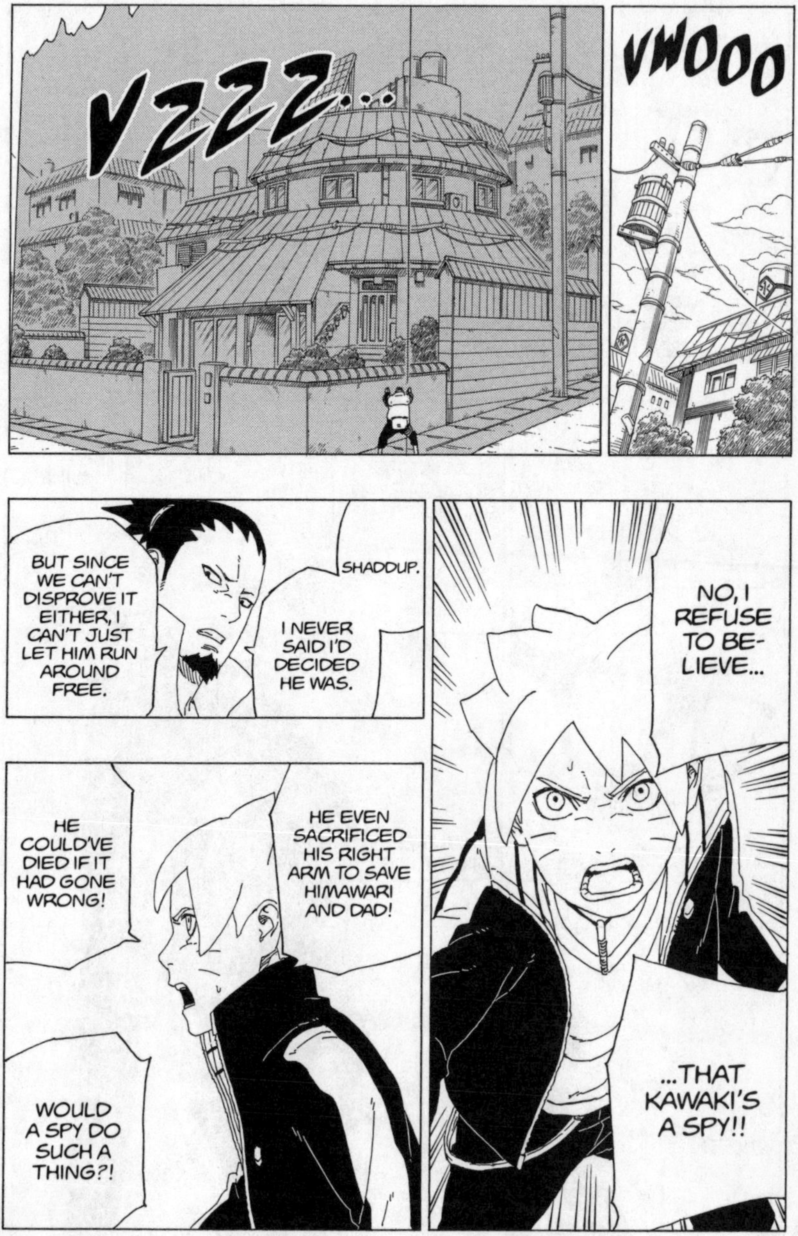
VWOOO
VZZZ...
NO, I REFUSE TO BE-LIEVE...
...THAT KAWAKI'S A SPY!!
SHADDUP.
I NEVER SAID I'D DECIDED HE WAS.
BUT SINCE WE CAN'T DISPROVE IT EITHER, I CAN'T JUST LET HIM RUN AROUND FREE.
HE EVEN SACRIFICED HIS RIGHT ARM TO SAVE HIMAWARI AND DAD!
HE COULD'VE DIED IF IT HAD GONE WRONG!
WOULD A SPY DO SUCH A THING?!

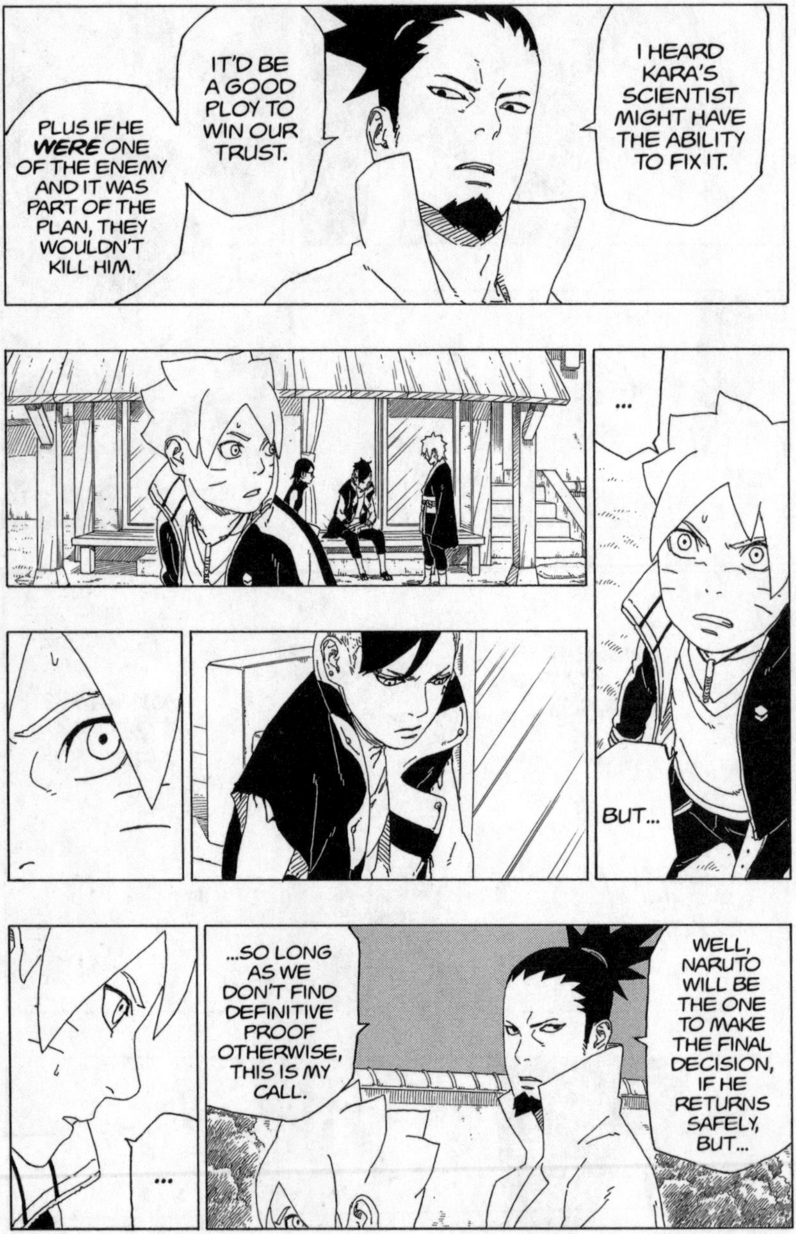
I HEARD KARA'S SCIENTIST MIGHT HAVE THE ABILITY TO FIX IT.
IT'D BE A GOOD PLOY TO WIN OUR TRUST.
PLUS IF HE *WERE* ONE OF THE ENEMY AND IT WAS PART OF THE PLAN, THEY WOULDN'T KILL HIM.
...
BUT...
WELL, NARUTO WILL BE THE ONE TO MAKE THE FINAL DECISION, IF HE RETURNS SAFELY, BUT...
...SO LONG AS WE DON'T FIND DEFINITIVE PROOF OTHERWISE, THIS IS MY CALL.
...

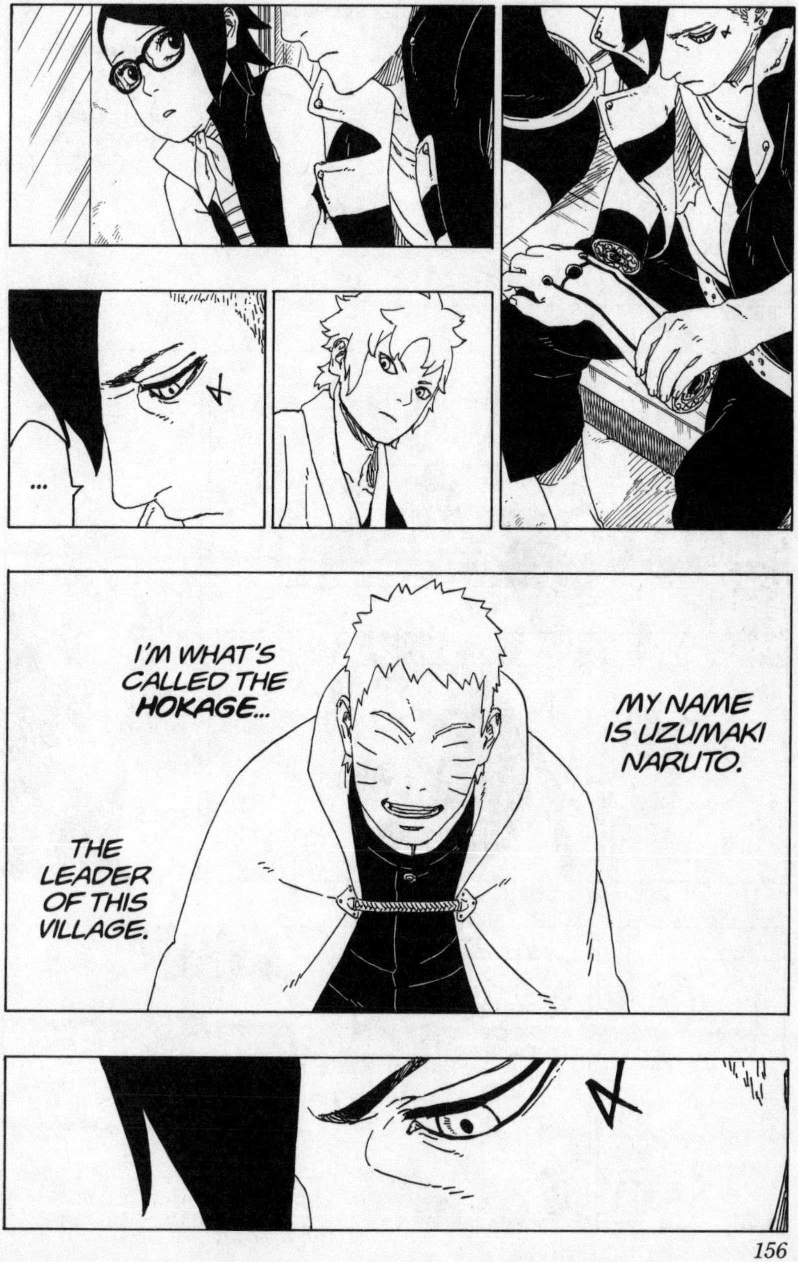
...
MY NAME IS UZUMAKI NARUTO.
I'M WHAT'S CALLED THE HOKAGE...
THE LEADER OF THIS VILLAGE.

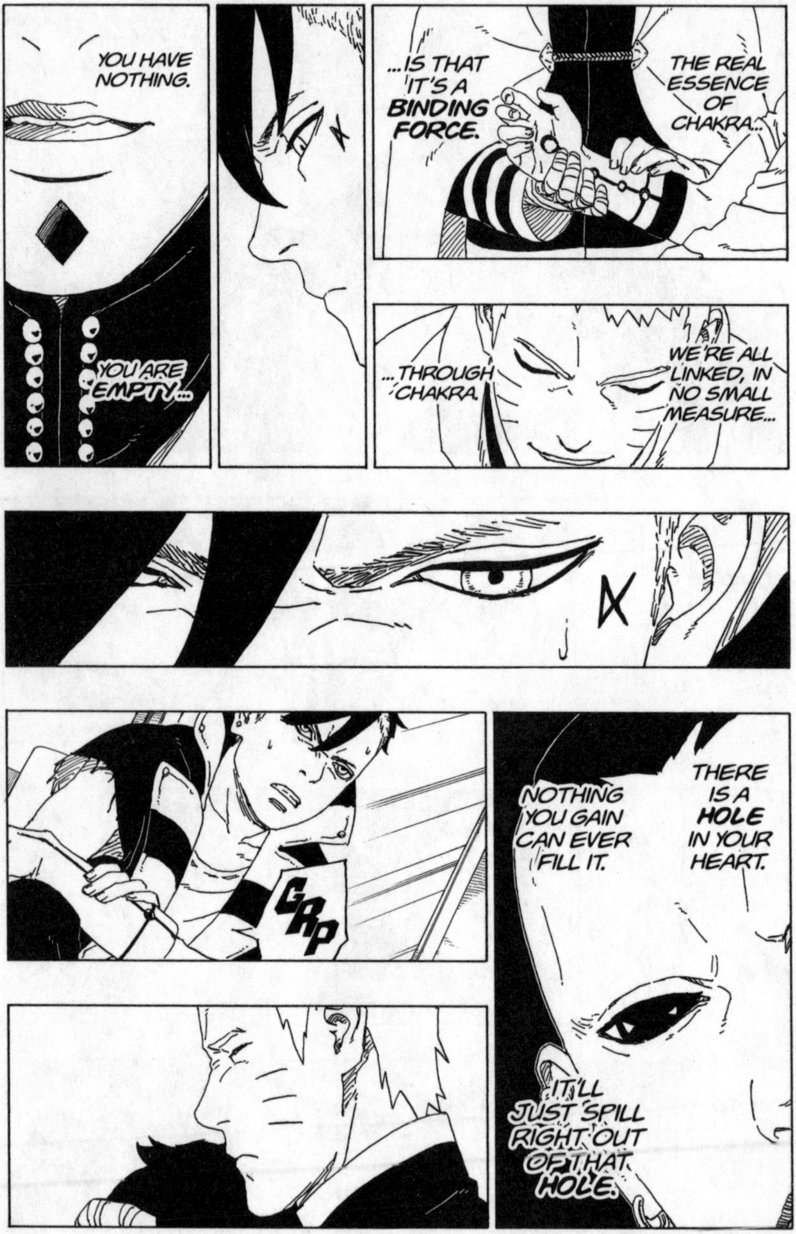
THE REAL ESSENCE OF CHAKRA...
...IS THAT IT'S A BINDING FORCE.
WE'RE ALL LINKED, IN NO SMALL MEASURE...
...THROUGH CHAKRA.
YOU HAVE NOTHING.
YOU ARE EMPTY...
THERE IS A HOLE IN YOUR HEART.
NOTHING YOU GAIN CAN EVER FILL IT.
IT'LL JUST SPILL RIGHT OUT OF THAT HOLE.
GRP

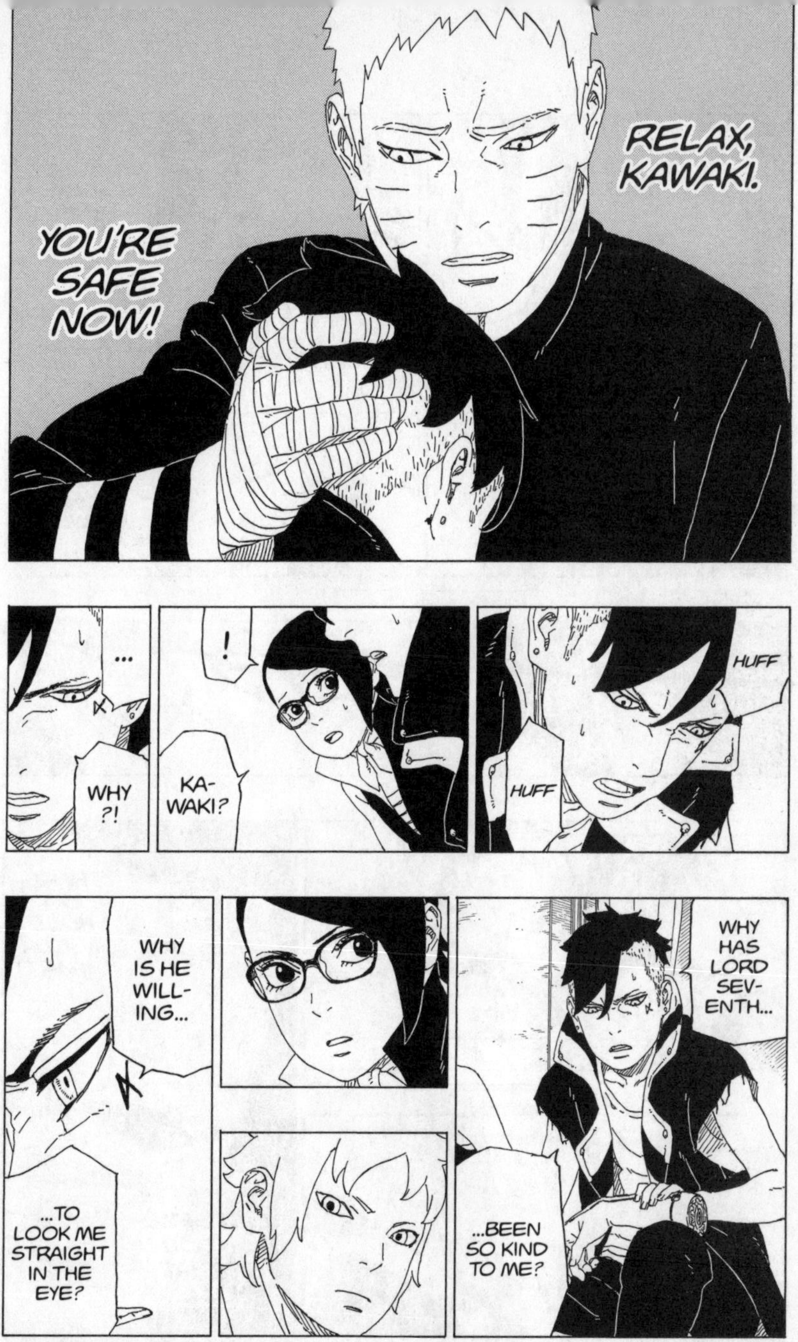
RELAX, KAWAKI.
YOU'RE SAFE NOW!
HUFF
HUFF
!
KAWAKI?
...
WHY?!
WHY HAS LORD SEVENTH...
...BEEN SO KIND TO ME?
WHY IS HE WILLING...
...TO LOOK ME STRAIGHT IN THE EYE?

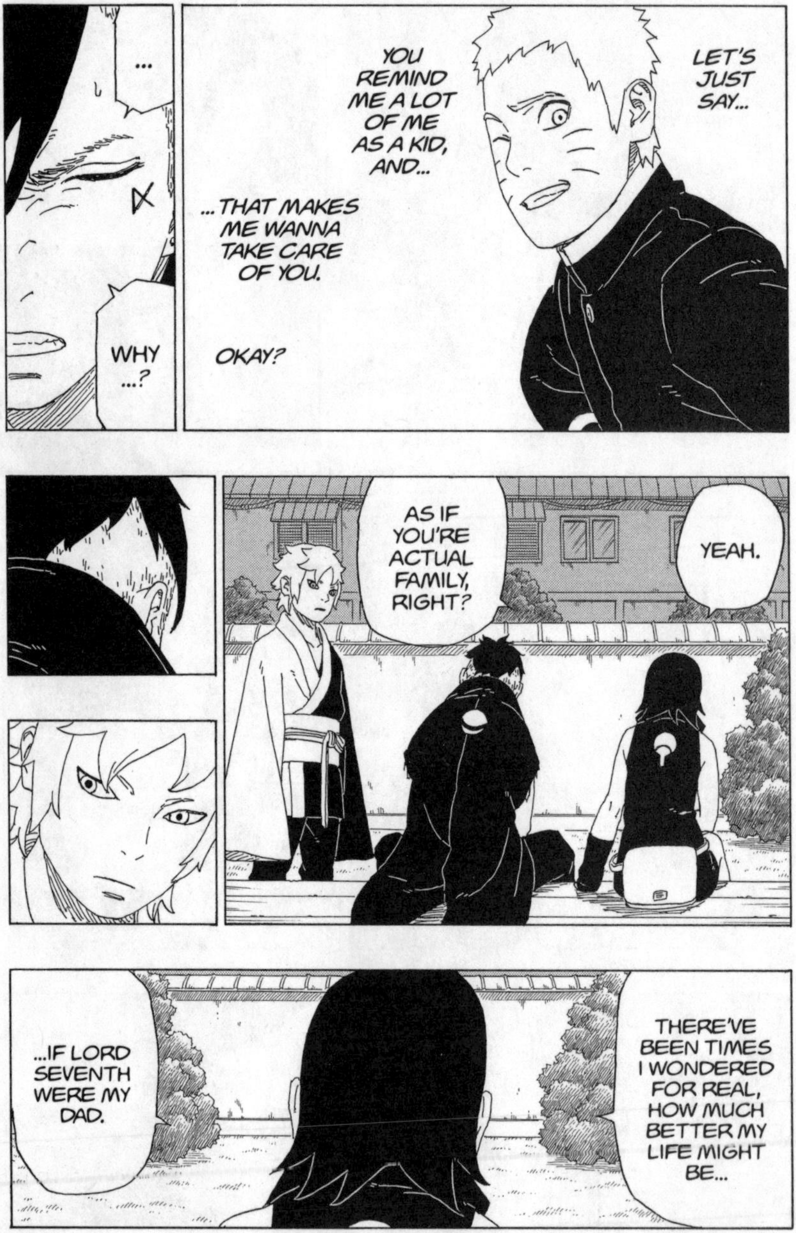
LET'S JUST SAY...
YOU REMIND ME A LOT OF ME AS A KID, AND...
...THAT MAKES ME WANNA TAKE CARE OF YOU.
OKAY?
...
WHY ...?
AS IF YOU'RE ACTUAL FAMILY, RIGHT?
YEAH.
THERE'VE BEEN TIMES I WONDERED FOR REAL, HOW MUCH BETTER MY LIFE MIGHT BE...
...IF LORD SEVENTH WERE MY DAD.

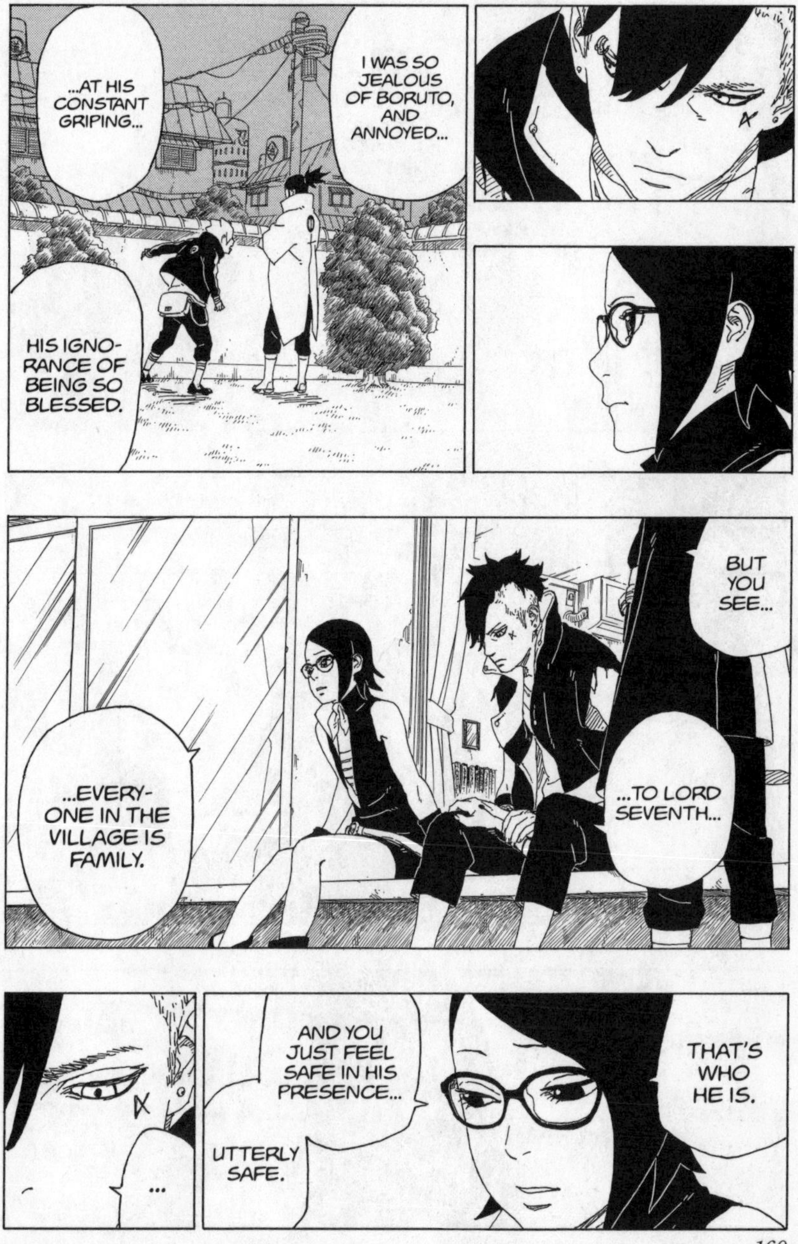
I WAS SO JEALOUS OF BORUTO, AND ANNOYED...
...AT HIS CONSTANT GRIPING...
HIS IGNORANCE OF BEING SO BLESSED.
BUT YOU SEE...
...TO LORD SEVENTH...
...EVERYONE IN THE VILLAGE IS FAMILY.
THAT'S WHO HE IS.
AND YOU JUST FEEL SAFE IN HIS PRESENCE...
UTTERLY SAFE.
...

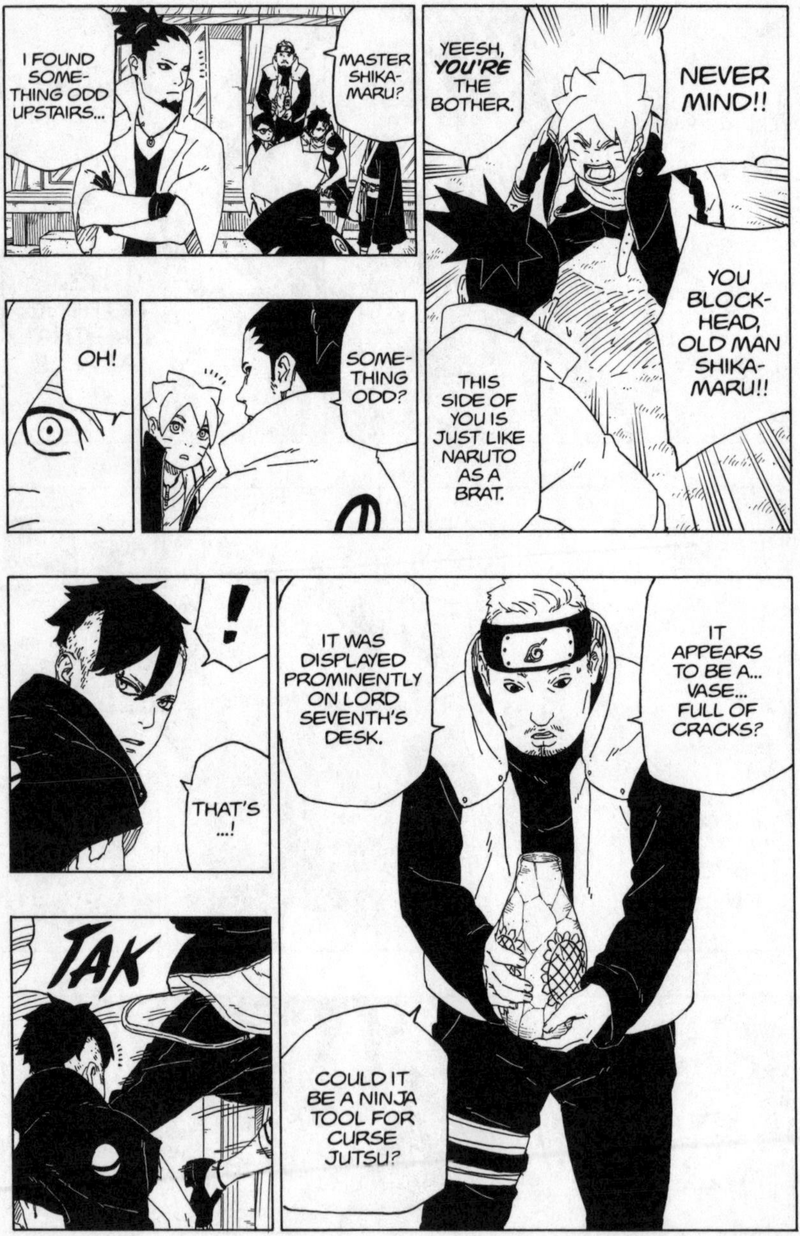
NEVER MIND!!
YEESH, *YOU'RE* THE BOTHER.
YOU BLOCKHEAD, OLD MAN SHIKAMARU!!
THIS SIDE OF YOU IS JUST LIKE NARUTO AS A BRAT.
MASTER SHIKAMARU?
I FOUND SOMETHING ODD UPSTAIRS...
SOMETHING ODD?
OH!
IT APPEARS TO BE A... VASE... FULL OF CRACKS?
IT WAS DISPLAYED PROMINENTLY ON LORD SEVENTH'S DESK.
COULD IT BE A NINJA TOOL FOR CURSE JUTSU?
!
THAT'S ...!
TAK

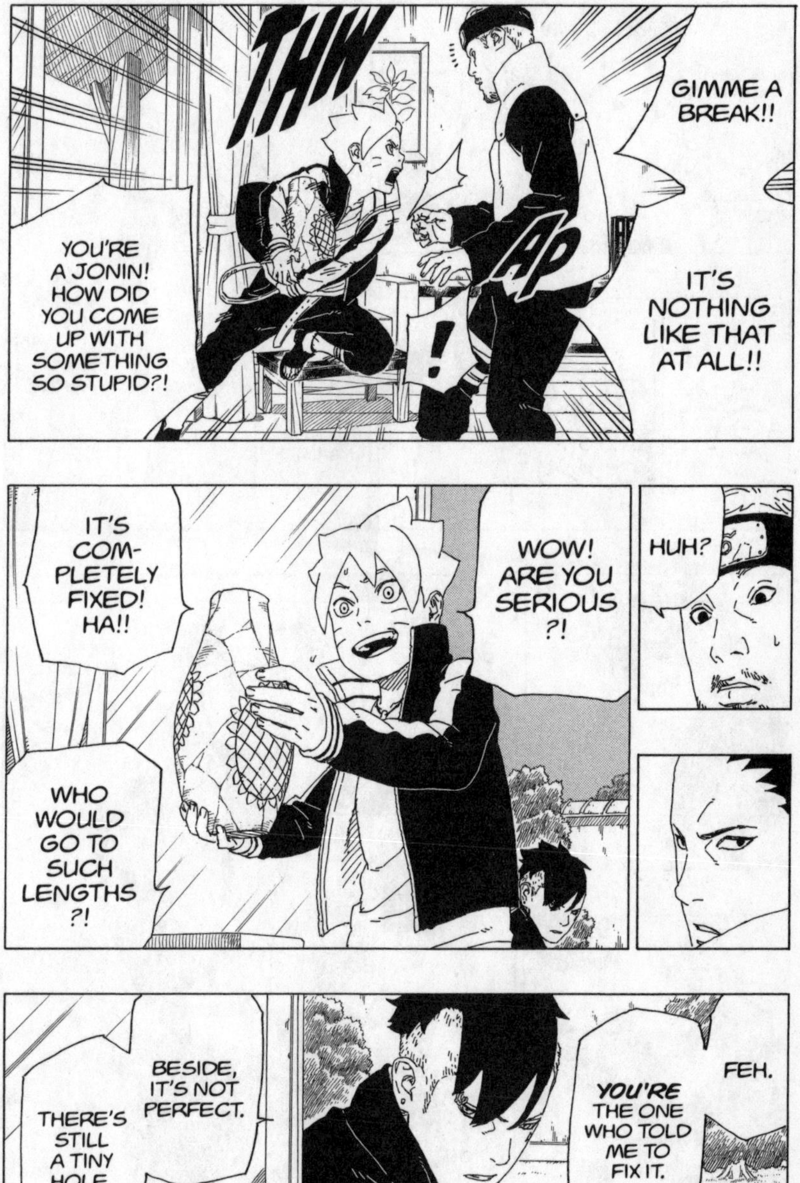
GIMME A BREAK!!
THW
IT'S NOTHING LIKE THAT AT ALL!!
AP
!
YOU'RE A JONIN! HOW DID YOU COME UP WITH SOMETHING SO STUPID?!
HUH?
WOW! ARE YOU SERIOUS?!
IT'S COMPLETELY FIXED! HA!!
WHO WOULD GO TO SUCH LENGTHS?!
FEH.
YOU'RE THE ONE WHO TOLD ME TO FIX IT.
BESIDE, IT'S NOT PERFECT.
THERE'S STILL A TINY HOLE.

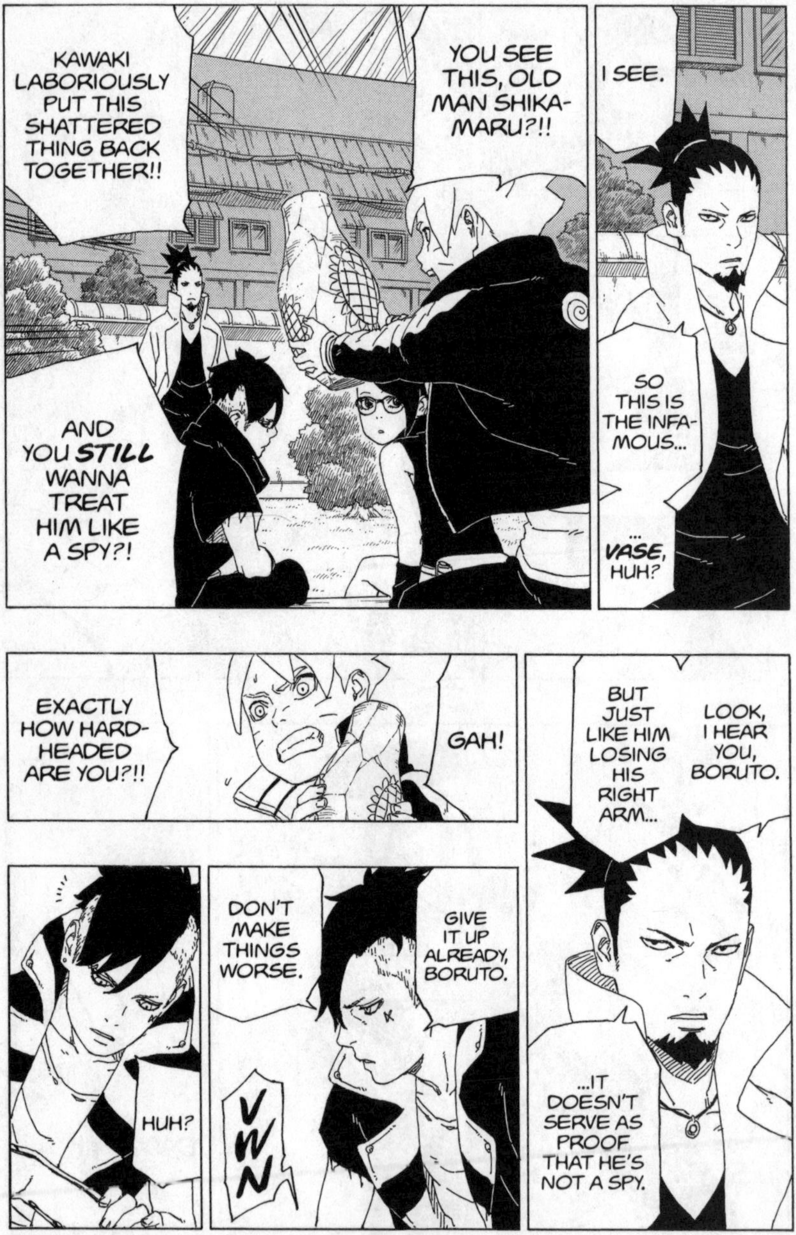
I SEE.
SO THIS IS THE INFAMOUS...
...VASE, HUH?
YOU SEE THIS, OLD MAN SHIKAMARU?!!
KAWAKI LABORIOUSLY PUT THIS SHATTERED THING BACK TOGETHER!!
AND YOU **STILL** WANNA TREAT HIM LIKE A SPY?!
LOOK, I HEAR YOU, BORUTO.
BUT JUST LIKE HIM LOSING HIS RIGHT ARM...
...IT DOESN'T SERVE AS PROOF THAT HE'S NOT A SPY.
GAH!
EXACTLY HOW HARD-HEADED ARE YOU?!!
GIVE IT UP ALREADY, BORUTO.
DON'T MAKE THINGS WORSE.
VWN
HUH?

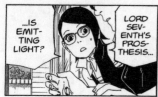

...IS EMITTING LIGHT?

LORD SEVENTH'S PROSTHESIS...

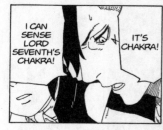

I CAN SENSE LORD SEVENTH'S CHAKRA!

IT'S CHAKRA!

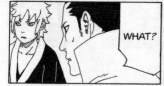

WHAT?

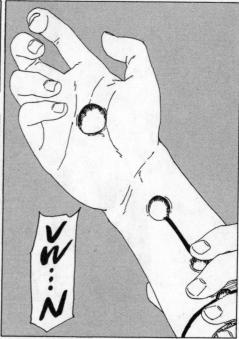

VW...N

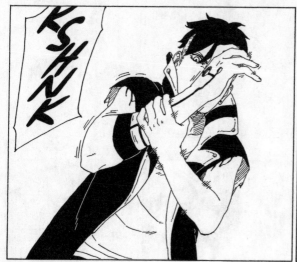

KSHNK

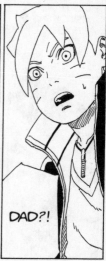

DAD?!

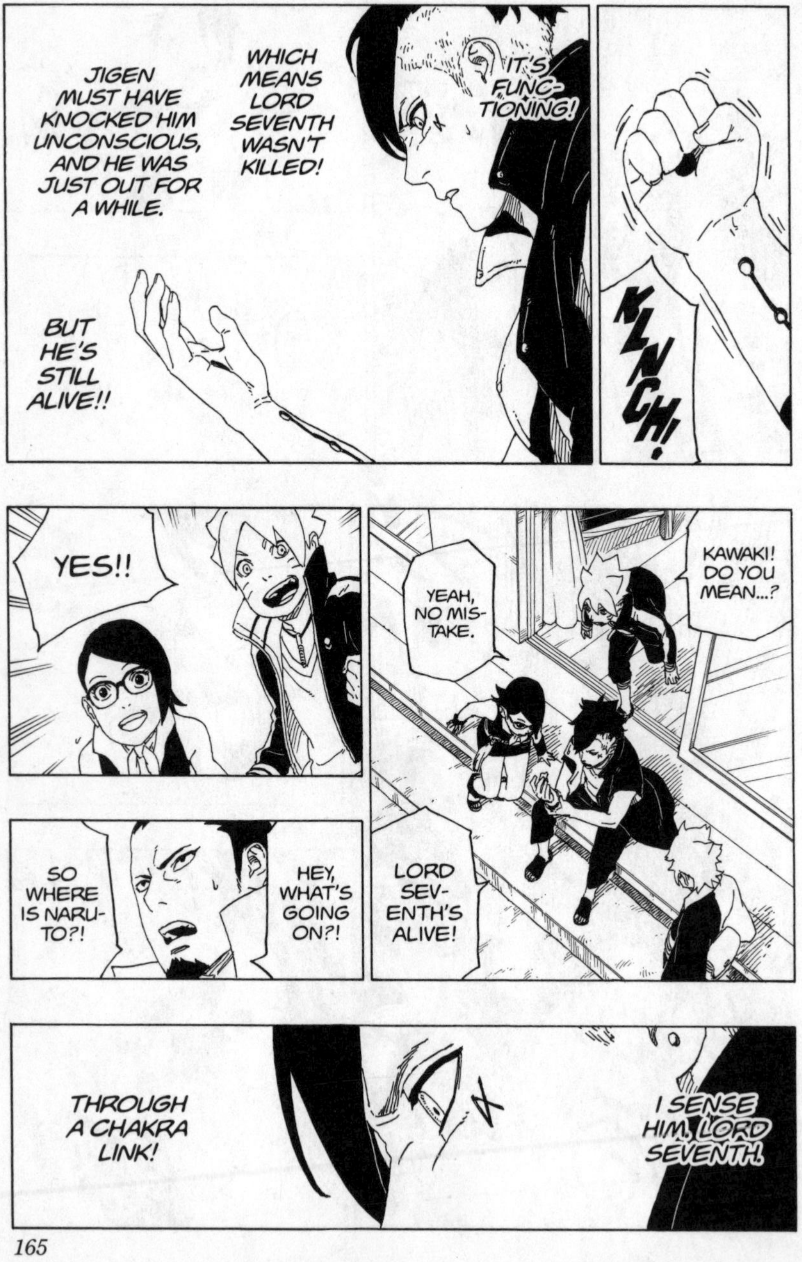
KLNCH!
IT'S FUNC-TIONING!
WHICH MEANS LORD SEVENTH WASN'T KILLED!
JIGEN MUST HAVE KNOCKED HIM UNCONSCIOUS, AND HE WAS JUST OUT FOR A WHILE.
BUT HE'S STILL ALIVE!!
KAWAKI! DO YOU MEAN...?
YEAH, NO MIS-TAKE.
LORD SEV-ENTH'S ALIVE!
YES!!
HEY, WHAT'S GOING ON?!
SO WHERE IS NARU-TO?!
I SENSE HIM, LORD SEVENTH.
THROUGH A CHAKRA LINK!

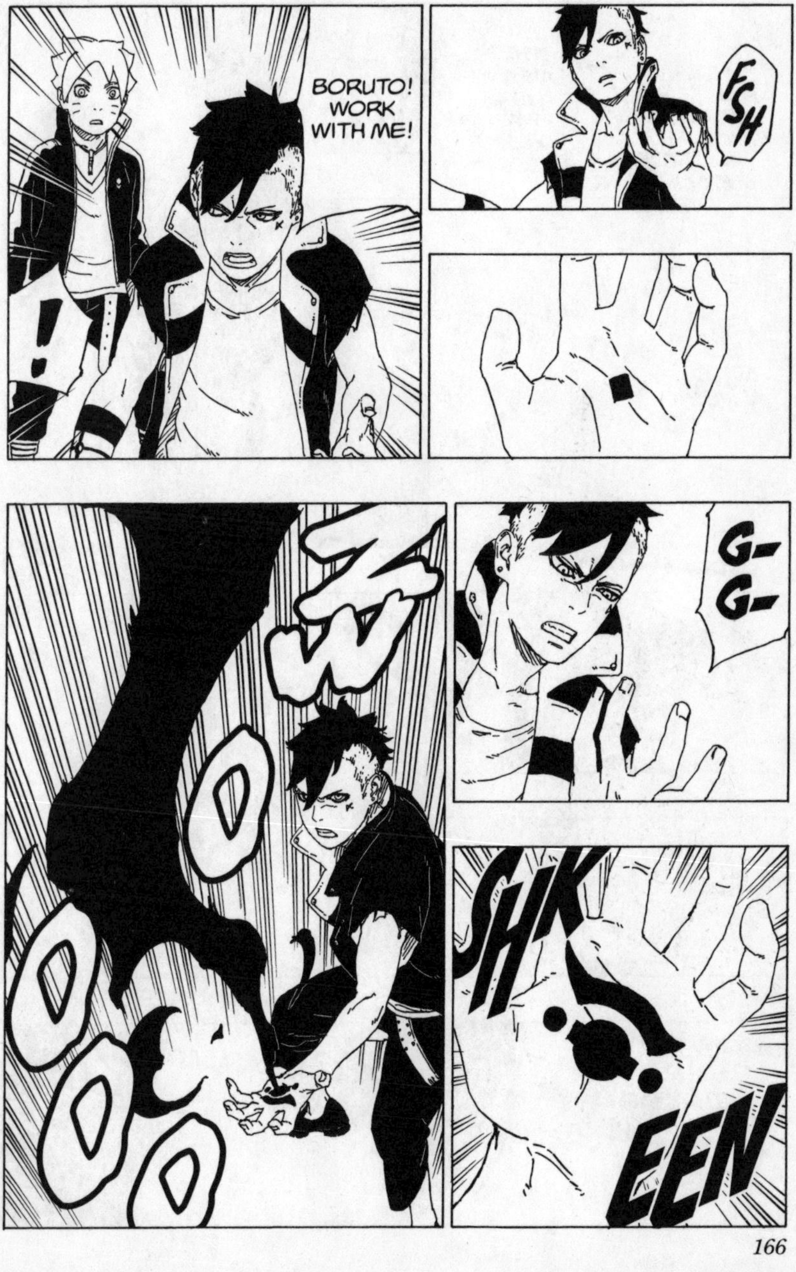
FSH
BORUTO! WORK WITH ME!
G- G-
SHKEEN
ZWOOOOO

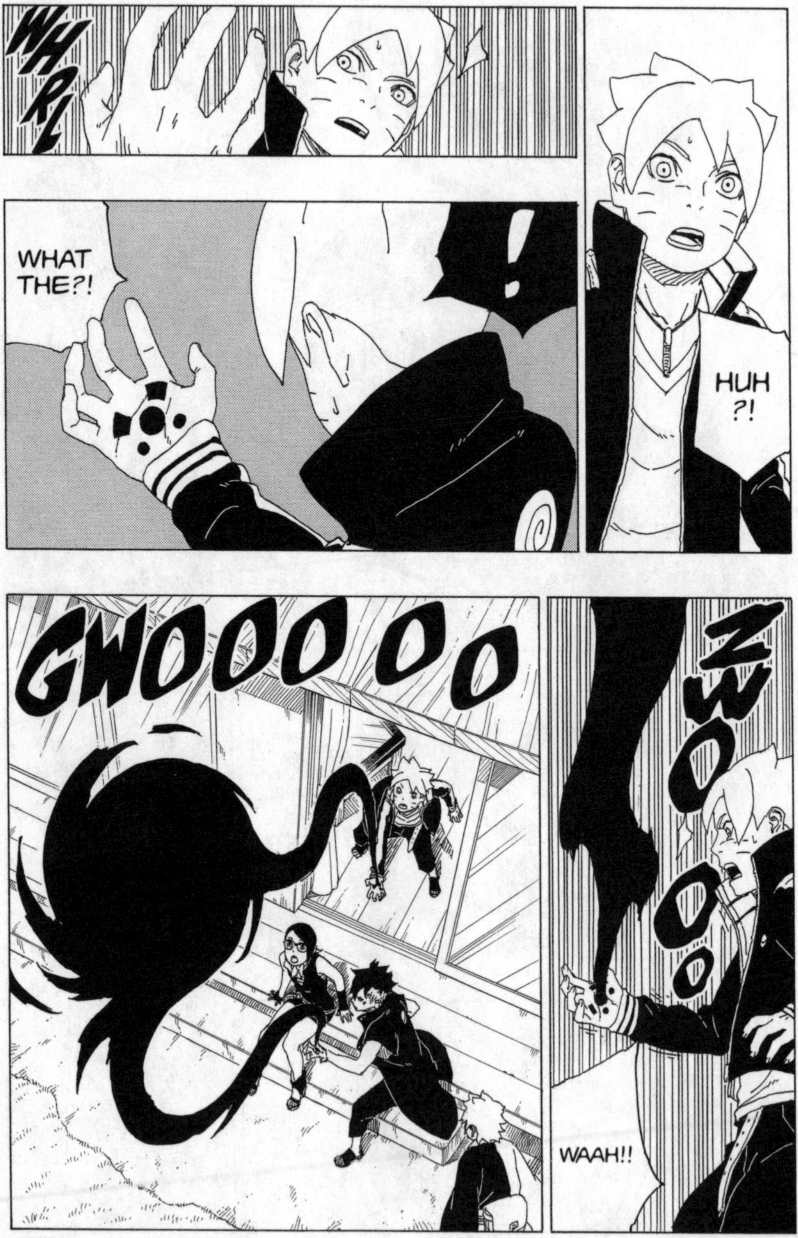
HUH ?!
WHRL
WHAT THE?!
!
ZWOOOO
WAAH!!
GWOOOOO

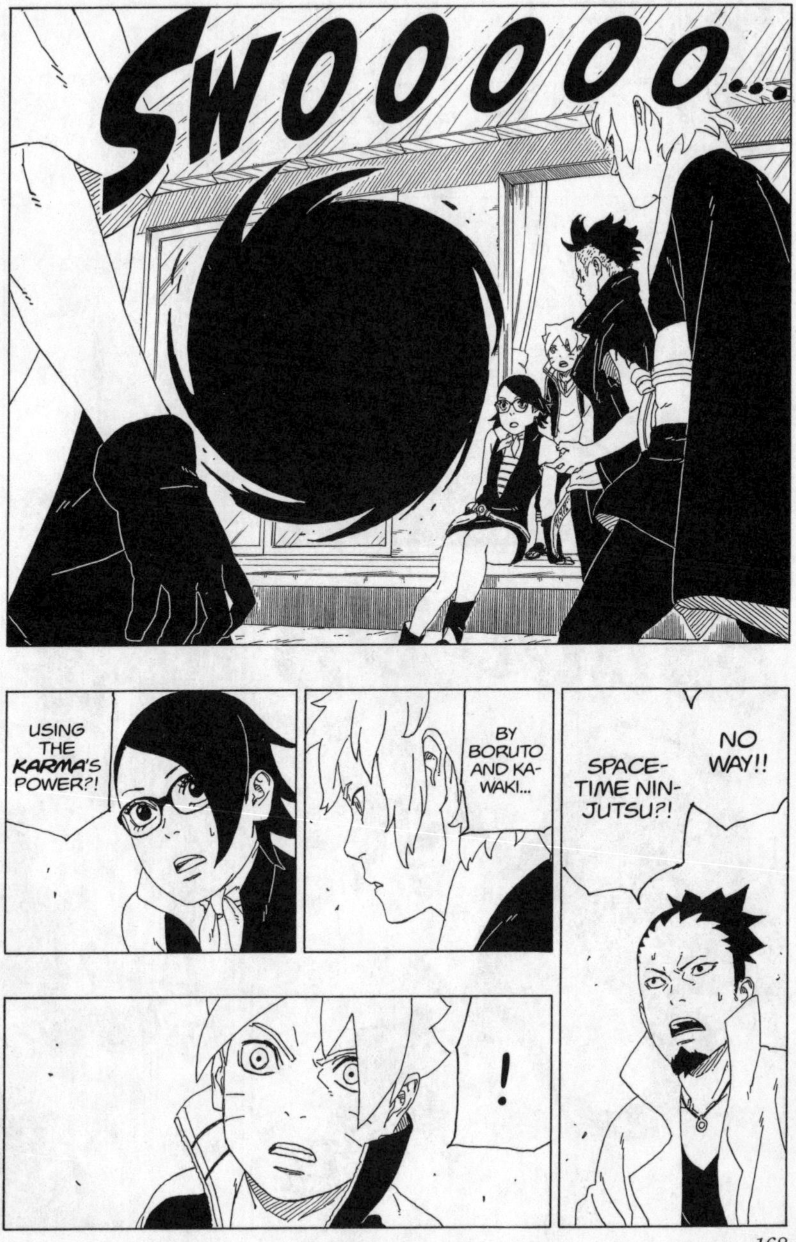
SWOOOOO...
NO WAY!!
SPACE-TIME NINJUTSU?!
BY BORUTO AND KAWAKI...
USING THE *KARMA*'S POWER?!
!

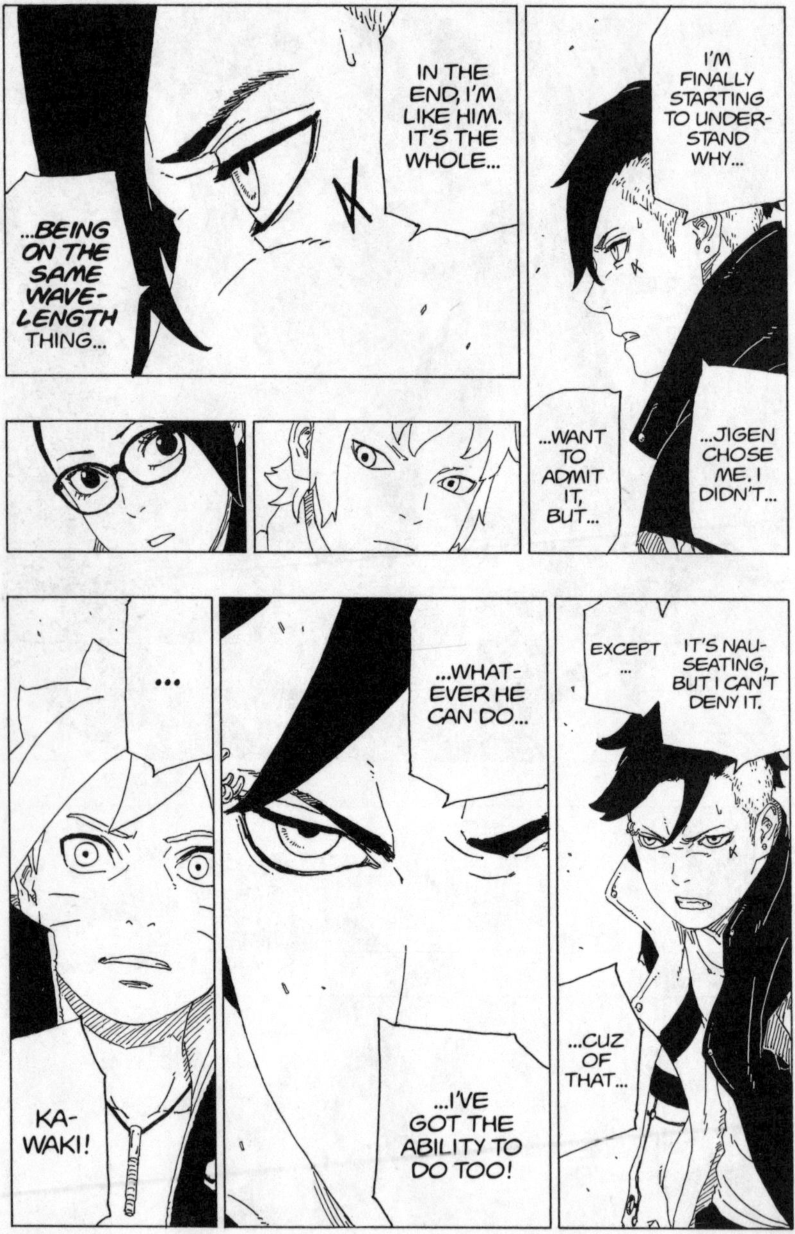
I'M FINALLY STARTING TO UNDER-STAND WHY...
...JIGEN CHOSE ME. I DIDN'T...
...WANT TO ADMIT IT, BUT...
IN THE END, I'M LIKE HIM. IT'S THE WHOLE...
...BEING ON THE SAME WAVE-LENGTH THING...
IT'S NAU-SEATING, BUT I CAN'T DENY IT.
EXCEPT...
...CUZ OF THAT...
...WHAT-EVER HE CAN DO...
...I'VE GOT THE ABILITY TO DO TOO!
...
KA-WAKI!

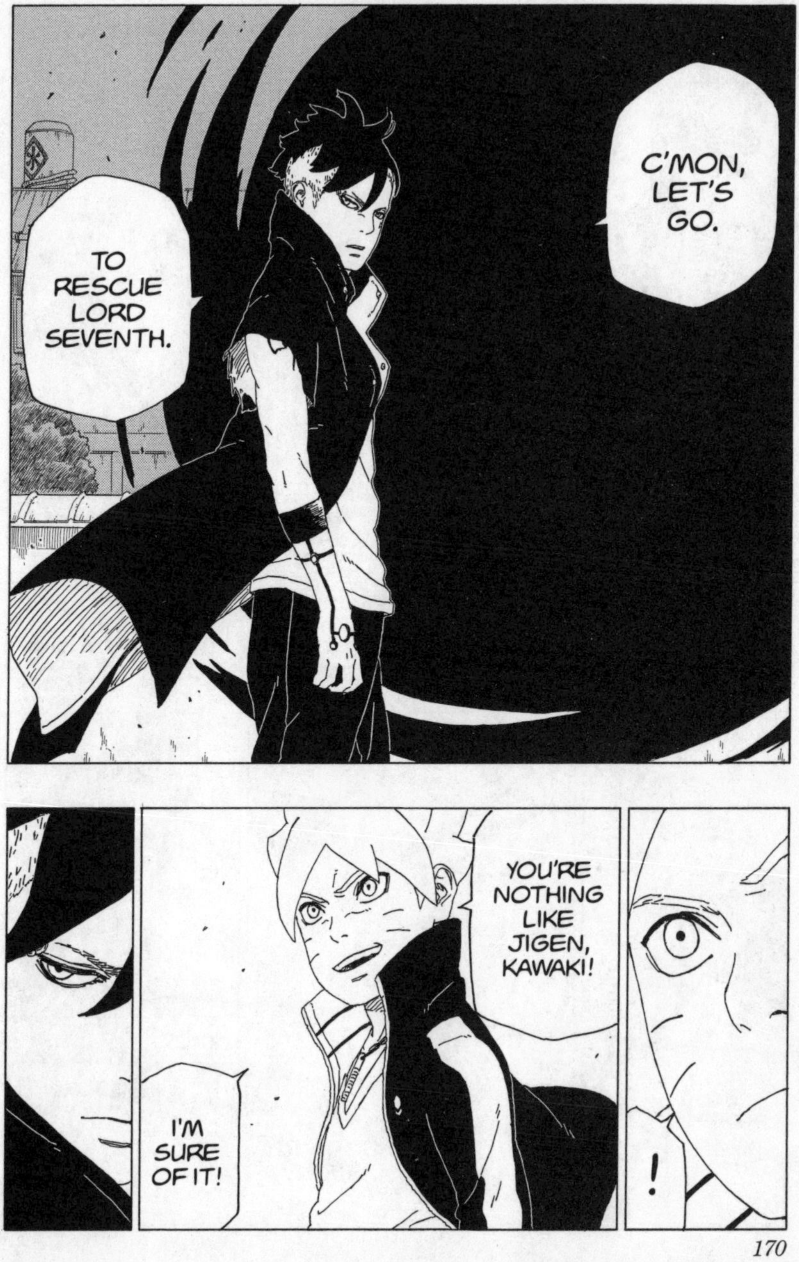
C'MON, LET'S GO.
TO RESCUE LORD SEVENTH.
!
YOU'RE NOTHING LIKE JIGEN, KAWAKI!
I'M SURE OF IT!

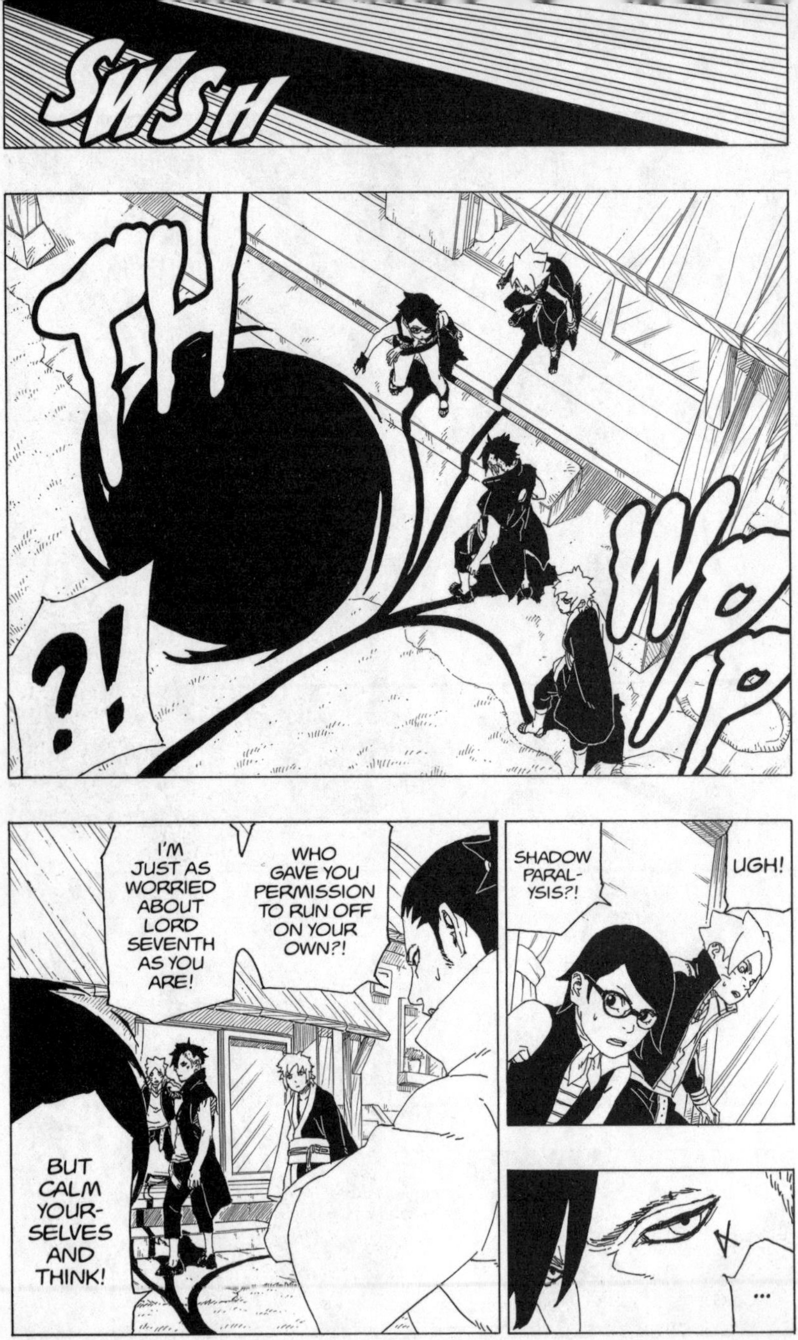
SWSH
TH
WOP
?!
UGH!
SHADOW PARALYSIS?!
...
WHO GAVE YOU PERMISSION TO RUN OFF ON YOUR OWN?!
I'M JUST AS WORRIED ABOUT LORD SEVENTH AS YOU ARE!
BUT CALM YOURSELVES AND THINK!

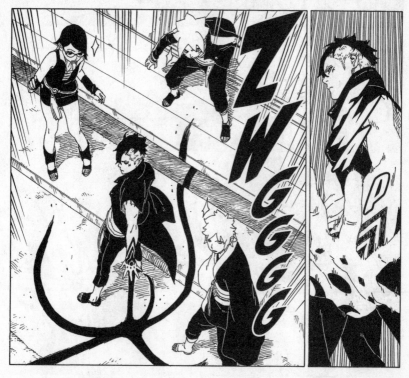

ZWGGGGG
BZP
!
UGH !!
!
I CAN MOVE AGAIN!
HURRY UP AND GO.
THE RIFT IS GONNA CLOSE.

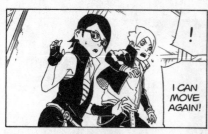

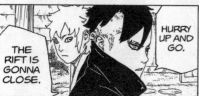

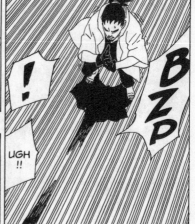

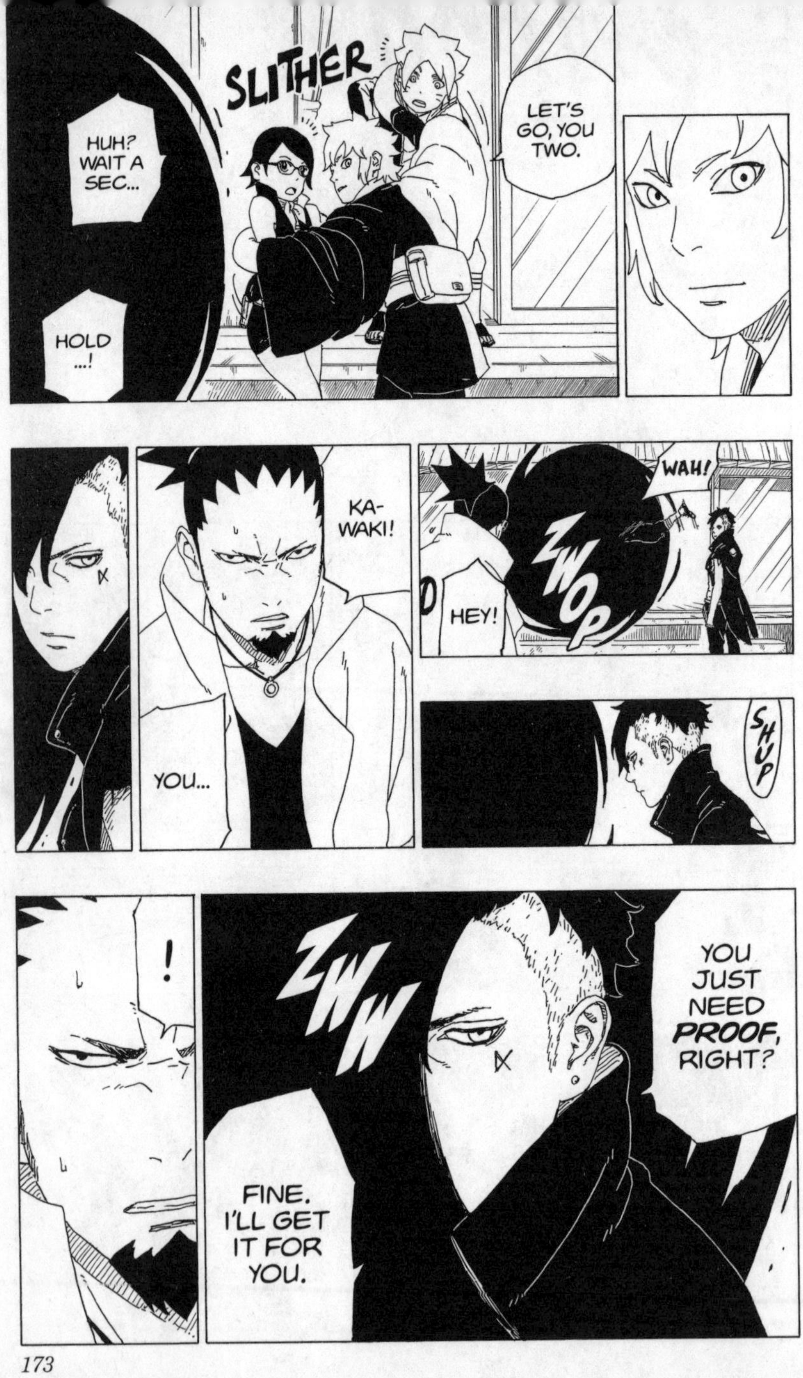
LET'S GO, YOU TWO.
SLITHER
HUH? WAIT A SEC...
HOLD ...!
WAH!
ZWOP
HEY!
SHUP
KA-WAKI!
YOU...
YOU JUST NEED **PROOF**, RIGHT?
ZWW
FINE. I'LL GET IT FOR YOU.
!

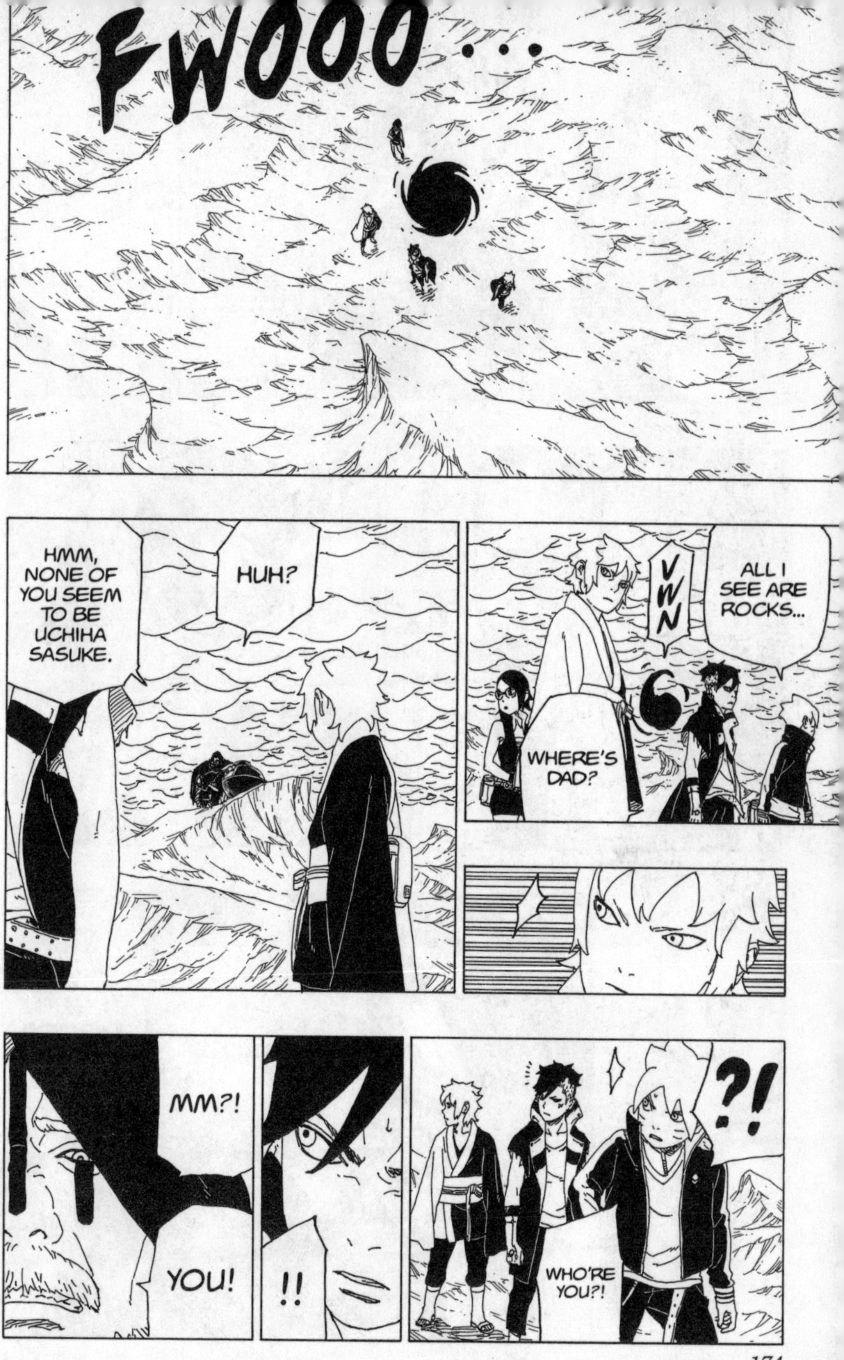
FWOOO...
ALL I SEE ARE ROCKS...
VWN
WHERE'S DAD?
HUH?
HMM, NONE OF YOU SEEM TO BE UCHIHA SASUKE.
?!
WHO'RE YOU?!
!!
MM?!
YOU!

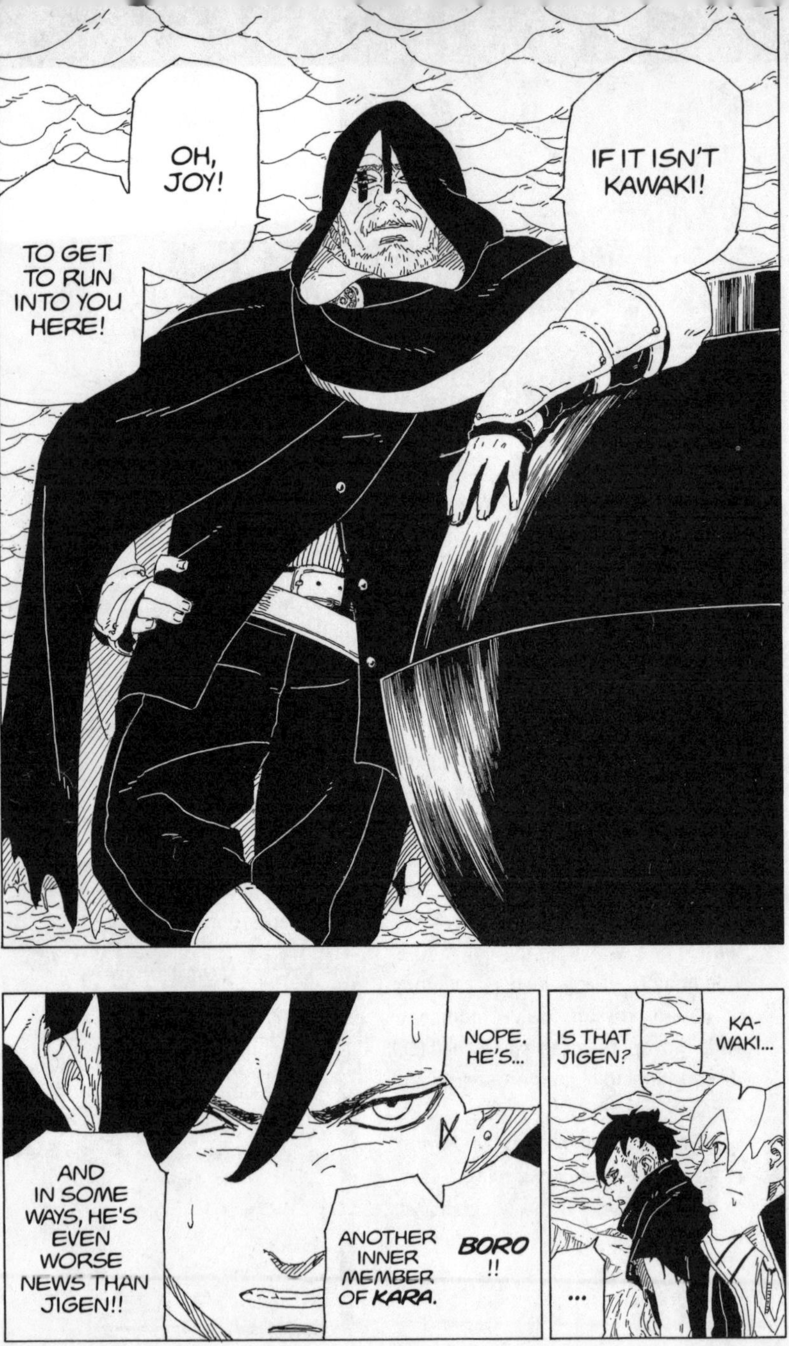
IF IT ISN'T KAWAKI!
OH, JOY!
TO GET TO RUN INTO YOU HERE!
KA-WAKI...
IS THAT JIGEN?
...
NOPE. HE'S...
BORO!!
ANOTHER INNER MEMBER OF KARA.
AND IN SOME WAYS, HE'S EVEN WORSE NEWS THAN JIGEN!!

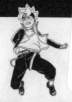

YOU'RE READING
IN THE
WRONG DIRECTION!!

WHOOPS! Guess what? You're starting at the wrong end of the comic!

...It's true! In keeping with the original Japanese format, **Boruto** is meant to be read from right to left, starting in the upper-right corner.

Unlike English, which is read from left to right, Japanese is read from right to left, meaning that action, sound effects and word-balloon order are completely reversed... something which can make readers unfamiliar with Japanese feel pretty backwards themselves. For this reason, manga or Japanese comics published in the U.S. in English have sometimes been published "flopped"—that is, printed in exact reverse order, as though seen from the other side of a mirror.

By flopping pages, U.S. publishers can avoid confusing readers, but the compromise is not without its downside. For one thing, a character in a flopped manga series who once wore in the original Japanese version a T-shirt emblazoned with "M A Y" (as in "the merry month of") now wears one which reads "Y A M"! Additionally, many manga creators in Japan are themselves unhappy with the process, as some feel the mirror-imaging of their art alters their original intentions.

We are proud to bring you **Boruto** in the original unflopped format. Turn to the other side of the book and let the ninjutsu begin...!

—Editor

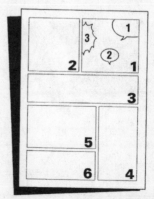